Windows on the World

Multicultural Festivals for Schools and Libraries

Alan Heath

The Scarecrow Press, Inc.
Lanham, Maryland, and London
2001

SCARECROW PRESS, INC.

Published in the United States of America
by Scarecrow Press, Inc.
4720 Boston Way, Lanham, Maryland 20706
www.scarecrowpress.com

4 Pleydell Gardens, Folkestone
Kent CT20 2DN, England

Copyright © 1995 by Alan Heath
First paperback edition 2001

British Library Cataloguing in Publication Information Available

**The Library of Congress Cataloged the cloth edition of this work as
follows:**

Heath, Alan, 1946–
    Windows on the world : multicultural festivals for schools and libraries /
Alan Heath.
           p.   cm.
    Includes bibliographical references and index.
    1.   Festivals—Study and teaching (Elementary).
    2.   Multiculturalism—Study and teaching (Elementary).
    3.   Festivals—Planning.   4. Festivals—Management.
    5.   Libraries—Cultural programs.   I. Title.

    Cloth edition copyright © 1995 by Alan Heath
    GT3930.H43   1995
    394.2′6—dc20   94-10032

♾ ™ The paper used in this publication meets the minimum requirements of
American National Standard for Information Sciences—Permanence of
Paper for Printed Library Materials, ANSI/NISO Z39.48-1992.
Manufactured in the United States of America.

ISBN: 0-8108-3958-x

for
Carl Kerr, a poet of rare gifts,
John Barker, scholar and raconteur,
and, of course,
Stephen and the Relish Sisters

Table of Contents

Table of Contents

List of Illustrations

A Word to the Reader

A writer, or indeed an observer of life, must approach cultures other than his or her own from within his or her own traditions, savoring the opportunities to explore the differences that enrich our society. Though an American, I come from English stock: a fact that not only nourishes my own cultural roots but also provides the treetop from which I look out upon the world. I beg that readers forgive me if my own understanding of another culture has led me unwittingly to use words or phrases that could give offense. Rest assured that they are unintentional. In my years as a teacher in a multicultural international school in a cosmopolitan city, I have come more and more to appreciate the texture, color and design that world cultures weave into our social tapestry. In my school of 1,500, over forty different nationalities harmoniously work and play side by side. We are not all alike, nor do we seek to be. I feel that it is essential not just to learn about other cultures, but to *preserve* them so that they continue to have their places on our common planet. *Windows on the World: Multicultural Festivals for Schools and Libraries* is offered with this end in mind: we celebrate the things we share while appreciating that there are things we don't share.

Introduction

Windows on the World: Multicultural Festivals for Schools and Libraries began during a coffee break at the American School in London when we teachers decided we wanted something special to enliven our wintry month of March. It had to be something that would involve the whole school, all 1500 of us. It had to be catchy, with lots of things to involve the imaginations of students aged four to eighteen. It ought to involve every classroom in both intimate self-contained events and larger projects for plenary indulgence! Who could possibly coordinate such a gargantuan project? The answer then was, "You could!" for at the time I was a librarian, with contacts throughout the school in reading programs, library classes, and artwork designed to promote the enjoyment of books. After several further coffee breaks for brainstorming, we organized our first festival. It was so much fun, with so many tangible, unifying results and rewards for everyone, that we did it again next year, and the next.

Our first festival was a weeklong celebration of science fiction, by coincidence scheduled for the London opening of the film *Close Encounters of the Third Kind.* We went on to celebrate ecology, wholefood (thus changing forever our school lunch program!), the Beatles (Paul McCartney lives around the corner, and we are a block away from Abbey Road), astrology, science, and several world cultures, such as China, Italy, Turkey, Egypt, and Britain. Our student body is made up of over forty nationalities and many ethnic and racial groups, so it seemed logical to take advantage of and to acknowledge the value of our component parts.

The idea behind the festival approach is to branch out from the regular curriculum and offer cross-cultural, cross-disciplinary activities for several age groups. The festivals center on the library but move about to include the theatre, classrooms, and other parts of the school through student seminars, outside speakers, films, plays, puppet shows, cooking demonstrations, feasts, art projects, music, and reading—all thematically related. The festival idea has also

1

grown to include events that cater to narrow age bands. The Beatles week, for instance, was for high school only, while the astrology festival was for middle school. We have been happy to host visiting teachers from several international schools and from the U.S. who have transported our festival ideas back to their own schools with great success.

Celebrating a Plural Society

The world has become a highly accessible, highly mobile place. Even when travel to foreign countries is not possible, television brings other cultures into the schools and living rooms of people everywhere. Ours is a multicultural planet, yet beneath varied costumes and customs, human hearts beat in the same rhythms from Peoria to Rawalphindi. America has been called a great melting pot of cultures. In recent years, immigrant national and ethnic groups have been proud to rediscover their old customs. Many regions now boast festivals that showcase the costumes, dances, foods, and folk arts of immigrant communities. How many cities celebrate Chinese New Year today? Is it easy to find a German Oktoberfest, a Lithuanian festival, or an Italian celebration? Native Americans are also proud to reassert pride in their history and customs, and many states are scenes of tribal and intertribal powwows and festivals. By studying and participating in a world cultural festival, students may see that the same sentiments occur in different forms in communities across the globe. In addition to commenting upon similarities, festivals can also value our differences and point out how they are shaped by climate, sociology and religion, and history. Through observing and participating in our similarities and differences, students can learn respect, tolerance and friendship for people from another culture.

Windows on the World: Multicultural Festivals for Schools and Libraries offers several organized approaches to involvement in multicultural learning. You may prefer, however, to select segments from several festivals to create a truly multicultural thematic unit, such as "Thanksgiving Around the World," "Winter Celebrations: What People Celebrate and Why," or "New Year Madness Around the World." Where the focus is on comparative culture rather than on one culture, a thread of similarity that runs through several religions, ethnic groups, or nations may be found. Since holidays are a universal ingredient of human life, world culture festivals can show students the essential similarity of people all over the planet. In Islam, for instance, the birthday of the Prophet Muhammad is a time of feasting. In Hinduism, Janmashtami recalls the birth of Krishna. In Christianity, Jesus's birthday is celebrated with carolling and gift giving. In the Taoist/Confucian tradition of China, the birthday of the Sun King is celebrated with candles, incense, sweet cakes, and storytelling. Most cultural celebrations are not religious in nature, but span the gamut of folklore, history, politics, art, and food.

A festival at school can give dramatic impetus to learning. Adding to the regular pace of day-in-day-out school work these will be special times for remembrance, feasting, dancing, and celebrating some of the good things in life.

When to Hold a Festival

A world culture festival can be held at any time, but these dates offer a handy peg on which to hand a thematic program:

July	—the month of U.S. Independence
October	—Canadian Thanksgiving Day
	—Columbus Day
	—British harvest festival
November	—U.S. Thanksgiving
November 11	—Armistice Day
December	—Hanukkah
	—Christmas and New Year

It may make greater sense to hold a festival during a "slack time" when there are no annual local celebrations or events scheduled. For us, that was the month of March, and it has become traditional to organize a multicultural festival then. Alternatively, celebrate the four seasons with elements from different cultures, choosing from among the following and other events and selecting appropriate secular manifestations of religious, spiritual, or seasonal occasions to illustrate how people the world over celebrate the joys of life.

Winter

1. The Hindu celebration of Makara Sankranti
2. The Jewish feasts of Purim and Hanukkah
3. The Christian seasons of Advent and Christmas
4. Valentine's Day
5. St. Patrick's Day
6. New Year's Day and Chinese New Year's Day
7. The Chinese celebration of the Birthday of the Sun

Spring

1. Hindu New Year's Day (Dhvajaropana)
2. Jewish Festival of Pesach
3. The Christian festival of Easter
4. The Muslim month of fasting, Ramadan
5. The Chinese Pure and Bright Festival

Summer

Because most schools are not fully operational in the summer, inclusion of these festivals could be transferred to term-time.
1. The Hindu Ratha Yathra
2. The Jewish Shavuot
3. The Christian feast of the Assumption

Autumn

1. The Hindu Diwali, or Festival of Lights
2. The Jewish Rosh Hashanah, Yom Kippur, and Sukkot
3. The Chinese Birthday of the Harvest Moon
4. The Chinese Kiteflying Day

In celebrations for the four seasons of the year, festival organizers may draw upon customs, holidays, and special commemorative events from various world cultures. Rather than try to observe a Hindu holiday when one's own beliefs are not Hindi, or rather than trying to celebrate Easter if one is not Christian, gather some of the secular manifestations of the religious festivals which could be enjoyed by everyone. While a Christmas tree or an Easter egg may give joy to many, a crucifix might not. The same is true with other religions and observances. And, as for other festivals in this book, if there is any serious doubt about promoting it, don't do it.

Activities

In each of the ten festivals which follow, participants will be encouraged to do some or all of the following:

1. Find out about the customs and beliefs of a country, people, or ethnic group
2. Read, listen to, or dramatize a folktale or piece of literature
3. Find out about a major holiday celebration
4. Create a work of art
5. Write creatively
6. Prepare and eat food from the culture
7. Hear an authority speak on the subject

Format

Each festival is organized within a chapter. At the beginning of each chapter is a precis of, or apologia for, the festival that gives background information and serves to introduce the participant to the activities. This precis may be used in publicity, such as in-school handout leaflets, brainstorming or committee meetings, or press releases about your events. A bookmark which may be reproduced on festival programs, as library handouts, or for publicity also accompanies each chapter. Suggestions follow for festival displays and bulletin boards, art activities, guest speakers, publications, foods to prepare, stories to read or perform, and other projects particular to certain topics.

Each chapter concludes with "Sources of Inspiration," books which have aided in the research and organization of the festival. While the books included for each festival are important, the lists are not exhaustive. Make use of the materials in your classroom and libraries, adding to them when necessary.

How to Organize a Festival

Organizing a festival can be simple, but there will be moments of intense planning and work. One person, for instance the librarian, can do all the work alone, limiting the festival to a colorful display, some storytelling, presentation of thematic books, and perhaps one special activity such as arts and crafts, creative drama, a video or film, an edible treat, or an invited speaker. On the other hand, an army of teachers, librarians, and parents can work together to plan, organize, and present a large festival spanning several days and including outside speakers, music, art, and other appurtenances. Determine the limits of time and space. Will the festival include the whole school building and all its denizens, or will it be held by the sixth grade only? Will it last a week, with events spread out over several days, or will it take place one afternoon?

A small committee of inspired teachers and librarians can organize a festival quickly in a single brainstorming session. The convenor, or facilitator of the festival, may present the theme he or she would like to explore, such as a week of African-American history, or members of the committee may offer their own suggestions. To begin, follow one of the festival outlines in *Windows on the World: Multicultural Festivals for Schools and Libraries.*

Someone will be devil's advocate, offering special insights into why the proposed idea won't work: not enough space, not enough time, not enough money; too much work, too many people involved, too many readers and not enough books; the theme hasn't enough scope for development here; the theme has far too much scope for development and will exhaust both itself and the audience. Learn what local limitations of time, space, materials are and plan the festival accordingly.

Research on the part of the organizer is essential. He or she must *know* or be willing to *learn* about the culture to be celebrated, either through personal involvement or through education. Books in "Sources of Inspiration" will help. Feel free to call on people with greater expertise so that the festival can include as many facets of the culture as possible. Although one dynamic person may organize a festival perfectly well, delegation of some responsibilities to others will help spread out the work load. The Festival Planning Sheet (figure 1) will help organize the components of the festival. Use it as a checklist, filling in the blanks with appropriate titles, organizers' names, and addresses. Photocopy this outline for use in your school.

How Much Will It Cost?

Most of the activities in the festivals which follow can be carried out with existing school materials: art supplies, books, notepaper and pencils. Some can be achieved with found or borrowed materials: cardboard boxes, grocery containers, half-empty cans of household paint. Sometimes, though, funds may be necessary to offer an author or a speaker an honorarium or travel expenses, to pay for cooking ingredients and photocopying, or to buy other special materials. Check your own school budget.

Scheduling

If the festival is organized by a classroom teacher for his or her own students, scheduling does not present a problem, but for a schoolwide festival, care must be taken to avoid scheduling an event to which nobody comes. It is essential to ensure that a core of students and teachers will be present at any given event. When organizing the festival, therefore, have the school timetable on hand and arrange activities accordingly, either during *appropriate classes* or in *free time*. To ensure a core audience, plan a speech or author's seminar for one particular English or science class, at the same time inviting others to attend if they can. Make sure the guest speaker isn't speaking to a class at the same time the teacher had planned an exam—make cooperative arrangements long in advance.

If the entire school is curricularly involved in the festival, events for different age groups and interests may occur simultaneously in various parts of the building. An author may prefer to talk cozily in a corner of the library to several small groups in one day or to one large assembly in the school auditorium (figure 2). A drama may be enacted once, perhaps in the evening, or several times throughout the festival in various locations. Artwork may be done in the library or classrooms, or in the art department. Music may be performed to a seated audience, as part of storytelling, or for casual listening. Scheduling depends entirely upon local needs and situation. Flexibility and cooperation are two key words.

When the festival agenda of speakers, seminars, art and cooking demonstrations, and displays has been finalized, print a schedule for distribution as a take-home handout. List the events by date and time, including place, even if they are not for the general public. If, for example, at two o'clock on Tuesday Mr. Smith's eighth grade art class is making a kachina for the Native American festival, include it in the agenda along with the booktalk on Native American history books for high school social studies, the demonstration of Native

(Figure 1)
FESTIVAL PLANNING SHEET

TITLE OF FESTIVAL _____

DATES _____

1. Event   Delegated   Phone
                                   Organizer   Number
                                                      & Address

    A. Speakers _____   _____

        Authors _____   _____

        Demonstrators _____   _____

        1. Fees _____

        2. Honorarium _____

        3. Travelling Expenses and Arrangements _____

    B. Storytelling _____   _____

    C. Booktalks _____   _____

    D. Films and Videos _____   _____

    E. Trips to Take _____   _____

    F. Music _____   _____

    G. Arts and Crafts _____   _____

    H. Food and Recipes _____   _____

2. Publicity

    A. Posters, handbills _____   _____

    B. Newspapers notices _____   _____

    C. Local radio and tv _____   _____

3. Festival Printouts

    A. Brochure of Events _____ _____

    B. Bibliography _____ _____

    C. Special publications:

        Recipe booklet _____ _____

        Student artwork _____ _____

        Student writing _____ _____

4. Cleaning Up Afterwards

    A. Repositioning of
       furniture _____ _____

    B. Vacuuming, mopping,
       litter pickup _____ _____

    C. Removing displays _____ _____

    D. Returning borrowed
       items _____ _____

5. Post-Festival Evaluation

    A. Organizers' Meeting _____ _____

    B. Written reports _____ _____

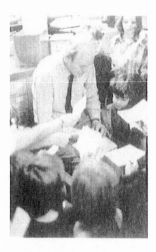

(Figure 2) The late Roald Dahl (left), author of *Danny the Champion of the World,*
Charlie and the Chocolate Factory. Kiss Kiss, and other novels enjoyed by old and young
alike, autographs copies of his book after speaking to a group of middle school
students. Katharine Hollabird (right), signs copies of her *Angelina* books during a
special dramatic adaptation and performance of *Angelina* stories by lower school
students at the American School in London. Most authors welcome this contact with
their reading public, and are happy to talk to youngsters.

American cooking for Ms. Haliburton's domestic science class, and
the Navajo rug maker's talk in the theatre. A printed brochure of
events makes the festival seem more solid and helps people keep up
with events.

Use the festival bookmark to illustrate the brochure or ask an art
student to draw a design for the cover. Put copies of the brochure in
all teachers' mailboxes; give them to each student; send them home
to parents; use them to entice neighboring schools to visit; send them
to the local newspaper.

Making the Festival Your Own

The following festival programs offer ideas to fill a significant period
of time with planning, organization, and presentation. Fit the
festival into your school or classroom realistically. If some of the art
ideas require too much time, dexterity, or space, whittle them down
until they can be accomplished on your terms. If you want to offer a

special week of African-American culture, it can be done with a bulletin board and some interesting book talks instead of the several activities offered in chapter six. On the other hand, the activities given here may not be *enough*. Let local needs open channels of creativity to fill in the omissions.

A Tree with Many Roots and Many Branches:
A Multipurpose Multicultural Display

A multicultural festival is a special period of time when we celebrate our ethnicity, our cultural differences, the things we share, and the things we don't share. This can be symbolized visually with a graphic tree that is adaptable to all of the festivals in this book. Since America is a nation composed of many cultures, the tree can symbolize that unity in diversity. Segments of the tree can be cut from different colors of construction paper to represent different national or ethnic origins, or for a small, photocopiable tree, differentiate the segments with varying graphic designs (figure 3).

What You Need:

Construction Paper (various colors)
Scissors
Staples or pins
Felt-tip pens

Make the tree as large as the display space allows. Line the display area with plain paper, and sketch on the tree shape. Cut segments from color paper to fit the sketch. Make as many branch segments as the festival requires, one segment per item to be represented. Make leaf templates for students to use when making leaves to add to the tree or provide paper for students to use to create their own leaf shapes.

For the opening chapter on stamps as windows on the world, the tree could represent all the continents. The leaves can show stamps from the countries in those continents that students have received through their research.

For festivals that feature religious groups (chapters eight, nine, and to some extent five), one branch of the tree can represent that group, while other branches stand for others. For festivals that celebrate national origins (chapters two through five), the branch representing the featured group should be highlighted with color or special texture. For a celebration of African-American history, use "people colors" of black, white, red, brown, and yellow to represent five different tree segments.

The leaves can represent the contributions from individuals of

A Multicultural Tree

Figure 3

various countries, religions, and ethnic groups, either by name or accomplishments. During a Hispanic festival, the tree could stand for the many contributions Hispanics have made to life in the United States: music, art, language, games, religion. During "Una Festa d'Italia," the tree could represent music in the United States, with different branches showing its origins in Africa, Japan, Latin America, and Italy.

The multipurpose multiethnic tree makes a good classroom or library display. In classrooms, students can use the tree as a visual aid in research. They can make small trees for their own records and add leaves to the large tree to commemorate guest speakers, field trips, books and films, and any other relevant experiences.

What's in a Name?
Titles for Activities

What shall we call the festival? Since a name lends character and definition, the following compilation of fifty-six appellations may help give variety, clarity, humor, or extra sparkle to various events within the festival or to the entire celebration itself. Why have a mere seminar when one could be part of a *conversazione?* Why go on a field trip when one could enjoy an *escapade?* And wouldn't a *wayzgoose* be much more fun than an ordinary picnic?

These terms are fun. Some are archaic, and some are poetic. Sometimes they can lend an exotic sound to an ordinary occasion. They are not always appropriate, but wise use of a few of the terms will more than broaden student and teacher vocabularies.

Beano: A noisy good time. (British)
Cabaret: Entertainment provided while participants are at table, eating or drinking.
Carnival: Festivities of unrestrained mirth, originally held before the Lenten fast.
Carol: Joyous song, originally with accompanying dance.
Carousal: Heavy revellry and feasting.
Ceilidh: Informal assembly in which anyone may join with song, music, speech, recitation, or dance. ([Gaelic] Pronounced: KAY–lih)
Charivari: A medley of sounds.
Conversazione: A learned social gathering. (Pronounced: Con–fer–zat–si–o–ne)
Convocation: A calling together in assembly.
Divertissement: A short act or entertainment between longer pieces.
Eisteddfod: Congress of Welsh bards, or any local gathering for music, speech, and communal entertainment. (Pronounced: Ice–ted–fod)
Escapade: An adventure contrary to ordinary activity.
Exhibition: Demonstration of art, literature, or produce.
Expo: A fair, exposition, or explanation, often used to describe huge world fairs.
Extravaganza: Fantastic production of music, literature, film, or other expressive art.
Fair: Periodical gathering of buyers and sellers with attendant entertainments and exhibitions.
Festival: Period of merry-making on a theme, with music, literature, food, books, and jollity.
Fête: Grand scale celebration. (Pronounced: Feht)

(Figure 4) Kids bring a festival to life! This group of seventh graders at the American School in London memorized thirty minutes of lively poetry by Shel Silverstein, Jack Prelutsky, and Ogden Nash to present a cabaret in the library called "The Fabulous Dancing Pants," with dancing, singing, and choreographed movement as main feature in a multicultural *Windows on the World* festival of stamps.

Fête champetre: Outdoor entertainment or country fair, with picnics, dancing, and rustic music. (Pronounced: Feht–sham–peh–tra)

Fiesta: A Spanish or Latin American festival.

Fleidh: An Irish jamboree with music. (Pronounced: flay)

Frolic: A dance or athletic occasion with merriment and pranks.

Gala: A special, often glitzy, occasion. (Pronounced: Gah–la; *not* gay-la)

Gymkhana: Assembly of horse-riders, car-drivers, or other persons with a common sporting goal. (Pronounced: Jim–ka–na)

Happening: All-inclusive event, suggesting planned spontaneity.

High Day: A festal day, sometimes with religious connotations.

Holiday: Originally "holy" day, but now any day on which work is suspended for recreation.

Hullabaloo: Confusing uproar, or much ado about something.

Levée: A dignified reception, often in the afternoon, in honor of a particular person.

Jubilee: A special anniversary or its celebration.

Masque: Dramatic, musical, dance revellries.

Mise en scène: A stage setting, or tableau, with actors and scenery. (Pronounced: Mees–ahn–sehn)

Moot: A gathering, often with opportunity for expression of individual opinions.

Mummery: A gaudy spectacle of a slapstick nature.

Pageant: A parade, procession, or several events in series.

Pleasance: Pleasure, enjoyment; dignified, sophisticated, leisurely entertainment.

Powwow: A Native American term for a special gathering.

Regalement: Sumptuous festivity.

Regatta: Boat race with appended entertainments.

Revel: A riotously merry feast with all the arts on show.

Rêverie: Abstracted musing, daydreaming, or fantastic theory, or a period during which these things occur.

Ridotto: A dancing party. (Pronounced: Ri–DOT–to)

Sardanapalian: A luxurious event in which the old Assyrian king Sardanapalus would be inclined to participate. (Pronounced: Sar–da–na–PAY–li–an)

Saturnalia: An unrestrained period of joy or celebration. (Pronounced: Sa–tur–NAH–li–a)

Soirée: An evening eclectic gathering. (Pronounced: Swa–RAY)

Solemnization: A celebration with ceremony.

Son-et-Lumiere: Entertainment by sound and light, usually in the evening, and often outside. (Pronounced: Saw–neh–loom–ih–eyr)

Spectacular: Sensational, eye-delighting, special event.

Spree: Unrestrained participation in an event.

Symphony: Great unison of sound or effort drawn for many parts.

Tableau: A picture or striking dramatic scene or group. (Pronounced: Ta–BLO)

Tattoo: A military festival, with drums and marching display, often with fireworks and cannon.

Tournament: A competition.

Wake: Merry-making, though its general contemporary usage has come to be limited to funeral vigils.

Wassail: Festive occasion with consumptions of beverage, especially on Twelfth Night and Christmas Eve. From the Old English *wes hal,* "Be of Good Cheer!" a drinking toast.

Wayzgoose: A publisher's or printing firm's annual staff party, usually in summer, with a picnic. (Pronounced: WAYS–goose)

Films for Festivals

Films and videos can form an integral part of any festival, providing entertainment, enrichment, and learning. Since new films are being made rapidly and old films being deleted, rather than list motion pictures for each festival in this book I suggest the following suppliers. They will happily provide catalogues with information arranged according to subject about sale and hire of films, videos, slides, and filmstrips. There is sure to be something to suit most festival themes.

Aims Media Film and Video Catalog
6901 Woodley Avenue
Van Nuys, California 91499

Barr Films
12801 Schabarum Avenue
P.O. 7878
Irwindale, California 91706-7878

BBC Television Distributors (Canada)
Suite 1220 Manulife Centre
55 Bloor Street, W.
Toronto, Ontario M4W 1A5

British Broadcasting Corporation (U.S.A.)
Films Incorporated
733 Green Bay Road
Wilmette, Illinois 60091

BBC Hire Library
The Guild Organization
Oundle Road
Peterborough PE2 9PZ, England

Disney Educational Productions
(Coronet, Distributors)
108 Wilmot Road
Deerfield, Illinois 60015

Educational Media International
(Health and Safety Videos)
25 Boileau Road
London W5 3AL, England

Educational Videos by Educators
Orange County Department of Education
Media Services Unit
P.O. 9050
Costa Mesa, California 92628-9050

Eye Gate Media
3333 Elston Avenue
Chicago, Illinois 60618

Films for Humanities and Sciences
Box 2053
Princeton, New Jersey 08543

Random House Media
Dept. 437
400 Hahn Road
Westminster, Maryland 21157

Society for Visual Education (SVE)
1345 Diversey Parkway
Chicago, Illinois 60614

Sunburst Communications
101 Castleton Street
Pleasantville, New York 10570

Viscom, Ltd.
Parkhall Road Trading Estate
London SE21 8EL, England

Walt Disney Educational Media Company
500 South Buena Vista Street
Burbank, California 91521

Weston Woods
389 New Town Turnpike
Weston, Connecticut 06883

Sources of Inspiration

Cavendish, Richard. *The Great Religions.* New York: Arco, 1980.
Well-illustrated with photographs, paintings, and drawings, this book traces the histories of Judaism, Hinduism, Islam, Christianity, and Buddhism from their origins to the present day and includes bibliographies of founders and leaders.

Cole, Ann et al. *Children and Children Are Children.* Boston: Little, Brown and Company, 1978.
This activity approach to learning explores the cultures of Brazil, France, pre-revolutionary Iran, Japan, Nigeria, and the former Soviet Union, offering games, projects, and recipes.

Cole, W. Owen. *Five Religions in the Twentieth Century.* Amersham, Buckinghamshire, England: Hulton Educational Publications, 1981.
Designed for British high school religious education studies, this book explains Hinduism, Judaism, Christianity, Islam and Sikhism today, giving impressions of the strengths of these faiths the world over.

Gaer, Joseph. *Holidays Around the World.* Boston: Little, Brown, and Company, 1953.
This book for younger readers compares festivals in various cultures, Chinese, Indian, Jewish, American Christian, Muslim, Parsi, Jainist, and concludes that all of the celebrations refect the age-old wish for "peace on earth, good will to human beings."

Harrowven, Jean. *Origins of Festivals and Feasts.* London: Kaye and Ward, 1980.
Harrowven records in a lively manner customs and superstitions and attendant games and recipes with roots in ancient Britain.

Waters, Derek. *A Book of Celebrations.* London: Mills and Boon, 1971.
A British headmaster creates festivals to fill the void between the repetitive cycles of Christmas and Easter in his school, using British history as a basis.

Chapter One

Windows on the World:
A Festival of Stamps

Postage stamps are "windows on the world": collectors can enjoy colors, scenes, and historic figures from at home and abroad; they can be inspired to learn about world politics and geography; and they can deepen their art appreciation through study of stamps. This festival, while focusing on postage stamps, can celebrate various world cultures, foods, music, and art-forms. It gives philatelists a chance to talk about and exhibit their interests and lets non-collectors ponder the hobby of stamp enthusiasts. The festival invites *everyone* to the fun of learning about postal history, early and contemporary stamps, foreign cultures and customs, and stamps as works of art. Stamps can be a springboard for jumping into the excitement of travel, even of the armchair variety. This festival can be held in just one afternoon, or it could cover a few days, depending upon the curricular involvement of geography classes, field trips, and student art participation. As may be seen in the following activity suggestions, this festival probably needs a core of stamp collectors in the school as a nucleus around which to form the program, so it may be worthwhile to organize a stamp club one year then organize the Windows on the World festival the next. Or, if the Festival is classroom contained, the teacher may plan preliminary activities (writing for stamps) early in the year, with Festival activities culminating at the end of the year to gather together the accumulated knowledge.

We will look at free or inexpensive sources for foreign stamps, ideas for a bulletin-board display, and activities inspired by stamp collecting, such as cooking and artwork. This festival is ideal for an in-class thematic study that can unite geography, art, music, language arts, and literature. It is also suitable for library sponsor-

22

At the beginning of every chapter, there is a bookmark to reproduce in your school or library. Prior to printing, add the name of the school, appropriate dates, or an agenda of festival activities in the blank space on the front or on the back. Give them away to everyone in the school community. Give them to bookstores to offer at the cash register. Enlarge the designs to make bulletin boards. Reproduce them on festival handouts, such as programs, activity sheets, admission tickets and bibliographies.

ship, so that several age and grade levels can participate in coordinated events and activities.

A Stamp Display

What You Need

Stamps, domestic and foreign
Stamp Collecting books
Travel Posters
National Geographic or travel magazines
Plain poster paper
Pencils and felt-tip pens
Ruler
Scissors

Since foreign stamps are windows onto another way of living, find a collection of them to display in a case or behind glass in a picture frame. Nearby, arrange books about stamp collecting (see "Sources of Inspiration" on pages 43–46). Balance the display of stamps with a poster from a foreign country (often available free from embassies and consulates, or from travel agents or airlines). Open photo-documen-

Festival of Stamps—A Stamp Display

tary articles about foreign cultures in *National Geographic* issues on the display area. Cut out or print a headline, such as "Stamps Open Windows Onto Other Cultures" to unite the various elements of the display which can involve wall space, tables, shelves, and floor. Another display (see page 24) can be drawn on poster paper or cut from color paper to make a collage. Beneath the heading "Open Windows on the World: Collect Stamps" draw a large stamp. From the list of sources at the end of this chapter choose one particular stamp and enlarge it, or invent a design and enlarge it to the size of a sheet of poster paper. Include the signs for foreign currency and the lines of the postmark. To highlight activities and events, save space on this display to advertise festival fashion shows, food samplings, stamp collectors' displays, and art exhibits.

Organize a Stamp Club

To generate interest in the world of stamps, organize a collectors' club. The adult sponsor need not be a collector but can act as a catalyst to instill enthusiasm in students. Stamps may be placed in albums made especially for that purpose, or they can be stored in small boxes, photo albums, or plastic wallets. Various activities, some of them scholastic others purely intrinsic, can involve members in learning about artists who design stamps, foreign countries represented in members' collections, and artistic ways of displaying stamps. Even if there is no stamp club in your school, you can still hold a stamp festival, encouraging an interest not only in postage stamps but also an awareness of the contacts these stamps can provide with the rest of the world.

Collecting domestic stamps is fun, and some children may be content to stick with United States stamps. Frequent commemorative issues ensure a rich, colorful, and interesting variety, and most post offices sell souvenir T-shirts, postcards, and even refrigerator magnets based on special domestic stamps.

Foreign stamps give a wider dimension. Some people in your community may have foreign relatives or business connections abroad. If so, there may exist a supply of stamps from outside the United States. Another source exists, however, which could provide not only foreign stamps, but also pen pals from several countries— the many international schools dotted around the globe.

Language Arts Assignment: Locating Foreign Stamps

An educationally exciting project for the stamp club (or for a class during the Windows on the World Festival or a geography unit) is to write to a foreign or international school, requesting pen pals and stamps. Each year libraries in American and international schools abroad receive hundreds of packages, magazines, and letters which, if they haven't been put through a franking machine, have been mailed with attractive, collectible stamps from faraway places. These private schools serve the English-speaking, often American, communities in which they are sited. Students' parents may be diplomats, business people, actors, or simply expatriates drawn to life abroad. Many of the schools reflect local culture through a partially native student body.

What to do

Write to "The Librarian" at one of the following schools, stating your interest in stamps. Ask if he or she would be willing to send some interesting ones your way. Offer to pay postage through an international postal order available at your local post office, but don't send U.S. stamps—remember that U.S. postage is not valid for letters sent outside the United States.

Creative writing can be an integral part of the festival if students compose the letters and mail them themselves. The librarian or teacher could, in fact, build an activity center which includes the letter writing project along with some of the activities which follow later in the chapter. The sample letter (page 27) is short and to the point. Some students may wish to enclose a photo of themselves or their school to stimulate a prospective pen pal.

Stamp Sources: Schools in Foreign Countries

Of the hundreds of American or international schools abroad, the following list contains enough to get a stamp search started in Europe, Asia, South America, and Africa. For a complete list of schools affiliated with the European Council of International Schools, write to:

Fieldwork, Ltd.
61 Grays Inn Road
London WC1X 8TL, England

Monroe Junior School
314 Green Valley Road
Deer Park, South Carolina 42997 USA
September 3, 1998

Use school stationery ...

... the date

The Librarian
American International School
Rue Orleans, 49
3900 Lyons, France

be sure to include street numbers ...

Dear Sir or Madam:

if you can, type ...

We are students in the fifth grade interested in collecting postage stamps from foreign countries. We read about your school in the book *Windows on the World,* and wondered if you have any stamps that you could share with us. Since you probably receive lots of mail from many different parts of the world, please keep us in mind and set aside a few interesting stamps for our project. As part of our stamp collecting club we are also finding out about life in foreign countries. The stamps you send us will be displayed in our school library along with our projects. We will be happy to pay for postage.

If there is a student who would like to write to us here at Monroe Junior School to tell us about your school and city, we would like to become pen pals. Thank you very much for helping us.

Yours sincerely,

Anita Craig and Charles Patterson
Grade 5 (II)
(Mr. Greene's Homeroom)

Sign clearly

Ask for the *International Schools Directory* for the current year, which in 1994 lists over 750 schools with comprehensive data about each, and costs about $40. Before sending them a check, you should write to confirm current prices and postage.

This is a partial list of international schools, arranged alphabetically by country within continents or geographical areas, to which you and your students may write.

Europe

The American International School of Vienna
Salmonsdorferstrasse 47
1190 Vienna, Austria

The Antwerp International School
180 Veltwijcklaan
2070 Ekberen/Antwerpen, Belgium

Copenhagen International School
Gammel Kongevej 15
1610 Copenhagen, Denmark

International School of Helsinki
Topeliuksenkatu 22
00250 Helsinki 25, Finland

The American School of Paris
41 Rue Pasteur
92210 Saint-Cloud, France

John F. Kennedy School
Telltower Damm 87–93
1000 Berlin 37, Germany

The American School in London
2/8 Loudoun Road
London NW8 ONP, England

The American Community School of Athens
129 Aghias Paraskevis Street
Ano Halandri
Athens, Greece

The American Overseas School of Rome
Via Cassia 811
00189 Rome, Italy

The American School of Florence
Villa la Tavernule
Via del Carota 16
Florence, Italy

The American School of the Hague
Doornstraat 6
The Hague, Netherlands

Stavanger American School
Nylundsgata 1
4000 Stavanger, Norway

American International School of Lisbon
Apartado 10
2795 Linda-a-Velha, Portugal

The Anglo-American School of Moscow
78 Leninsky
Moscow, Russia

The American School in Aberdeen
Craigton Road
Cults
Aberdeen, Scotland

The International School of Belgrade
Temisvarska 19
11040 Belgrade, Serbia

The American School of Madrid
Apartado 80
Madrid, Spain

The American School of Mallorca
Calle Oratorio 9
Portals Nous
Calvia, Mallorca, Spain

The International School of Geneva
La Chataigneraie
1297 Founex, Switzerland

Africa

The American School of Algiers
5 Chemin Cheikh Bachir
Brahimi, Alger, Algeria

Northside Primary School
POB 397
Gabarone, Botswana

The International School of Kenya
POB 14103
Nairobi, Kenya

American Embassy School
c/o United States Embassy
New Delhi, India

The American School of Novakchott
c/o American Embassy Novakchott, Mauretania
Dept. of State
Washington, DC 20520

Rabat American School
c/o United States Embassy
1 Avenue de Marrakech
Rabat, Morocco

The International School
Mereweather Road
New England
POB 85
Free Town, Sierra Leone

The International School of Moshi
POB 733
Moshi, Tanzania

The International School of Ouagadougou
BP 35
Ouagadougou, Upper Volta

The International School of Lusaka
POB 50121
Ridgeway
Lusaka, Zambia

Asia and the Pacific

St. Joseph International School
85 Yamate-cho
Naka-tu
Yokohama, Japan

The Canadian Academy
3-1 Nagaminedai 2-chome
Nada-ku
Kobe 657, Japan

Singapore American School
60 King's Road
Singapore 10, Malaysia

The International School of Kuala Lumpur
POB 2645
Kuala Lumpur, Malaysia

The International School of Manila
CCPO Box 323
Makati 3117
Metro Manila, Philippines

The Middle East

Bahrain American School
POB 934
Jufair, Bahrain

Walworth Barbour American International School
Rehov Hazorea
Kfar Shmaryahu, Israel

South America

The American School of Rio de Janeiro
Estrada de Gavea 132
22451 Rio de Janeiro, Brazil

The American School of Lima
Apartado 247
Miraflores, Lima 18, Peru

Through stamps, students can get to know another region's games, food, animal life, artwork, and customs, fostering a kinship with and an appreciation for other places and cultures. Through postage stamps and independent research on a particular country, students can present demonstrations of cooking, drawings of national costumes, or pictures of wildlife. Although each nation has its own peculiar characteristics, the following activities can be used for the study of any country.

Travelog

Television programs, even entire channels, are devoted to travel around the world. Students at all levels can produce their own school-based travel show, either on video or live before a festival audience of their peers.

While displaying stamps from a chosen country, a student talks abouts its cities, farms, schools, and natural resources, particularly if they are illustrated on the stamps. Using postcards, travel brochures, souvenirs, or sketches based on research in reference books, the student can not only tell about the country, but also why particular plants, people, geographical features, or other objects appear on the nation's stamps. Students who find difficulty in speaking confidently before an audience can psychologically shift the emphasis from him or her self to the documents and artwork. The library may have slides, filmstrips, or documentary videos to turn the travelog into a lengthy foreign journey. The student can draw a map of the country for display and show where the country is on a globe.

Fashion Show

Using resources such as encyclopedias, magazines, travel brochures, and a history of costume, students can again borrow from the world of television by presenting a historical fashion show, or a Parade of Costumes. Younger students may improvise costumes from a prop box or attic that would give an immediate idea of what people wear (or wore) in other countries or regions. Most people in the West dress similarly today, but some traditional costumes still survive. If the library has a recording of folk or other music from those countries, students can play it for background atmosphere.

There should be a student master of ceremonies for the fashion show to introduce each of the participants as they appear. This Emcee could read a scripted narrative, describing the country and the costume, or the participants themselves can do this.

For an in-class festival, all students can be expected to participate. Besides helping to visualize the costumes of other cultures, dressing up is fun. For a school festival, the fashion show could be limited to two or three students from each class, or it could be made an optional activity for "extra credit" or just for fun.

Some modes of foreign dress will be familiar to students through television, films, and the press; the desert robes of Arabs; the saris of Indian women; the Mao suits of the Chinese; kimonos from Japan; lederhosen from Bavaria and the Tyrol; fur hats from Russia; and sarongs from the Far East. An important part of a festival that compares other cultures to that of America is developing an understanding of *why these modes of dress occurred*—of understanding that robes protect the wearer from hot sun and sand storms; that lederhosen provide rugged apparel for mountain walking and climbing; that though they may appear odd to other cultures, these patterns of dress are logical where they are used.

A Tabletop Costume Parade

What You Need:

Poster board or stiff cardboard
Scissors
Felt (optional)
Glue
Drawing paper
Coloring media (felt-tips, crayons, pencils)
Reference materials (encyclopedias, magazines)

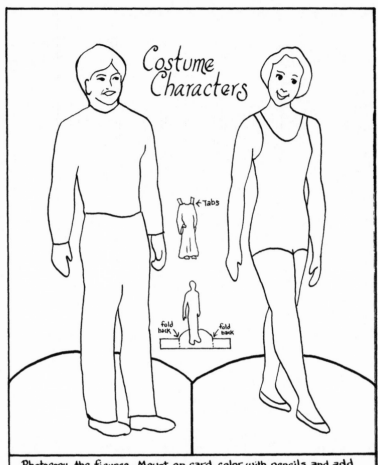

Costume Characters

←Tabs

fold back fold back

Photocopy the figures. Mount on card, color with pencils, and add wings to base which, folded back, will make them stand up. Cut the figures out carefully. Display stamps from around the world with these costume manikins to show how people in different countries and climates dress. Use cut-outs as templates for drawing clothing. Costumes may be glued onto manikins, or hung onto their shoulders by adding fold-back tabs before cutting out.

(Figure 7) Festival of Stamps—Fashion Show

A variation on the live fashion show is models made from stiff cardboard or heavy poster board. Photocopy the characters in figure 7 (page 34), cut them out, and glue to stiff card or poster board. When the glue is dry, cut around the characters, leaving a bit of extra space along the bottom as shown to serve as wings to keep the manikins upright. An optional extra (with extra work involved) is gluing felt, cut to exact size, onto the character, so that the paper costumes will stick to it without adhesive or tabs. Another option is blanking out the faces of the characters in figure 7 so that students can vary hairstyles and racial or ethnic features.

Using available reference sources, students should design national costumes for their two stand-up characters. By tracing lightly around the characters, students can make the costumes to size. If they have not applied felt to their stand-up character, they should make tabs, as illustrated, so the costumes can hang from the shoulders or head.

To help those who will look at the display, students should write a brief description of their work on a 3" × 5" notecard, indicating country, reasons for the development of this type of costume (if known), and whether this type of dress is still worn today.

Storytelling

Combine the fashion show with a story or folktale from a foreign country or its continent or region. Check the library card catalog. There may be no folktales in your collection from, say, Tanzania, so a student may have to generalize with a tale from Africa.

Teachers, librarians, and other adults should read internationally-flavored folktales aloud often during the Festival. They could, for instance, introduce a reading of *Aesop's Fables* by asking how many in the audience have collected stamps from Greece. They can also do some preliminary scouting to find out what countries the students have collected stamps from. If someone has some stamps from Denmark, then a story from Hans Christian Andersen would fit in well with the theme. If someone has collected some of the U.S. state stamps, such as the "My Old Kentucky Home" issue, then how about a story of Daniel Boone?

Student participation can include dramatic readings, theatrical improvisations, retellings in their own words, illustrations through artwork, or character dress-ups.

Treats to Eat

Present some edible treats (figure 8), either as part of an international buffet meal or to accompany the travelog, story, or fashion show. Prepare a simple food item that might be served in a country from which there is a collection of stamps. If possible, bring the ingredients to school and demonstrate how to prepare the dish. To keep it very simple, tie in a special food item with a folk tale or story: for Aesop's Fables, particularly the "Sour Grapes," fable, a bowl of freshly washed grapes; for Hans Christian Andersen, a tin of Danish cookies; for Kentucky, a dish of southern cookies; or for Italy, a tray of home-made pizza.

International Friendship Day

Some or all of the preceding activities could happen on a special day of the festival devoted to world peace and international understanding during which every student presents his or her researched project to the classroom or festival audience. Find out when classes in your school are doing a project on any foreign countries, folklore, or world geography. Tie the stamp festival into the curriculum by holding it as the foreign study unit culminates.

Create a festival atmosphere by making flags of the nations to hang in hallways, classrooms, and the library. Fancy a bit of noise? Dressed in improvised national costumes, younger students can attach their paper flags to broom handles or sticks to carry in an International Friendship Parade around school hallways and campuses as they march to the beat of homemade percussion instruments: dried beans or unpopped popcorn in a clean coffee can with lid or in a washed and dried plastic margarine tub.

What You Need:

Drawing paper
Pencils
Coloring media (crayons, pencils, felt-tips)
Reference books for locating pictures of flags
Washed and Dried Coffee Cans with lids (optional)
Washed and Dried small plastic containers with lids, such as margarine tubs (optional)
Dried beans and unpopped popcorn (optional)
Broomsticks, dowel rods (optional)

(Figure 8) What better food to prepare for International Friendship Day than vegetarian pizza—especially if you have collected stamps from Italy. Food, too, can be a window on the world.

At an activity center in the library or classroom, provide blank paper and drawing tools. Give students instructions for finding pictures of their chosen country's national flag in an encyclopedia or other book. Ask them to make a big color copy the size of the paper. These flags can decorate hallways, the classroom, and the library. Students can also make miniature versions to accompany the Tabletop Costume Parade characters or to include in their stamp collections.

As part of International Friendship Day, invite a foreign resident, a member of an embassy or consul staff, or someone who has travelled or lived abroad to talk about the experience, perhaps showing slides and pictures. Find out if a stamp dealer or collector in the area would bring in some foreign stamps to show to students.

Stamps as Art: Create an Art Gallery

Special stamp issues, both domestic and foreign, can be very attractive. They are often designed by artists with special interpretive skills that can capture a heroic moment, a special pose, or a certain look. Students can make a gallery of stamp art with simple hand-made paper frames. Framed, the stamps will have the added dignity of being seen as "art." The framed stamps will look good with the Tabletop Costume Parade, but they will also be very attractive on their own, on a wall in the classroom or library.

What You Need:

Stamps
Color paper, approximately 3″ × 4″ (7.5 cm × 10 cm)
Scissors (or artist's craft knife with adult supervision)
Old magazines to provide work surface
Cellophane tape or masking tape
Ruler
Pencil

Select an attractively designed stamp that appeals to you. Choose a piece of color paper, perhaps one that coordinates with one of the colors in the stamp. Fold the color paper in half (figure 9) by bringing one of the **short** ends toward the other and creasing in the middle. From this folded piece of paper, make a folder-frame in which to display the stamp.

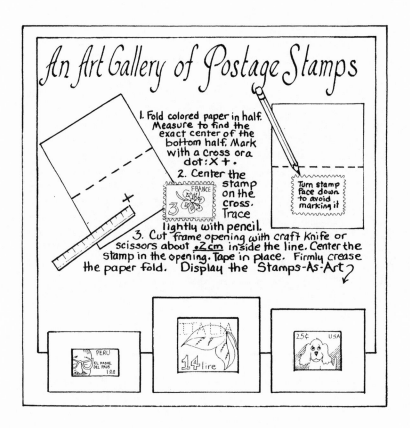

Figure 9

Work on the **inside** of the folder. With the ruler, find the center of the folded sheet by measuring the width and length. Mark the center with a pencil. Place the stamp over the center mark. Try to center it exactly. Lightly trace around the stamp with pencil. Set the stamp aside. With the ruler and pencil, draw lines slightly **inside** the trace lines. This will form the window opening for displaying the stamp.

To open this window frame use either the artist's craft knife (with adult supervision) to cut along the lines, or use scissors. When using a craft knife, place the paper on an old magazine to avoid cutting into the work surface. To use scissors to cut the opening successfully without gouge marks showing, place the frame folder open on the desk. Start the cut by placing the point of the scissors in the center of the window box. Gently pull the paper up toward the scissors: this pressure will cause the paper to pull up around the scissors, so use gentle exertion. When the scissors have pierced the paper, cut as normal until the window frame has been thoroughly opened.

Place the stamp behind the open window. When the stamp is centered to your satisfaction, use a small piece of tape to hold it in position. Pin these folder frames on the wall to make an interesting display. Avoid haphazard arrangements. Try putting the filled folder frames along a straight line formed by stretching a length of string between two pins placed at equal distance from the floor. Create a harmonious display by confining the folder frames to a rectangular area formed by several horizontal lines, one over the other, limited to a set length.

Design a Stamp

Organize a competition to find new stamp designs. If the project is not confined to one classroom or to one grade, the competition should be arranged by age levels, with "winners" at every category. You can establish certain rules, asking all entries to be drawn on standard sized paper (such as 2' × 4', a piece of typing paper, or a 3" × 5" card) to make the display easier to mount and judge, or you may let each contributor choose the size. Students may also select the medium: watercolor, black ink, tempera, color pencil. Bear in mind that black ink designs reproduce most easily and with greatest success on photocopy machines. Therefore, "all entries in black and white only" would be a sensible rule.

Here are some ideas to give the Design a Stamp competition focus:

1. Design a commemorative stamp for the United States, using a holiday, historic event, invention, plant, bird, animal, person, or building as your theme.
2. Design a stamp for a foreign country of your choice, using one of that country's finest features or achievements as the theme.
3. Design a stamp to be used for interplanetary delivery.
4. Design an "in-house" stamp to be placed on all internal mail: notes from teachers to students, notes from the librarian, memos from the office.

Award appropriate prizes for the best entries, based on creativity and skill. Some possibilities: frame winning entries for permanent display in the school; give small prizes, such as a collection of stamps, a book, vouchers for a book or school supplies; art materials; a visit to an exhibition, museum, or film. Provide ribbons or certificates for all winners and runners up, or be generous—give them to all entries!

Build a Model

Add interest to a display of international stamps by making models of foreign buildings and villages based on photographs in encyclopedias, travel and publicity brochures, and books. Use found items, such as grocery containers, cardboard boxes, twigs and stones, cloth, and paper. Stamps from the British Isles might inspire the assembly of a cardboard castle. Stamps from India could begin the building of a Hindu temple or a mosque. Stamps from Thailand could stimulate the construction of a Buddhist temple, a spirit house, or a house on stilts. What kinds of found materials could a student use to build Moscow's St. Basil's Cathedral to accompany a display of Russian stamps? (see pages 85, 210, 340)

For display, students should identify their models with a short description on a card that includes name of the building, country of origin, materials it might be made from in real life, age of the original building, and the student's name.

Visit a Post Office

Organize student visits to the local post office. You may be able to get a guided tour that will explain how letters are delivered with automated processing machines, computerized dispatchers, and a huge fleet of trucks, trains, and planes. Prepare students beforehand by reading and learning about the postal system. Students should go armed with questions: Who invented the postage stamp? Who invented the zip code system? How much does a post-office box cost? How long does it take a letter to travel? How often are new commemorative stamps issued? Does mail ever get lost? If a field trip isn't feasible, invite a postal carrier to talk to students about his or her job.

Sources of Inspiration

Bateman, Robert. *The How and Why Wonder Book of Stamps.* London: Transworld Publishers, 1970.
From the British beginnings of the modern world-wide postal system to the commemorative stamps of today, this book gives an overview of the world of the mail.

Cabeen, Richard M. *Standard Handbook of Stamp Collection,* 3rd ed. New York: Harper and Row, 1979.
This comprehensive reference book is an excellent work for the serious collector or for a student who wants to learn more about definitive stamps up to the late 1970's.

Evans, Donald. *The World of Donald Evans.* New York: Harlin Quist, 1980.
The artist creates postage stamps as well as a geography, history, and culture for imaginary countries.

Felix, Ervin J. *Identify Your Stamps.* Racine, Wisconsin: Whitman Publishing, 1967.
Felix shows how stamps portray a vast era of civilization and offers extensive historical and comparative information.

Forster, R. K. *World Postmarks.* London: Batsford, 1973.
From the earliest known "postal marks" 5000 years ago in Egypt to English ones in 1661 to the millions today around the world, this book traces many things to be discovered in collecting not just stamps, but actual postmarks.

Gibbons, Stanley. *Stamps of the World.* London: Stanley Gibbons Publications, 1983.
This detailed, illustrated guide for collectors includes the history of changes of paper, perforation, shade, and watermarks.

Hobson, Burton. *Getting Started in Stamp Collecting.* New York: Sterling, 1963.
Find out how and where to buy or trade for the most interesting stamps—airmails, first day covers, blocks, foreign.

Melville, F. *Stamp Collecting.* London: English Universities Press, 1963.
Enter a journey of discovery by following the directions in this hobbyist's manual.

New, Anthony B. *The Observer's Book of Postage Stamps.* London: F. W. Warne, 1977.
Learn how stamps are printed in a press after reading the illustrated history of how stamps came to be used in their modern form.

Olcheski, Bill. *One Hundred Trivia Quizzes for Stamp Collectors.* State College, Pennsylvania: American Philatelic Society, 1982.
Fun, games, and teasers for the well-immersed philatelist show how engrossing stamp collecting can be.

Renfield, Fred. *Commemorative Stamps of the U.S.A.* New York: Crowell, 1956.
This handy small volume illustrates all United States "picture stamps" up to the mid-'50's and gives a history of the events they illustrate.

Scheele, Carl H. *A Short History of the Mail Service.* Washington, D.C.: Smithsonian Institution, 1970.
Through rain, hail, snow, sleet and other discomforts, the mail must go through! This history reveals how rural free delivery, among other postal things, came to be a vital part of American life.

Sutton, R. J. *The Stamp Collectors Encyclopedia,* 6th rev. ed. New York: Philosophical Library, 1959.
Serious collectors will enjoy this volume, and it proves a reliable source of identification and history for students who happen to come across old stamps.

Torbert, Floyd. *Postmen the World Over.* New York: Hastings House, 1966.
Torbert reveals how mail service has developed from early to modern times.

Villiard, Paul. *Collecting Stamps.* New York: New American Library, 1974.
This young person's guide to the hobby tells how to mount or display stamps, how to know if stamps are worth money, and how to swap with friends.

Williams, Leon Norman. *Scott's Guide to Stamp Collecting.* New York: Simon and Schuster, 1963.
This excellent handbook with glossary shows how where to collect and how to locate stamp clubs.

Young, Walter, *Stamp Collecting, A to Z.* San Diego: A. S. Barnes, 1981.
Authoritative, practical philatelic information with black and white illustrations, telling the story of stamps, how to lay out an album, how to preserve stamps, and why some stamps are rare.

Nevin, David. *The Expressmen.* New York: Time-Life, 1974.
Thrill to the excitement of the pony express as it moved the mail in the pioneer West.

Stamp Collectors' Magazines

American Philatelist. American Philatelic Society, Inc., Box 800, State College, Pennsylvania 16801.
This monthly, indexed magazine, with a circulation of over 45,000, contains good book reviews to keep libraries abreast of what's new in the field.

Canadian Stamp News. McLaren Publications, Ltd., 1567 Sedlescomb Drive, Mississauga, Ontario L4X 1MS, Canada.
Published twice a month, this informative news magazine has articles about rare stamp prices, display, and fairs.

Stamp Collector. Van Dahl Publications, 520 E. First Street, Albany, Oregon 97321.
This weekly magazine has 25,000 collectors on its mailing list and offers news about stamp artists, collecting rarities, auctions and stamp fairs, and advertisements from stamp dealers that would be of interest to students.

Stamp Fun. Benjamin Franklin Stamp Club, Box 746, Washington, D.C. 20044.
Since this promotional magazine is free, and appears eight times a year, it makes sense to get in touch for assistance in aiding and abetting the stamp club at school.

Stamp Monthly. Stanley Gibbons Magazines, 391 The Strand, London WC2R 0LX, England.
With over 50,000 regular readers, this monthly magazine features most of what there is to know about British and European stamp collecting.

Stamp News. Sterling Street, Dubbo, New South Wales 2830, Australia.
14,500 readers, mostly Australian, read this stamp collectors news magazine from down under, and it is worth buying just to capture the international flavor of stamp enthusiasts from another part of the world.

World Stamps. Solway Publications, 4 Buccleuch Street, Dumfries, Scotland.
This magazine has pre-publication reviews of stamp books along with good photographs of stamps and on annual index.

For International Activities

African Children's Games for American Children. Ubana, Illinois: University of Illinois Press, 1975.
The perfect accompaniment to a folktale on Friendship Day, this book offers illustrated, concisely-written details of games to play.

Arnold, Arnold. *The World Book of Children's Games.* New York: World Publishing, 1972.
Highlight "International Friendship Day" with games from around the world, which are well-explained with illustrations and text in this book.

Arnott, Kathleen. *African Myths and Legends.* New York: Henry Walck, 1963.
Another good source for tales of mighty animals, of Anansi, and of the wise people of Africa.

Courlander, Harold. *The King's Drum and Other African Stories.* New York: Harcourt Brace Jovanovich, 1962.
While not every African country is represented, there are exciting tales here, full of music, heart, and trickery.

Dobler, Lavinia. *Customs and Holidays Around the World.* New York: Fleet Press, 1968.

This is a good source of inspiration for bringing international ambience to a festival. Use it to find dances, foods, games, costume, and decoration.

Johnson, Lois. *Happy New Year Around the World.* Chicago: Rand McNally, 1963.

Find out how people across the globe ring in the New Year and borrow ideas for celebrations any time.

McWhirter, Mary Esther. *Games Enjoyed by Children Around the World.* Philadelphia: American Friends Service Committee, 1970.

East to follow instructions make this illustrated book a welcome addition to any elementary school program.

Chapter Two

First on the Land: A Festival of Native Americans

When Europeans began settlements along the eastern shores of America, first in a trickle, then in an undammable flood, the native inhabitants of the continent had long maintained a harmonious relationship with the land. Living in tribes and villages throughout the vast country, with diverse cultures, habits, and languages, these people who came to be known as Indians had to give up their homes and hunting grounds to the ever-increasing white usurpers. Often, friendships between the two races were formed, but more frequently the European colonists and the Native Americans waged war. Eventually, the Indians gave way to the new order, settling on reservations in the West, and dreaming of the old days of myth and legend.

Most states had proud native cultures, though few traces may remain today. This festival honors the original inhabitants of the North American continent, and may, in a general way, give an overview of the diversity of Indian life. On the other hand, the festival organizers may wish to focus on local Native American life, using entirely regional resources, ar-

47

Native American Bookmark

tifacts, and personnel. It is not uncommon even today to uncover flint arrow heads in the dry streambeds of the Dakotas or in the fertile farmlands of the Tennessee Cumberland plateau. Festivals centered on local tribes can make use of these instruments of the past to make days gone by more vivid and more immediate.

Perhaps the abundance of print material on Native Americans reflects a latter-day awakening of consciousness, an emergent wish to honor those who once ruled the virgin American forests and plains. Ample resources are available for a festival on specific tribes. Catalogues will reveal recordings of Indian chant and dance, block-buster films and little-known documentaries, books, magazine articles, charts, maps, and statistics. Many writers have portrayed Native Americans sympathetically in fiction, and there is a wide choice of Indian legends and tales in print.

A Native American festival could be tied into curricular studies, or it may serve to highlight an area that is not very well covered by the school's course offerings. It could be held prior to the Thanksgiving holiday in November, since many children like to re-enact that first thanksgiving when the English settlers and the local Indians shared a meal. Other timely occasions include commemoration of the Cherokee Trail of Tears through Tennessee and Arkansas in the early 19th century, or the Battle of Little Bighorn near the beginning of the 20th. Anytime, in fact, is suitable to remember the heritage of the original Americans.

The Festival should incorporate student art projects, dramatic readings, guest speakers, films, storytelling, and food to create a broader appreciation for the past and deeper resolutions for the future.

Displays to Reflect Tribal Differences

What You Need:

Books about Native American culture
Paper
Drawing Materials
   Pencil for sketching
   Black felt-tip pens
   Colored felt-tips (optional)
Scissors

Identify one item of Native American craft or art—a basket, spear, feathered bonnet, ceremonial pipe—to serve as both theme of the festival display board and a logo for reproduction on the brochure of events. Study photographs and drawings from books in the "Sources of Inspiration" at the end of this chapter. From the Northwest come magnificent totem poles. From the Southwest are kachinas and turquoise and silver jewelry. Further south, from the Mexican peninsula, come Aztec and Mayan statuary. In Florida, the Seminoles make colorful woven objects. In the southern Appalachians, the Cherokee weave split oak baskets and make shirts of hide. Select an example of Native American art and enlarge it to make a bulletin board. Through art projects and other activities, Festival participants will realize that the diversity of native American culture can not be summed up by one logo: for a totem pole would not represent tribes from outside the Pacific Northwest, and a kachina would not make sense to a Sioux.

By enlarging the Festival Bookmark at the beginning of this chapter, a bulletin display board can conglomerate two or more items associated particularly with native Americans. Each item, such as the kachina and the totem pole, the wigwams and the adobe pueblo, can be drawn separately and attached to the display to make a collage, either in black and white or in color. Black and white can be a powerful medium, since with crosshatching, it can be made to resemble old copperplate etching. Color can be added in the border, which in this instance was borrowed from the belts and pottery designs of the tribes in New Mexico.

First, make a sketchy outline in pencil of the items to be drawn, either chosen from the bookmark or from books. Make adjustments to the drawing in the pencil stage. Then go over the outline with felt-tips. Cut out the drawing. If there is only one, attach it to the board with the title of the Festival (use stencils to make cut-out lettering or write the title on another piece of paper), and put up a border design. When creating the collage with two or more drawings, spread them out on the floor in their approximate positions before pinning them individually to the board.

Totem Poles and Kachinas: An Art Project

What You Need:

Books and Photographs of Native American Art and Crafts
Cardboard tubes from:
   paper towels
   toilet paper
   kitchen foil and plastic wrap
Corrugated cardboard boxes
Plaster-impregnated cloth (from art supply shop) or
   Papier Mâché (newspaper, wallpaper paste)
Scissors
Craft Knives
Pencils
Tempera paints
Brushes
Wooden beads, fake fur, feathers (for kachina)
Thread or string (for attaching beads)
Newspapers to cover work surface

No single art form will represent all the Native American tribes, so the festival organizer and art teacher will decide upon one or two projects for the Festival. The following totem pole and kachina projects will take several art periods to complete, so if they are to be on display during the Festival, they will need to be started long in advance.

First, ask students to save and collect cardboard tubes. Any sizes will do, from toilet paper rolls to carpet tubes. Second, familiarize the students with Indian design and style through sharing of books and professionally printed artwork and photographs of totem poles and kachinas. Discuss the symbolism, function, and design of the totem poles, and ask students to find out the purpose of kachina figures.

Third, students should decide whether they want to make a totem pole or a kachina (figure 11), and draw several designs on paper to use as guides when beginning the modelling project. These designs may be reworked later in felt-tip pen for wall-mounted displays of graphic art and make an ideal background for the completed sculptures.

What to Do: Totem Poles

Using the cardboard tubes, either singly or taped together, we will form the bodies of the totem poles. A totem pole can be make quite

(Figure 10) Students make totem poles and kachinas from found materials and papier mâché. In photograph one, the framework for a totem pole has been made from cardboard tubes and boxes. In the second photo, boys add a layer of papier mâché. In the third photograph, a student begins to paint her kachina. The final photograph shows a display of colorful kachinas and totem poles in front of a butcher paper mural painted with sponges and brushes by fifth graders.

tall by locking several tubes together with protruding wings, noses, and arms slotted for connecting the segments together (figure 12, section 3). Exceptionally tall totem poles will need to have large foot projections and may even require a base on which to secure the feet. Refer to the diagrams and photographs for step-by-step procedures.

What to Do: Kachinas

Basically, each kachina will need two toilet roll cardboard tubes for the legs, and half a tube for the head. Tubes and/or rolled newspaper may be used for the arms (figure 10). To ensure that they will stand up without leaning or falling, students will need to make a back brace, disguising it as part of the kachina's outfit. Refer to the illustrations for complete instructions (figure 13).

(Figure 11) Hopi kachinas are interesting to study during a Festival of Native Americans. These, collected by Montgomery County, Maryland, teacher Wade Coplen, are from pueblos in New Mexico.

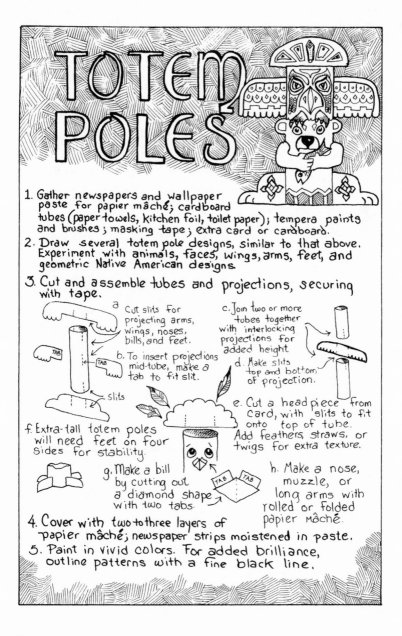

TOTEM POLES

1. Gather newspapers and wallpaper paste for papier mâché; cardboard tubes (paper towels, kitchen foil, toilet paper); tempera paints and brushes; masking tape; extra card or cardboard.

2. Draw several totem pole designs, similar to that above. Experiment with animals, faces, wings, arms, feet, and geometric Native American designs.

3. Cut and assemble tubes and projections, securing with tape.

   a. Cut slits for projecting arms, wings, noses, bills, and feet.

   b. To insert projections mid-tube, make a tab to fit slit.

   c. Join two or more tubes together with interlocking projections for added height.

   d. Make slits top and bottom of projection.

   e. Cut a headpiece from card, with slits to fit onto top of tube. Add feathers, straws, or twigs for extra texture.

   f. Extra-tall totem poles will need feet on four sides for stability.

   g. Make a bill by cutting out a diamond shape with two tabs.

   h. Make a nose, muzzle, or long arms with rolled or folded papier mâché.

4. Cover with two to three layers of papier mâché; newspaper strips moistened in paste.

5. Paint in vivid colors. For added brilliance, outline patterns with a fine black line.

Figure 12

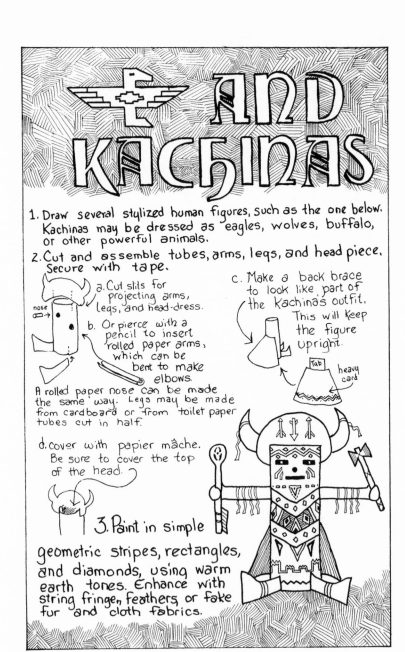

⟨eagle⟩ AND KACHINAS

1. Draw several stylized human figures, such as the one below. Kachinas may be dressed as eagles, wolves, buffalo, or other powerful animals.

2. Cut and assemble tubes, arms, legs, and head piece. Secure with tape.

   a. Cut slits for projecting arms, legs, and head-dress.

   nose →

   b. Or pierce with a pencil to insert rolled paper arms, which can be bent to make elbows.

   A rolled paper nose can be made the same way. Legs may be made from cardboard or from toilet paper tubes cut in half.

   c. Make a back brace to look like part of the Kachina's outfit. This will keep the figure upright.

   Tab   heavy card

   d. cover with papier mâché. Be sure to cover the top of the head.

3. Paint in simple geometric stripes, rectangles, and diamonds, using warm earth tones. Enhance with string fringe, feathers, or fake fur and cloth fabrics.

Figure 13

Ceremonial Masks: An Art Project

What You Need:

Books of pictures for reference (see Sources of Inspiration, page 67)
White art-room paper
Cardboard and string (for *tablitas*)
Pencils
Tempera paints
Brushes
Black felt-tip pens
Scissors
Glue
Staples and staple gun
Paper clips

Ceremonial masks form integral parts of rituals, dances, and games among many Native American tribal groups. The Hopi wear head-dresses, called *tablitas*, in dances to celebrate feast days in pueblos of the Southwest. Zunis celebrate a forty-nine day Shalako festival to invoke blessings on the earth and wear bird masks during dances to represent the messengers of the rain. Plains dwellers wear buffalo masks during hunt dances, just as eastern Iroquois wear grotesque wooden masks with intentionally humorous crooked features during healing rituals of the False Face Society. Students can make wearable paper masks based on authentic designs. The masks make a very attractive wall display. They can also be used in dramatizations of Native American myths and legends, examples of which can be found in "Sources of Inspiration" on page 70.

What to Do

Discuss the original purposes of masks and share pictures from reference sources. Read a Native American legend aloud or rewrite it as a play with speaking parts for every student. Determine roles by writing the names of all the characters on a piece of paper, inventing some if necessary, or by dividing characters into two people to make sure everyone has a part. Students then choose one from a hat. To present the dramatized story as part of the festival, students will make a mask to represent their randomly selected characters. Of course, it isn't necessary to act out a play to make a mask. Students can decide whom they wish to represent (an animal or spirit character: deer, eagle, buffalo; the wind, thunder, sun) based on study of the reference pictures. In fact, once the masks are completed, they themselves could inspire the students to make up their own dramas, combining myths, legends, and stories creatively.

The adult should make templates for the masks by enlarging the sample in figure 14. Basically, the mask is a large circle with a belt extending from each side. Make the belt as long as the sheet of paper, for each artist will shorten it to fit his or her own head by stapling and gluing the ends together when the project is finished. Students can trace around the templates on their own sheets of paper. Students should adjust the location of the eyes and mouth to fit their own faces. Various eye and mouth shapes can be drawn in and cut out, depending upon the type of mask being designed. Almond shaped eyes look calm. Round eyes can express fright or a state of alertness. A round mouth can express exclamation or surprise, while a stylized rectangular mouth can emulate that of a kachina. The cut-out shape is not as important, however, as the designs to be drawn on and painted in the next stage.

When the templates have been traced and the eyes and mouths drawn on, students should cut the two slits, top and bottom. These will be folded back, stapled, and glued to make the mask three dimensional before drawing on the design.

When the student has determined who the mask is going to represent, an appropriate nose piece can be drawn. The teacher can provide several templates, but students should be encouraged to develop their own. Noses can be beakish, cylindrical, or snout-like, depending upon the way the paper is cut and folded. Experimentation will achieve remarkable results! Glue and staple the nose onto the mask.

Now the mask is ready for its design. Students should practice first on a separate piece of paper. Emphasize that strong, bold lines will work best as a basis for the mask, though some details may be added. When the design is ready, draw it lightly on the mask. Don't worry about mistakes, for they will be painted over. Choose a native American pattern to make a repetitive design on the belt too.

Paint in the details, one color at a time, to create sharply defined edges. Paint large areas first, smaller areas last. When the colors are completed, use either a thin brush with black tempera or a black felt-tip pen to outline the color areas. This makes the mask even bolder.

If the masks are going to be displayed on a wall, don't glue or staple the belt together. To wear the mask and display it when not in use, attach the ends of the belt with paper clips to fit the head.

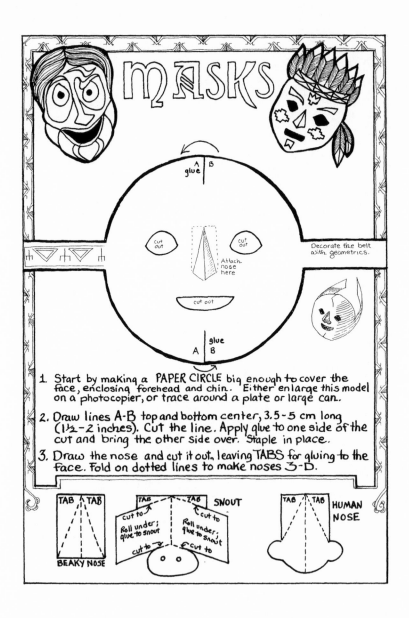

MASKS

Decorate the belt with geometrics.

1. Start by making a **PAPER CIRCLE** big enough to cover the face, enclosing forehead and chin. Either enlarge this model on a photocopier, or trace around a plate or large can.

2. Draw lines A-B top and bottom center, 3.5-5 cm long (1½-2 inches). Cut the line. Apply glue to one side of the cut and bring the other side over. Staple in place.

3. Draw the nose and cut it out, leaving **TABS** for gluing to the face. Fold on dotted lines to make noses 3-D.

Figure 14

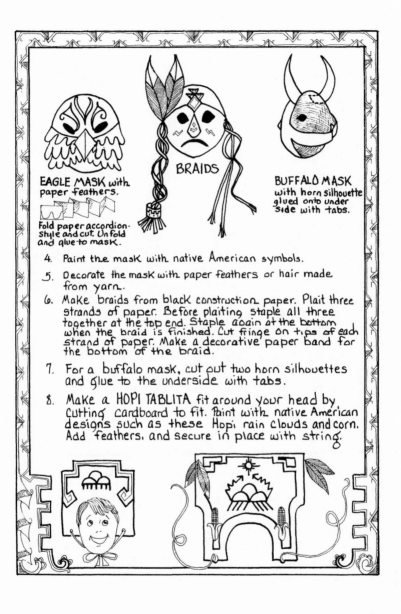

EAGLE MASK with paper feathers.

Fold paper accordion-style and cut. Unfold and glue to mask.

BRAIDS

BUFFALO MASK with horn silhouette glued onto under side with tabs.

4. Paint the mask with native American symbols.

5. Decorate the mask with paper feathers or hair made from yarn.

6. Make braids from black construction paper. Plait three strands of paper. Before plaiting staple all three together at the top end. Staple again at the bottom when the braid is finished. Cut fringe on tips of each strand of paper. Make a decorative paper band for the bottom of the braid.

7. For a buffalo mask, cut out two horn silhouettes and glue to the underside with tabs.

8. Make a HOPI TABLITA fit around your head by cutting cardboard to fit. Paint with native American designs such as these Hopi rain clouds and corn. Add feathers, and secure in place with string.

Figure 14 (cont'd)

Guest Speakers: Native Americans and Historians

If you live near a Native American village or reservation, invite a tribal elder, a chief, or other representative of the tribe to speak during the festival. The speaker may want to talk about the history of his or her own people, prospects for the future, or Native Americans in general. He or she may be able to bring along costumes, jewelry, weapons, and musical instruments to illustrate the speech. Ideally, the speech should be held campfire-style in the classroom, with students seated on the floor.

If there are no Native American speakers nearby, try to find a knowledgeable librarian, a university historian, or a local collector of arrowheads. These might even lead to a successful field trip to an area rich in arrowheads and other artifacts.

To give students practice in oral communication, encourage teachers to assign research projects in conjunction with the festival that could form short public seminars or lectures. Try these for topics:

Native Americans of This Area (or city, or county, or state)
Arrowheads and/or Other Artifacts I Have Found
Tribes of the Plains (or East Coast, or other area)
The Buffalo (or other animal important to native culture)
The Wigwam (or pueblo, or bark shelter)

These and other topics could be shared by students of different age and grade levels for oral presentation in class and in public festival gatherings.

Creative Writing: Legends and Stories

Publish a **festival magazine** to stimulate students' creative writing. During classroom or library story sessions with lower and middle schoolers, read native American myths and legends or the "Hiawatha" epic. Discuss the religion of the Native Americans, their creation myths, and ceremonies. Encourage students to read Native American legends, poetry, and fiction, first, simply to learn and to enjoy, secondly, to be able to tell about their reading in their own words (oral or written book report), and finally, to be able to create literature of their own. Use the sources at the end of this chapter and sources available in your school for selecting readings.

Offer small prizes, such as books, to winning essays, stories, and articles: fictitious accounts of individual Native Americans in their own region; histories or frontier battles from the point of view of the native inhabitants whose homes, hunting grounds, and livelihoods were at stake; poems; annotated bibliographies of available books, set in the framework of "The Ten Best Books in our Library about Native Americans." Another interesting project for a group of middle or high school students is the dramatization of a novel or legend, beginning with improvisations, following up with a narrative and script, and ending with a rehearsed reading or performance. A good vehicle for group dramatic interpretation is the poem "Hiawatha."

Younger students can be given themes upon which to write poetry or stories from the Native American point of view, such as:

My first lesson in horse riding
The coming of the white man
Our house of bark
My father's wigwam
The buffalo hunt

In addition to publishing the winning entries, display the written work on walls or tables to make it an integral part of the festival. Combine written work with art and books for a textured display.

Who will judge the written work? If the project becomes part of classroom assignments or enrichment, then individual teachers can make selections. If the creative writing project is open to all by choice and not by assignment, then the festival organizer should form a small team of judges who are willing to spend the time necessary.

And publication? If funds allow, the magazine could be printed professionally, but with desktop publishing available in most schools, a journalism class, a keyboarding class, or even the library staff could take on the project, making masters for the photocopy machine.

What's in a place name? Do local towns and cities, rivers and natural features carry centuries-old Native American names? Provide reference sources so that students can find names of towns, counties, mountain ranges, or other sites that are called by their original names. Draw a large mural map of your region or state and place it on an accessible wall so that new discoveries may be added as they are found. Students can carry this project a step further by writing short histories of Native American place names on note cards. Attach the note cards to the side of the map and connect them to the actual map location with a string or color yarn. Broaden the scope by working on a large mural map of the entire United States. Use different colors of yarn to represent different tribal contributions to place names today.

Create a competition to accompany the place-name map. Offer small prizes (extra credit in a social studies unit; an edible treat; a book) to the first complete worksheet turned in, or to the first correct answers pulled from a hat, or to the most comprehensive answers to questions such as:

1. Name five U.S. Rivers that still are known by Native American names.
2. Name five U.S. states that bear Native American names.
3. Name twenty U.S. towns that have Native American names.
4. Which states have the most Native American place names? Why?
5. Which tribes have contributed the most place names to American sites?

Native American Foods: Corn

From the new world to the old, Native American foods have enriched the diets of many world cultures. Native Americans introduced British settlers to maize, or corn. Many popular American dishes come from this versatile food, including cornbread, popcorn, tortilla chips, and grits. To celebrate this contribution to world culinary culture, demonstrate some of the uses of corn, either through cooking demonstrations during the festival or through making samples of food available during events.

A Cornbread Contest

There are many recipes for this typical southern and mid-western bread, all of them derived from a Native American foodsource. Some cornbread recipes are based on water, while others use milk and egg. Some cooks use sugar, while others add spicy chilis. A "Cornbread Contest" will reveal many different variations on the theme, from spoonbread to hoe-cakes. A schoolwide baking contest needs a few rules: (1) Anyone may enter; (2) All entries must be accompanied by the recipe (including ingredients and procedures), written clearly on paper; (3) All entries must be prepared by the student. Publish a selection of the recipes at the end of the festival as part of the literary magazine.

Establish one day for the event. All entries should be brought to a central location, such as the library. Teachers should be available to help arrange the entries and the recipes. Select a team of tasters/ judges to include students and teachers. Set a time for a judging based on appearance, texture, and taste. Give prizes for different age levels and different types of bread (sweet, spicy, traditional, unusually shaped) so that as many entrants as possible can go home with a prize (which can be a certificate, a ribbon, or another token: set of measuring cups, a cookbook). Ask all contestants to collect their entries for a cornbread feast in their classrooms at the end of the day.

We have chosen cornbread as a festival food because of the readily available ingredients and ease of baking, but festival organizers could well expand into a more complete celebration of Native American foods. The black walnut, the tomato, the peanut, several varieties of bean (tepary), the turkey, melons and squashes, sunflowers, tomatillos (or ground cherries), and dandelions originated in the New World and were cultivated, cooked, and eaten before the arrival of Columbus. A Native American Feast, then, would offer samples of foods other than corn, and an energetic festival organizer could organize cooking competitions on a grand scale.

Festival Recipe: Buttermilk Corn Bread

This basic cornbread recipe provides a tasty treat at the end of a storytelling session or the conclusion of an art project. It also makes a good demonstration dish for making with students.

What You Need:

1 cup yellow or white cornmeal
1/3 cup flour
1 tsp baking powder
1/2 tsp salt
1/4 tsp soda
1 beaten egg
1 cup buttermilk

3–4 tbsp butter or olive oil
Mixing bowls
Spoons
Baking pan or cast-iron skillet

Preheat oven to 400° F.

Place baking pan in oven to preheat. In this pan, melt the butter or heat the oil: do *not* allow it to smoke.

Combine all the dry ingredients in a bowl and mix well. Add the egg and milk, mixing ingredients well. Take the baking pan from the oven and tilt so that the surface is coated with butter or oil. Pour hot liquid into the cornbread batter and stir.

Pour cornbread batter into the baking pan and bake for 20–25 minutes or until golden brown. Serve hot or cold. (Optional recipe additions: 1 tbsp honey, or 1/3 cup whole kernel corn, or 1/2 cup grated Cheddar cheese, or 1/4 cup chopped green pepper)

Trips to Take

Schools in the United States Southwest are lucky in that Native American sites are usually within comfortable driving distance: taking students to learn firsthand about ancient cultures is relatively easy. Most states, however, have sites of importance to the discovery of pre-Columbian civilization. Some sites include ancient ceremonial or burial mounds, while others consist of archeological digs, historic salt licks, or trading route crossroads.

Hints for Successful Outings

1. Become knowledgeable about local Native American sites and lead an excursion of students. Brief them beforehand about the archeology and history. If there are collections of Indian artifacts in a local museum, go there. Focus the visit by requiring detailed sketches of chosen objects, such as costumes, weaponry, agricultural tools, or jewelry. The museum may provide a student activity sheet or study guide: if not, make one yourself prior to the trip to help students get more from the experience.
2. If there is a reservation nearby, find out about arranging a visit. Small numbers might be much more welcome than busloads of students, so a personalized visit by some school journalists or history students might be more worthwhile than wholescale tourism. These students could

report their discoveries in the school paper or in a public seminar during the festival, and include a display of photographs.

3. Most people enjoy make-believe, but smaller children really get into it. Even students up to seventh grade level can participate in this activity with a great deal of sophistication. Take students on a picnic in the woods, having divided them into two groups—white settlers and native inhabitants. One set of teachers can head one group, while another set takes the rest. Dress in improvised costumes. Each group should establish its territory, its village life, its hunting ground or farm. Points to improvise: how do the two groups get along? What happens if the European settlers encroach upon the natives' hunting ground? How does the tribe react if the Europeans suffer crop failure and have no food? Is it necessary to use force to get one's way? The make-believe sojourn could finish on a high note with foods that early pioneers and Native Americans might have shared: vegetables, wholegrain bread, cornbread, milk, berries, apples, and fowl such as turkey or duck. Follow-up back in the classroom with discussions about territorial possession, sharing space, assimilation of minorities into the majority culture, and safe-guarding minority rights.

4. Schools within visiting distance of Cherokee, North Carolina, high in the Smokey Mountains National Park, can watch the outdoor perfor- mance of "Unto These Hills," the story of the Trail of Tears and that band of the tribe which hid in the mountains, avoiding deportation across the Mississippi. For information about tickets and accommoda- tion contact:

The Cherokee Historical Association
Cherokee, North Carolina 28719
(Telephone 704-497-9195)

Also ask for information about the Museum of the Cherokee Indian and the Oconaluftee Indian Village, a recreation of a 1750's Chero- kee town with live demonstrations and tours of crafts and skills.

Plays to Perform

For many, a rich vein of imagination is empowered by romantic legends of the American West. Novels, films, and television series have embellished the stories of European expansion into Native American territory with wagon trains winding across tallgrass prairies, cowboys driving herds through dusty gulches, and sheriffs taming the rough and rowdy elements around crossroads settlements. Where do the natives fit into this picture? Are they "good guys"?

With the help of the drama teacher, encourage improvisations on the theme of the romantic Old West. From collections of Indian myths and legends, select short stories to read aloud dramatically. Rearrange one of the stories as a readers' theater presentation. Use the art project masks during the presentation, either for characterizations or set decoration. From history books, choose a disagreement between Native Americans and white settlers and, with some research, present it as a courtroom trial with arguments for and against both sides. End it with a pronouncement from the "judge."

There are also some good plays designed for stage performance that would provide a fitting high point for the festival. Sufficient preparation would have to be given, of course, to casting, rehearsals, set design, and publicity prior to the festival: organizers will need to discuss this months in advance with the drama department. Rehearsed public readings of the plays can eliminate much of the preparation, allowing both players and audience to create the ambience of the drama in their imaginations.

Three particular plays are eminently suitable for school actors and audiences. Since most students will be familiar with Longfellow's "Hiawatha," they may be interested in presenting parts of it as readers' theater. There is an adapted version by Michael Bogdanov that has been successful in both professional and school theater. Arthur Kopit's "Indians" is also a marvelous play for high schools, and Christopher Sergel's "Black Elk Speaks" dramatizes the tale of the Battle of Wounded Knee.

Sources of Inspiration

Informational Books About Native Americans

Adams, Howard. *Prison of Grass: Canada from the Native Point of View.* Toronto: New Press, 1975.
Native Canadians describe their feelings about life and their homeland.

Ashbranner, Brent. *To Live in Two Worlds: American Indian Youth Today.* New York: Dodd, Mead, 1984.
The shared experiences of young Indians across America opens awareness of the opportunities and problems facing them today.

Barbour, Philip. *Pocahontas and Her World: A Chronicle of America's First Settlement in Which Is Related the Story of the Indians and the Englishmen—In Particular Captain John Smith, Captain Samuel Argall, and Master John Rolfe.* Boston: Houghton, Mifflin, 1970.
The life and times of Pocahontas take her from the colonies to her untimely death by disease in England.

Brown, Dee. *Bury My Heart at Wounded Knee: An Indian History of the American West.* New York: Holt, Rinehart, and Winston, 1971.
An account of Custer's last stand from the Native American point of view raises awareness of deceit and misadventure.

Clifton, James A. *The Potawatomi.* New York: Chelsea House, 1987.
This is a seven-chapter history of the canoe-travellers who lived near the Great Lakes waterways and are now dispersed in scattered locations from Oklahoma to Ontario.

Collins, Henry B. et al. *The Far North: 2000 Years of American Eskimo and Indian Art.* Washington: National Gallery of Art, 1973.
This catalogue of an exhibition held at the National Gallery of Art is a valuable source of illustrations.

Debo, Angie. *And Still the Waters Run: The Betrayal of the Five Civilized Tribes.* Princeton: Princeton University Press, 1972.
In spite of solemn promises that were to endure "as long as the waters run," nothing stopped the liquidation of the independent republics of Choctaws, Chicasaws, Cherokees, Creeks, and Seminoles.

Deloria, Vine, Jr. *Custer Died for Your Sins.* New York: Macmillan, 1969.
The much-abused Indian speaks of betrayal, twisted legend, and broken promises.

Eastman, Charles. *Indian Boyhood.* New York: Dover Press, 1971.
Eastman describes the skills, tribal ceremonies, and games learned during his fifteen years with the Sioux.

Feest, Christian F. *Native Arts of North America*. Rev. ed. New York: Thames and Hudson, 1992.
  Photographs, drawings, maps, and charts relate the arts of over 1000 tribes and 200 language groups.

Fehrenbach, T. *Comanches—The Destruction of a People*. New York: Alfred Knopf, 1974.
  Fehrenbach tells poignantly of the 19th-century encroachments of whites upon the unity and integrity of this mighty tribe.

Freedman, Russell. *Indian Chiefs*. New York: Holiday House, 1987.
  Six western Indian tribal chiefs who led their people against the encroaching European civilizations are included in this biographical collection.

Highwater, Jamake. *Many Smokes, Many Moons: A Chronology of American Indian History Through Indian Art*. Philadelphia: Lippincott, 1978.
  Learn about Indians' perceptions of their history through pottery, wood carving, and painting.

Holm, Bill. *Indian Art of the Northwest Coast: A Dialogue on Craftsmanship and Aesthetics*. Vancouver: Rice University Press, 1980.
  Photographs and drawings of totem poles and other significant cultural art expressions of the Northwest Indians make this a valuable resource during student art projects.

Hungry Wolf, Beverly. *The Ways of My Grandmothers*. New York: Morrow, 1980.
  This documentary record of the author's Blackfoot tribe combines personal history, legend, myth, and rare photographs.

Jahoda, Gloria. *The Trail of Tears: The American Indian Removals 1813–1855*. London: Allen and Unwin, 1976.
  Leading directly across Tennessee and Arkansas, from the Smokey Mountains into Oklahoma, the Trail of Tears led the Cherokees from their ancestral stronghold to a new life of deprivation. This is a well-documented account, with maps and illustrations.

Josephy, Alvin. *Red Power: The American Indians' Fight for Freedom*. New York: American Heritage, 1971.
  Documents from the 1960's Indian movement chronicles the struggle for equality, freedom, and repossession of land.

Klein, Bernard, ed. *Reference Encyclopedia of the American Indian*. Rye, NY: B. Klein, 1967.
  Klein's guide gives materials on museums, associations, films, government publications, periodicals, and books.

Niethammer, Carolyn. *American Indian Food and Lore: 150 Authentic Recipes*. New York: Collier (Macmillan), 1974.

Recipes for main dishes, fruits and vegetables, desserts, breads, medicines, dandelion wine, and corn whiskey are accompanied by an alphabetical dictionary of over fifty desert plants which are important as food and ritual items.

Osinski, Alice. *The Chippewa.* Chicago: Childrens Press, 1987.
For young readers, this is an illustrated history and account of modern life among the Chippewa around the western Great Lakes.

Rosenstiel, Annette. *Red and White: Indian View of the White Man, 1492–1982.* New York: Universe Books, 1983.
Indian writings from North and South America portray their relations with white people.

Rozin, Elisabeth. *Blue Corn and Chocolate.* New York: Alfred Knopf, 1992.
Native American food products appear in 175 varied recipes featuring corn, potatoes, tomatoes, chocolate, peppers, and turkey, along with anecdotal stories of how each food gained acceptance in the Old World.

Seven Families in Pueblo Pottery. Albuquerque: Maxwell Museum, 1989.
This is a basic primer of Southwest Indian pottery art which proliferates in the pueblos of the region.

Silverberg, Robert. *Home of the Red Man: Indian America Before Columbus.* Boston: New York Graphic Society, 1963.
This book presents a comprehensive survey of diversified cutures of pre-Columbian America.

Trimble, Stephen: *Talking with the Clay: The Art of Pueblo Pottery.* Santa Fe: School of American Research Press, 1989.
This is a well-illustrated documentary look at contemporary Pueblo potters: their art, technique, and traditions.

Warner, Rita. *Dancing Indians.* Mesa, Arizona: Mesa Creations, 1976.
Bold black-and-white graphic drawings of ceremonially-dressed Indians are bordered with appropriate motifs and symbols and are accompanied with a short history of the dance, the tribe, and costume.

Wetmore, Ruth. *First on the Land: The North Carolina Indians.* Winston-Salem, North Carolina: John F. Blair, 1975.
This comprehensive chronicle of Indian life begins 10,000 years B.C. and ends with tourism in the western Carolina mountains. Included is information about ceremonies, war preparations, legends, culture, and agriculture.

Worcester, Donald. *The Apaches, Eagles of the Southwest.* Norman, OK: University of Oklahoma Press, 1979.
Before the Spanish conquest and beyond the American encroachment of the 19th century, the Apaches have been a proud and noble people.

Wright, Barton. *Hopi Kachinas: The Complete Guide to Collecting Kachina Dolls.* Flagstaff, Arizona: Northland Publishing, 1988.

Illustrated with color photographs, this book gives essential background history of the Hopi and their kachinas and detailed descriptions of over 100 separate works of art.

Wyatt, Edgar. *Cochise, Apache Warrior and Statesman.* New York: McGraw-Hill, 1953.

Wyatt presents the true story of a brave 19th-century American.

Native American Myths and Legends

Bierhorst, John, ed. *The Fire Plume—Legends of the American Indians.* New York: Dial Press, 1969.

These stories and fables of adventure and romance were first heard by white settlers in the early 1800's.

Day, David. *Many Voices: An Anthology of Contemporary Canadian Indian Poetry.* Vancouver: J.J. Douglas, 1977.

Thirty-four Native Canadians from the Salish, Carrier, Shoshone, Algonquin, and Micmac tribes present work founded in tradition, storytelling, and religion, covering politics, poverty, disease, and love of the land.

Erdres, Richard, ed. *American Indian Myths and Legends.* New York: Pantheon, 1984.

One hundred and sixty previously unpublished stories from over eighty tribal groups give this collection power and immediacy.

Gillham, Charles. *Medicine Men of Hooper Bay: More Tales from the Clapping Mountains.* New York: Macmillan, 1955.

Eskimo stores of wolves, ice, blubber, seals, and caribou tell of the beauty of the Alaskan landscape.

Grey Owl. *Tales of an Empty Cabin.* Toronto: Macmillan of Canada, 1975.

First published in the 1930's, this is an Indian's epic story of the vast North Land, its people (both Indian and white), and its animals, trees, rivers, and weather.

Haviland, Virginia. *The Faber Book of North American Legends.* London: Faber and Faber, 1979.

The first part of this book contains fourteen Indian legends, followed by African American, European immigrant, and "Tall Tale" stories. The Indian section is largest and reflects the poetic imagery of creation myths, water, and fire.

Parker, Arthur C. *Skunny Wundy: Seneca Indian Tales.* Chicago: Albert Whitman and Co., 1979.

Twenty-eight exciting legends, tales, and fables, collected by a member of the Iroquois tribe, were first published in 1926.

Fiction: Featuring Native Americans

Banks, Lynne Reid. *The Return of the Indian.* New York: Doubleday, 1986.
Omri finds himself trapped between fantasy and reality as he tries to save his Indian friend Little Bear in the French and Indian Wars.

Barnouw, Victor. *Dreams of the Blue Heron.* New York: Dell, 1969.
A young Chippewa boy in Wisconsin is caught in fierce conflict between his traditional forest-dwelling grandparents and his father, who works in a white man's sawmill.

Baver, Marion. *Tangled Butterfly.* Boston: Houghton Mifflin, 1980.
While on the rest-cure in Minnesota, a disturbed white girl meets a young Native American.

Brown, Dee. *Creek Mary's Blood.* New York: Holt, Rinehart, and Winston, 1980.
Proud and beautiful Creek Mary dominates a saga that spans tne years from the American Revolution to World War I and includes such characters as Tecumseh, Crazy Horse, Sitting Bull, and Teddy Roosevelt.

Collura, Mary Ellen. *Winners.* New York: Dial Press, 1986.
After years in foster homes, 15-year-old Jordy Threebears finds himself caught between worlds when he returns to his grandfather's primitive prairie cabin on the Siksika Reservation.

Cooper, James Finnimore. *The Last of the Mohicans.* New York: Penguin, 1986.
A classic story of the French and Indian Wars, this is a sad account of friendship, betrayal, and battle.

Eckert, Allan W. *Johnny Logan, Shawnee Boy.* Boston: Little, Brown, 1983.
A young Indian is torn between his own people and the powerful white men who are taking over his Ohio territory in the early 1800's.

George, Jean Craighead. *Water Sky.* New York: Harper and Row, 1987.
The legend of the white-tailed whale leads a young man on a quest from Massachusetts to the Inuits of Alaska.

Highwater, Jamake. *Legend Days: Part One of the Ghost Horse Cycle.* New York: Harper and Row, 1984.
A young Native American girl draws upon her secret gifts when she is abandoned by her tribe during a smallpox epidemic.

Houston, James. *Ghost Paddle—A Northwest Coast Indian Tale.* San Diego: Harcourt Brace Jovanovich, 1972.
A party of unarmed braves follow Chief Sea Wolf into enemy territory to make peace with the river people.

Jackson, Helen Hunt. *Ramona.* New York: Avon, 1970.
    A young Indian girl leaves her wealthy stepfather's ranch to be with Alessandro, a poor sheep farmer, in this book, which upon publication over 100 years ago raised Americans' consciousness about maltreatment of the Indians.

La Farge, Oliver. *Laughing Boy.* New York: Washington Square Press, 1962.
    This is a story of a time recently gone among the Navajo: of modern American encroachment on an older, simpler way of life.

O'Dell, Scott. *Sing Down the Moon.* Boston: Houghton Mifflin, 1970.
    A young Navajo girl maintains hope, even after white soldiers have captured her tribesmen and threatened her way of life.

————. *Streams to the River, River to the Sea.* Boston: Houghton Mifflin, 1986.
    This is based on the true story of Sacagawea, the young Shoshone girl who guided the Lewis and Clark expedition.

Paulson, Gary. *The Night the White Deer Died.* Nashville: Thomas Nelson, 1978.
    Janet, the only white girl in her age group, is troubled by dreams of a white deer and seeks help from an Indian town loafer.

Shorris, Earl. *The Death of the Great Spirit.* New York: New American Library, 1971.
    This is the story of a proud and wise culture, marked by tragedy, usurpation, and engulfment by Europeans.

Sneve, Virginia. *Driving Hawk: When Thunders Spoke.* New York: Holiday, 1974.
    A sacred Indian relic starts to bring luck to a Sioux family.

Speare, Elizabeth George. *The Sign of the Beaver.* Boston: Houghton Mifflin, 1983.
    A young Indian helps eleven-year-old Matt survive in the 18th-century wilderness.

Wallin, Luke. *In the Shadow of the Wind.* New York: Bradbury, 1984.
    Clashes between the Creeks and the whites in 1832 thwart the unlikely love between frontiersman Caleb McElroy and Pine Basket, a Creek maiden.

Wilcox, Eleanor. *The Cornhusk Doll.* Eau Claire, Wisconsin: E. M. Hale, 1956.
    Sally Redpath is captured by the Shawnee after the French and Indian Wars, and is saved from being sold into slavery by a freak accident.

Drama: Native Americans

Bogdanov, Michael. *Hiawatha.* London: Heinemann, 1981.
    This powerful adaptation of Longfellow's classic poem unites legend, myth, song, and ritual dance to give an exciting opportunity for actors and actresses.

Kopit, Arthur. *Indians.* London: Methuen, 1969.
This is a tale of Wild Bill Hickok and the decimation of both buffalo and Indians.

Sergel, Christopher. *Black Elk Speaks.* Chicago: Dramatic Publishing Company, 1976.
Indians tell their version of the Battle of Wounded Knee.

For Further Information

American Indian Art Magazine
7314 E. Osborn Drive
Scottsdale, Arizona
Find out about current trends in silver, weaving, pottery, and carving and where to see and buy Indian art in specialist shops, galleries, and auctions.

American Indian Culture Research Center
Blue Cloud Abbey
Marvin, South Dakota 57251
Telephone 605-432-5528
This organization specializes in teaching the non-Indian public about culture and philosophy of native Americans. They offer resources such as photos, books, films, records, and tapes, while supporting Native American leaders in rebuilding the Indian community.

Indian Art and Craft Board
Room 4004
U.S. Department of the Interior
Washington, D.C. 20240
Telephone 202-343-2773
Write for a source directory of Indian, Eskimo, and Aleutian-owned arts and crafts galleries in the United States. In Room 1023 of the U.S. Department of the Interior Building (1800 C Street, N.W., Washington, D.C.) there is an Indian craft store, similar to one in nearby Georgetown at 1050 Wisconsin Avenue, N.W.

Society for American Indian Studies and Research
P.O.B. 443
Hurst, Texas 76053
Telephone 817-281-3784
For those interested in promoting research and teaching about Native Americans, the Society for American Studies and Research promotes discovery, collection, and preservation of materials and publications in anthropology, history, and literature. They maintain a monograph library on special research subjects.

Chapter Three

The Sceptered Isles:
A Festival of Britain

Changing the guard at Buckingham Palace, afternoon tea with scones and jam, Anglican choristers in medieval choir stalls, yachting in the Solent, mountain climbing in Snowdonia or the Cumbrians, 1960's Beatles records, paintings by Constable, Turner, and Hockney, poems by Shakespeare, Keats, and Betjeman, novels by Trollope, Dickens, and Benson . . . Britain, for so small a cluster of islands, possesses an inordinate amount of that illusive quality, culture, that defines attitudes to life through daily habits, artwork, sports, and humor. Perhaps more than any other single source, Britain has influenced the United States: its language, literature, democratic system of government, and sense of fair play. Because America's ties with its mother country are so strong, it is appropriate to honor the relationship with a "Festival of Britain," whose scope for celebration is so wide that planning sessions will be devoted to limiting items rather than creating them (figure 15).

Since American literature is largely rooted in that of the British Isles (England, Scotland, Wales, and Ireland), a

British Bookmark

(Figure 15) Begun in 1675 and finished in 1710, the Cathedral Church of Saint Paul, by Sir Christopher Wren, is one of the most famous landmarks in the City of London. Witness to British history since the 17th century, Saint Paul's was damaged by air-raids in World War II but with financial aid from Britons and Americans was completely restored. There is an American chapel behind the High Altar.

Photo by Jonathan Newman, 1989
Student, American School in London

festival may appropriately focus on great authors—poets, novelists, playwrights, essayists, diarists—whose works are the touchstones of modern thought and writing. Authors such as Shakespeare, Marlowe, Pope, Newman, Addison, Eliot, Keats, Shelley, Lear, Benson, Greene, Moorcock and Garfield (figure 16) span several centuries of writing, philosophy, purpose, and style. A "Festival of Britain" can focus on genre, such as science fiction, in which students could enjoy, among others, John Wyndham, Michael Moorcock, and Mervyn Peake or adventure, with writers as varied in style and subject as Thomas Hardy, Robert Louis Stevenson, and Rosemary Sutcliff, or poetry, from Geoffrey Chaucer, William Shakespeare, John Keats, and John Donne to Edward Lear and John Betjeman. Bram Stoker and Mary Shelley are still remembered for their horror stories. William Horwood, A. A. Milne, Richard Adams and Beatrix Potter are masters of the animal story. Children's writers, from John Newbery to Lewis Carroll to Graham Oakley, have led the field. Dramatists from Shakespeare to Oscar Wilde to Alan Ayckbourn are performed around the world. Indeed, in nearly every literary subject,

(Figure 16) British author Leon Garfield, center, talks to a group of high school students, all of whom had read at least two of his books prior to the informal session in which the writer spoke about his life and work. Garfield, the author of several historical novels set in London, wrote the screenplays for the acclaimed animated Shakespeare in 1992.

British writers have been, and are, at the forefront, publishing intelligent, witty, and enjoyable books that are read all over the world. Festival organizers will have more on their plates than they can eat, so judicious elimination, however difficult with so rich a menu, will be in order.

British music likewise offers unlimited scope. Early liturgical composers, such as John Taverner, Thomas Weelkes, William Byrd, and Thomas Tallis often had to straddle theological struggles, composing at one moment for the Roman Church and the next for the Reformed. Failure to please or to toe the line could have resulted in a swift and deadly end. Orchestral composers, from Frederick Delius to Edward Elgar and Malcolm Sargent, also composed "part" songs appropriate for a school choir to perform during a festival of Britain. British immigrant George Frederick Handel's oratorios are performed frequently in concert halls and churches throughout the British Isles and America. Benjamin Britten wrote a young people's cantata based on the life of St. Nicholas which, although easier to perform than his powerful musical drama *Noye's Fludde,* still offers scope for soloists, choir, and orchestra or keyboard. Andrew Lloyd Webber spans the world today in popular musicals such as *Joseph and the Amazing Technicolor Dreamcoat, Jesus Christ Superstar* (figure 17), and *Cats.* Pop groups from the British Isles often dominate Western teenage culture—Oisean and Da Danaan from Ireland, the Beatles from Liverpool, the Rolling Stones and Elton John from London. Folk music, sung and played over the centuries in pubs and around family hearths, has been popularized by musicians such as The Chieftains and Mary O'Hara from Ireland, The Kings Singers from England, and the McAlmans from Scotland. Composers from Ralph Vaughan Williams and Edward Elgar to Cat Stevens and Benjamin Britten have arranged folk songs for choirs.

British art manifests itself in stately homes designed by John Nash, gardens planned by Inigo Jones, portraits by Gainsborough, watercolors by Edward Lear, and sculpture by Henry Moore. Castles in Ireland, Scotland, the Isle of Man, Wales, and England, half-timbered Elizabethan houses, thatched roof cottages, medieval churches and cathedrals all testify to a magnificent architectural heritage. Folk artists in Wales still carve intricate love spoons; East Anglian basketmakers use local willow and reed to carry out an age-old craft; potters in the southern coastal town of Rye export their work to America; stained glass artists in London supply churches

(Figure 17) Sir Andrew Lloyd Webber's musical *Jesus Christ Superstar* has played to audiences around the world. In this British production, Stephen Miles sang the title role. Photograph by permission of Stephen Miles.

throughout Europe. The Royal Academy of Art in London's Piccadilly is one of the major innovators in exhibition and promotion of all the graphic arts in the western world.

British food, once limited in the popular imagination to fish and chips, roast beef, and over-boiled vegetables, is delightfully cosmopolitan, drawing upon the cuisines of its immigrant population and the influence of its European neighbors. Every community supports independent bakeries, fish shops, butchers, green grocers, and restaurants that make British dining not only pleasant and tasty, but healthy as well. Britain consumes more tea than any other country in the world. Four o'clock in England, Scotland, or Wales is one of the most pleasant times on earth when delicate cakes, hot-buttered crumpets, light scones, and assorted sandwiches of brown bread and cucumber, salmon, and York ham, accompanied by bottomless pots of rich, dark tea, provide a fulfilling interlude between a late pub lunch and dinner at eight.

A festival of Britain can be observed on a number of occasions—St. George's Day (Patron Saint of England, April 23); St. Andrew's Day (Patron Saint of Scotland, November 30); St. David's Day (Patron Saint of Wales, March 1); St. Patrick's Day (Patron Saint of Ireland, March 17); the birthday of an author; or at any other time, since the choice of material is so vast and can be arranged to suit any theme. It may be desirable to limit celebrations to one part of the United Kingdom, such as Scotland or Wales, or, more for political than geographical considerations, to hold an entirely separate festival for Ireland. With so much to choose from—music, foods, literature, traditions—a school could plan annual festivals from the British Isles for the next century without risk of repetition.

Who Should Celebrate This Festival?

A festival of Britain is appropriate anywhere in America but perhaps slightly more so in places such as these:

a. An Episcopal school—to honor the religious heritage of the Church of England, mother church of the Anglican communion, with its associated British literature and culture.

b. A Methodist school—to honor the work of John Wesley, British founder of the Methodist movement.

c. A Quaker school—to honor the early Quaker movement in England which fostered the development of Quakerism in America.

d. Any school which wishes to focus on any aspect of British culture, such as literature or music: a mini-festival of Charles Dickens or J.R.R. Tolkien, a festival of British children's literature, or a festival of British composers.

e. A town with an English name—to research the reasons why the early settlement was named after a British or Irish town and to renew links with people living in the original place. Names such as Birmingham, Winchester, Norwich, Manchester, Boston, York, Newark, Plymouth, Bangor, and countless others have their beginnings in the old country.

A Festival Display: Map and Flags of the United Kingdom

What You Need:

Construction Paper (varied colors)
Pencils
Color felt-tip pens
Reference map of the British Isles
Pins, staples

Enlarge an outline map of the British Isles (figure 18) on white construction paper, cut out the islands, and secure them to a background of blue. Label the political divisions with the names of the countries and national symbols:

England: St. George's flag, a red rose
Scotland: St. Andrew's flag, a thistle, a bagpipe
Wales: St. David's flag, a leek, a harp
Ireland: St. Patrick's shamrock, a snake, a harp

Draw in some major cities, especially London, Edinburgh, Belfast, Dublin, and Swansea, and some geographical features, such as the River Thames, the Cumbrian and Welsh mountains, the Scottish Highlands, and the Irish lakes.

A festival logo could be a small version of the outline map, with one of the symbols from each country at each compass point.

Guest Speakers: Travellers and Cricket Players

1. Invite a **university professor of English literature or history** to talk about one selected literary or historic theme, such as the novels of

(Figure 18) Britain Festival Display

Thomas Hardy, Charles Dickens, or Iris Murdoch. Naturally, it would
be essential to choose the audience carefully after consultation with the
school English and history departments so that students could prepare
for the lecture with prior reading.

2. Invite an **authority on British children's literature** to talk to lower
   school teachers or students. This authority could be a local librarian or
   professor or a member of the school faculty.

3. Ask a good **storyteller** to prepare some English folktales or children's
   stories to present to an audience of lower or middle schoolers.

4. A **travel agent** or a local **person who has travelled extensively in the British Isles** could speak, show slides, and offer brochures about Ireland and Britain. Topics could include customs, holidays, cities, cathedrals and churches, universities, rail travel, canals, lakes, mountains, foods, or other items.
5. Find a **cricket player or enthusiast** to explain how this ball game differs from baseball. Ask him to organize an exhibition team to play or to help a group of students to play. Similarly, ask a soccer or rugby coach or player to talk about those British sports.
6. Locate a local **British immigrant** who would enjoy telling students about his or her home country, how it differs from America, and what life is like there.
7. Listen to tapes, films, and other recordings of various **British accents.** Ask students to discuss the differences in vowel sounds and speech rhythms that exist not only between British and American usages, but also within regions of the British Isles themselves. What types of British accents can students identify? What role does education play in formulating accent? What is Cockney rhyming slang?
8. **Demonstrate the festival art projects.** Make the project ahead of time but demonstrate how to assemble it from scratch with pre-cut parts. Offer a how-to-do-it handout at the end of the demonstration.

Festival Design: Art Projects

The first two projects require only student art materials, some reference sources, and creativity spurred on by a prize for the winner. The other projects make excellent artroom or in-class activities, and they also make good public demonstrations as part of the festival speakers program.

What You Need:

Art-room paper
Drawing and coloring media of individual choice
Reference materials

Design a Travel Poster

Students involved in this project would need to write to consulates for posters, pamphlets, and brochures, investigate reference books, and thumb through some British magazines. Help students narrow down their choices to **one** castle, **one** bridge, or maybe even to a single flower symbolic of the British love of beautiful gardens.

Offer prizes to winning artists in various categories, such as age level or destination: castle, county, stately home, garden, city, or geographical region.

Design a Book Jacket

Students could choose any British book, from Wyndham's *Day of the Triffids* or Stoker's *Dracula* to Dickens's *Great Expectations* or Gibbons's *Cold Comfort Farm*. Lower school students could choose a British children's book, from *Paddington Bear* to Brian Wildsmith's *ABC*. Middle schoolers could illustrate a work of Leon Garfield, Alan Garner, or Susan Cooper.

Display the designs in the library. Award ribbons from a panel of judges. Select the best jackets for framing and permanent exhibition.

Build a British Castle (figure 19).

What You Need:
Pictures of castles from reference sources
Cardboard boxes
   All sizes of grocery boxes
   Cocoa boxes
   Round salt boxes
   Paper towel and toilet paper tubes
   Match boxes
Pencils
Craft Knife
Glue
String for drawbridge
Construction paper scraps (for turrets, banners, flags)
Toothpicks for flag poles
Tempera paints
Brushes

First, look at as many pictures of castles as possible in books and magazines. Meanwhile, collect cardboard boxes and tubes from foil and paper towels and, if possible, from carpets.

To make a simple castle, draw a crenellated edge along the top of a box and cut it out with the craft knife. Middle school students can do this themselves with close supervision. With a pencil, draw a few

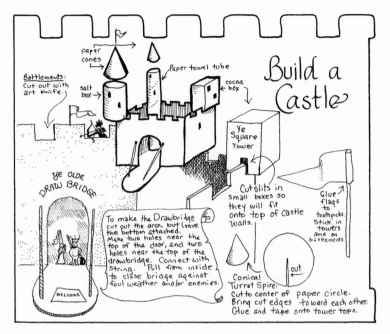

paper cones

Battlements:
Cut out with
art knife.)

salt box →

Paper towel tube

cocoa box

Build a
Castle

Ye
Square
Tower

YE OLDE
DRAW BRIDGE

Cut slits in
small boxes so
they will fit
onto top of castle
walls.

Glue
flags
to
toothpicks.
Stick in
towers
and on
battlements

To make the Drawbridge
cut out the arch, but leave
the bottom attached.
Make two holes near the
top of the door, and two
holes near the top of the
drawbridge. Connect with
String. Pull from inside
to close bridge against
foul weather and/or enemies.

Conical
Turret Spire:
Cut to center of paper circle.
Bring cut edges toward each other.
Glue and tape onto tower tops.

cut

WELCOME

Figure 19

small windows and a drawbridge gate. Cut out the gate, leaving the
bottom edge intact. To make the drawbridge, make two holes at each
edge of the door and two corresponding holes in the castle wall.
Thread string through the holes and seal with a knot.

Draw a portcullis (heavy iron gate, usually with sharp spikes at the
bottom, which can be lowered behind the drawbridge for further
security) on cardboard or poster board. Cut it out. Assign a group to
devise a pulley system behind the drawbridge gate to raise and lower
the portcullis.

To make castle towers, glue the cardboard tubes to the corners of
the box, fitting them onto the box with slits for greater stability. Cut
crenellations into the tops of the towers. Add a roof by pressing a
circular cut-out slightly larger than the tube into the top opening.

Inside the castle wall, build a medieval fortress from smaller
boxes. Paint the entire thing gray. Use a sponge to add highlights in
dark gray, white, and black. With a fine brush, delineate stonework.
Paint in windows and doors with black paint.

Design a Family Crest or Coat of Arms

What You Need:

Reference pictures of heraldic shields
Ditto sheets or photocopies of blank shields
Art room paper
Pencils
Tempera paints
Brushes
Scissors

Study the origin and meaning of family crests and shields, how they were represented in art, and where they were displayed. Ask students to invent a crest for themselves (figure 20), picking out personal hobbies or academic interests, favorite vacation sites, hometowns, or state symbols to incorporate in their design. The art project helps students think about their uniqueness through self-enhancing questions while learning about the historic development of coats of arms. Other choices for inclusion in the coat of arms are:

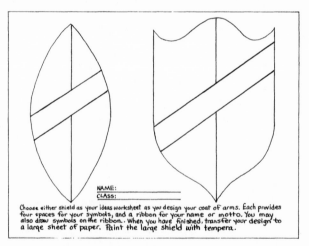

NAME:
CLASS:

Choose either shield as your ideas worksheet as you design your coat of arms. Each provides four spaces for your symbols, and a ribbon for your name or motto. You may also draw symbols on the ribbon. When you have finished, transfer your design to a large sheet of paper. Paint the large shield with tempera.

(Figure 20) Interpreting traditional designs, students can create personal coats of arms that incorporate favorite hobbies, vacations, pets, or seasons, and make personal statements about themselves. The close-up (right) reveals a girl's interest in riding horses and playing the violin. Others (left) portray national or regional origins, pets, and interests in music, drama, and gymnastics.

1. The things I am good at
2. My proudest moment
3. My pet
4. The best thing that ever happened to me
5. What I'd like to become good at
6. What profession I want to follow when I grow up
7. What I'd like to be remembered for
8. If I died today, these are the three words I'd want to be said of me

Provide photocopied blank shields for students to use in making their preliminary designs in pencil (figure 21).

To make the shield, give each student a large piece of art paper, which they should fold in half. To make a symmetrically shaped shield, they can draw one half of the design, centered on the fold (figure 22). By cutting the folded paper, they will have a complete shield. Alternately, provide students with a template to trace. Coats of arms need not be traditionally medieval in shape. They can be round like ancient Chinese shields, or almond-shaped, like African shields.

A shield may be divided in several ways: quartered, halved, halved and divided, halved and quartered. There are several standard decorative devices, too, that can add interest to blank spaces— diagonal stripes, colored dots, chevrons, fleur-de-lis, checkerboards—but students should be encouraged to invent their own, especially if their ethnic origin is other than European.

When the designs are completed, students fill them in with tempera paints, using one color (or mixed color) at a time to avoid unintentional blurring. With glue mount the finished crests on color-coordinated construction paper. Careful students can cut out animal designs, feathers, leaves and crowns to add individuality to their mounts.

Make a Welsh Love Spoon

Intricately carved and highly finished wooden spoons are still carved in the mountains of Wales, though they are more likely today to be sold in a craft shop than given by the carver to the lady of his choice. We can make replicas of these traditional British spoons with cardboard and papier mâché (figure 23).

Figure 21

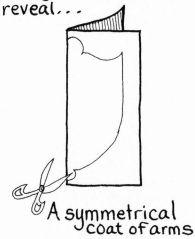

Fold your paper in half. Draw
half the shield so that its
center lies on the fold. Cut
through both halves to
reveal...

A symmetrical
coat of arms

Figure 22

What You Need:

Cardboard boxes
Glue
Craft knives
Pencils
Papier mâché (wallpaper paste and torn strips of absorbent paper)
Tempera paint
Varnish
Brushes
String or yarn

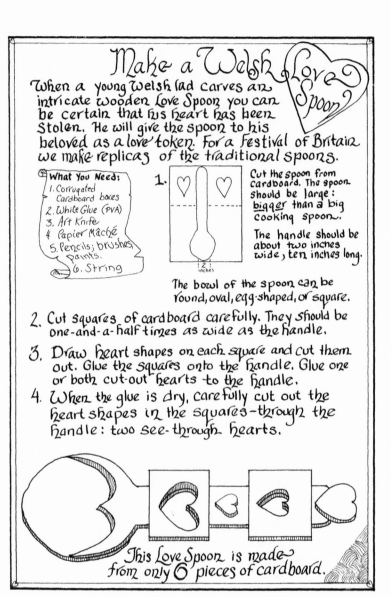

Make a Welsh Love Spoon

When a young Welsh lad carves an intricate wooden Love Spoon you can be certain that his heart has been stolen. He will give the spoon to his beloved as a love token. For a Festival of Britain we make replicas of the traditional spoons.

What You Need:
1. Corrugated Cardboard boxes
2. White Glue (PVA)
3. Art Knife
4. Papier Mâché
5. Pencils; brushes, paints.
6. String

1.

Cut the spoon from cardboard. The spoon should be large: bigger than a big cooking spoon.

The handle should be about two inches wide, ten inches long.

2 inches

The bowl of the spoon can be round, oval, egg-shaped, or square.

2. Cut squares of cardboard carefully. They should be one-and-a-half times as wide as the handle.

3. Draw heart shapes on each square and cut them out. Glue the squares onto the handle. Glue one or both cut-out hearts to the handle.

4. When the glue is dry, carefully cut out the heart shapes in the squares—through the handle: two see-through hearts.

This Love Spoon is made from only 6 pieces of cardboard.

Figure 23

5. Trace the bowl onto cardboard. Cut out the traced duplicate bowl.

Option: PIERCE TOP HEART FOR STRING TO HANG SPOON ON WALL.

6. Cut out a "rat's tail", or heart, design from the original bowl. Glue the second bowl onto the bottom.

7. For a smooth, solid-looking spoon, layer it three times with papier mâché, taking care to cover corrugated edges well.

8. Paint the spoon light brown. Then drag a dry brush with undiluted dark brown and black paint along the spoon from bottom to top to simulate wood grain. Finally, when dry, coat with protective polyurethane varnish.

Make a Larger Design

1. Draw half design on folded newspaper. Cut out. Trace onto cardboard.

2. Draw on vine. Cut out berries, leaves, bird.

3. Cut pot from scrap cardboard. Glue on.

4. Follow steps 5 to 7, above.

5. Glue string onto handle to make raised vine.

6. Paint.

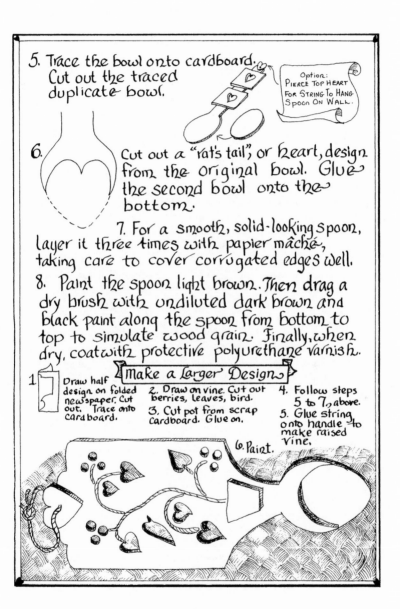

Figure 23 (cont'd)

To Make the Spoons:

1. Cut a spoon shape from corrugated cardboard, supervising children carefully if they are using craft knives. If in doubt, rely on sharp scissors or do the cutting yourself. Although there is no standard size, make the spoon somewhat larger than an ordinary cooking ladle to enable young artists to cut and glue with ease.
   a. Make the stem at least 5 cm (2 inches) wide and 25 cm (10 inches) long.
   b. Make the bowl of the spoon round, oval, or egg shaped.
2. Cut squares of corrugated cardboard to make the decorative bas-relief hearts. The squares should be at least one-and-a-half times as wide as the stem.
3. Draw heart shapes on the cardboard squares and cut them out. Glue the squares onto the stem of the spoon. If there is room on the stem, glue the hearts in between and on top of the squares.
4. When the glue is dry, carefully cut the heart shapes from the stem, creating see-through spaces.
5. To give the spoon realistic depth, trace the bowl of the spoon onto another piece of cardboard, and cut out the traced shape.
6. Draw a design, such as a crescent or traditional rat's tail, on the first bowl at the base of the handle. Cut out along that line. To make it more realistic, cut on a sloping angle. Glue the traced bowl to the bottom of the remaining spoon handle.
7. Dip the torn paper strips into the wallpaper paste, and appy a single, smooth layer to the entire spoon, molding it to fit into the cut-out spaces. Add up to three layers of papier mâché, and allow to dry.
8. Paint the spoon with brown tempera to approximate wood. With a fine artist's brush, paint on wood grain in a darker or lighter shade. When dry, apply a coat of protective gloss varnish.

To Make a Wide Spoon:

1. Make a template from plain paper. Fold the paper in half, and draw half the spoon, as in the coats of arms project (figure 22). Trace the design onto cardboard, and cut out with a craft knife.
2. Draw a curving vine onto the wide handle with pencil. Add leaves and berries. Cut out the leaves and berries.
3. Draw a flower pot on scrap cardboard, cut it out, and glue it to the base of the vine.
4. Follow steps 5–7 above.
5. Cut a length of heavy string, twine, or yarn to the fit the vine. Dip the

twine in glue, and place it over the vine shape. Cut out a heart shape (or use one of the leaf cut-outs) and glue it to the top of the handle.
6. Paint the spoon as in step 8 above or experiment with other colors, painting the vine realistically over a bright background.

To hang these love spoons on a wall, incorporate a long piece of string into the top of the handle by piercing a hole.

Crack Open a Cracker (figure 24)

English candy-maker Tom Smith invented the Christmas cracker in 1847 and spent the next twenty years making it a British holiday tradition. Basically, the Christmas cracker is a brightly wrapped tube that "cracks" when it is pulled open to reveal a small gift, a joke, riddle, fortune or motto, perhaps some candy or nuts, and a party hat. Why wait until Christmas to make these festive gifts? Call them trinket tubes and give them away as birthday treats or as prizes in the travel poster or book jacket competitions (projects 1 and 2).

What You Need:

Cardboard tubes (from toilet rolls)
Bright wrapping paper
Tissue paper
Glue or glue stick
String or thread
Ruler
Pencils and pens
Typing paper cut into strips
Scissors and pinking shears
Craft knife
Ribbon
Small gifts (such as erasers, pens, crayons, figurines)
Miniature packages of edible treats
Sequins, cut-outs, paper doilies, glitter

1. Begin with two cardboard rolls. Cut one of them precisely in half.
2. Think of a short joke or riddle, or make up a fortune, and write it on a strip of paper. Roll it up and put it in the uncut cardboard roll, along with a small toy and a small package of nuts or candy.
3. Place the cardboard tubes end to end and roll them up in two pieces of tissue paper cut 2.5 cm (1 inch) longer than the total length of the tubes

The Great British Cracker in six easy steps

1. Cut one cardboard tube in half.

2. Place small treats in the big tube.
   WHY DID THE CHICKEN
   Peanut Bits

3. Roll in tissue paper...

4. ...and gift wrap.

5. Wind thread tightly around the two spaces where tubes meet.

6. Decorate with ribbons, cutouts and stickers.

Figure 24

and 1.5 cm (1/2 inch) wider than the circumference. Secure the tissue paper in place with a small amount of glue.

4. Roll the tubes up in wrapping paper cut 1.5 cm longer than their total length (to allow the tissue paper to show at each end). Cut the edge of the wrapping paper with pinking shears for a decorative effect. Secure in place with glue.

5. Wind thread around the two spaces where the tubes meet to bring the tissue and wrapping papers together to seal in the treats. Remove the two half-tubes at either end and cut fringes on the ends of the tissue paper.

6. Decorate the trinket tube with ribbons, glitter, cut-outs, or paper doilies.

Play the Sweetheart Game

Sometimes called the "Sweetheart Game," the object of this party pastime is to form couples through skillful observation of a ball being passed behind the backs of players. It can also be called the "Friendship Game" or "Pick a Pal Game" to avoid romantic allusions. Recorded music may be played to establish rhythmic shoulder and body movements to help trick the sweetheart. Before playing, practice passing the ball (or fruit) so everyone can get the hang of it.

1. Ideally, an equal number of players is required, seated or standing, alternately boy–girl–boy–girl. Players should face into a tight circle, shoulders almost touching, their hands behind their backs.

2. One player begins by becoming the "sweetheart" (or friend, or pal), and going into the center of the circle. A group leader may determine the new sweetheart or pal, or a clockwise rotation may be established before play starts.

3. After the sweetheart has gone into the center, those in the circle have to pass a small ball (or apple, orange, or lemon) from one to another, trying not to let the sweetheart see who has it. Players can disguise the movement by twitching their shoulders even when they don't have the ball, or by being as still as possible when they do.

4. The sweetheart may guess aloud at any time. If the choice is correct, the sweetheart and the chosen one become a pair and retire from the game (to have refreshments, to watch the others, or to carry on with schoowork). For incorrect guesses, there is a penalty: the sweetheart changes places with the wrongly-guessed person, and the "wrong" player becomes the sweetheart. (Variation: give the sweetheart three chances before trading places.)

5. The circle becomes tighter as each couple leaves so that as little space as possible exists between each player.

Plant an Herb Garden: A Festival Project

Plan and plant an English herb garden, either on the school campus or in a private plot in the community. Refer to English and colonial American gardening books and find out from a local nursery which herbs grow well in your area. The mild British climate means that many herbs that would need protection or re-seeding in parts of America survive there year-round. If there is no outdoor space, try making an indoor garden on a windowsill.

When cultivating rosemary, thyme, sage, parsley, garlic, fennel, cumin, tarragon, and other culinary, medicinal, and fragrant plants, try pronouncing "herb" the British way by sounding the initial "h," as in the man's name.

Research the history of herbs in folk medicine and cooking. Find out which herbs are used in modern medicine. Learn about homeo-pathic medicine. For an organized presentation on herbal fact and lore, write the names of herbs on strips of paper, and place them in a box. Students can draw a title at random which they research using a worksheet like that in figure 25. Include unfamiliar plants along with well-known culinary ones, poisonous or dangerous ones along with benign or beneficial ones. Display the finished activity sheets along with potted herb plants. Include bowls of fresh or dried leaves of aromatic plants such as rosemary, mint, sage, tarragon, and marjoram that students can crush in their fingers.

Compare Appalachian and British Songs

Find some Appalachian folk songs, such as "Barbara Allen" and "Foggy, Foggy Dew." Experts say these songs came from the British Isles with settlers in the 17th century. Join with friends in singing these songs with guitar, celtic harp, piano, or fiddle.

Research the origins of the tune of "My Country, 'Tis of Thee," which originated in Great Britain, and is, in fact, the British national anthem with, of course, different words.

Find British Place Names in America: Research

Research the British origins of towns in your state. Learn about the settlers who named the towns and where they came from. Study the original counties, towns, and cities in the British Isles that bear these names.

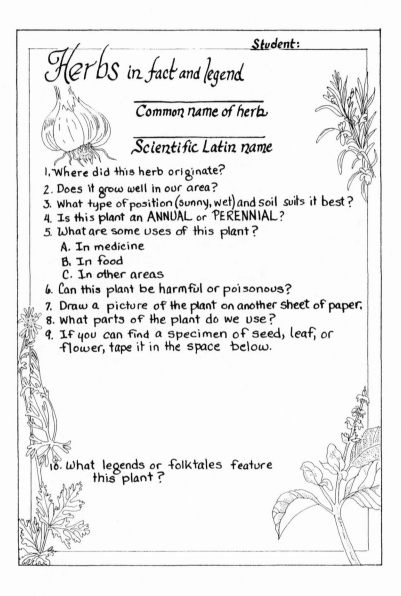

Student:

Herbs in fact and legend

Common name of herb

Scientific Latin name

1. Where did this herb originate?
2. Does it grow well in our area?
3. What type of position (sunny, wet) and soil suits it best?
4. Is this plant an ANNUAL or PERENNIAL?
5. What are some uses of this plant?
   A. In medicine
   B. In food
   C. In other areas
6. Can this plant be harmful or poisonous?
7. Draw a picture of the plant on another sheet of paper.
8. What parts of the plant do we use?
9. If you can find a specimen of seed, leaf, or flower, tape it in the space below.

10. What legends or folktales feature this plant?

Figure 25

a. Write to the Chamber of Commerce (often called "Board of Trade") in the British town of your choice, asking for brochures, pamphlets, or the name of a school that could lead to correspondence with children there. This will give first-hand information about the area and could lead to visits.

b. Organize a large mural painting, in which buildings and people of both the English and American "twin towns" are illustrated, either together (including historical figures as well as contemporary ones) or separately, one half being British, the other half American, separated by a small strip of Atlantic ocean.

Teatime in Britain: Five Regional Recipes

Tea is a visual experience, as well as a tasty one. Since it is usually an intimate affair, tea should be served at separate small tables, rather than one large one, onto which dainty white cloths have been laid and topped with small vases of flowers. Arrange cutlery, napkins, plates, tea cups and saucers (never mugs), creamers and sugar bowls. (During a festival, where many people will be eating, it is not inappropriate to serve the tea buffet-style, standing.)

Tea in the British Isles is served strong and hot, fresh from the teapot (which may be a "brown Betty," that storybook brown clay teapot, available in the U.S. from Conran; a Spode heirloom; a Georgian silver masterpiece; or anything in between), alongside which is placed a jug of just boiled water to refresh the tea as cups are poured. The teapot may also be sheltered beneath a cozy, a padded cover that keeps the contents hot. Local custom and thought differs from hill to dale about which should be poured first, the tea or the milk, and in the final analysis, matters little. Some people, in fact, prefer lemon or a sprig of mint, or nothing at all to dilute the tea itself. Sugar is usually offered, but rarely taken.

In addition to the following representative foods from the four countries of the British Isles, one should offer strawberry jam, butter, and whipped cream (to add to the jam and butter-filled scones), as well as any sponge cakes or cookies (called "biscuits" in Britain) one desires. These may all be preceded by delicate sandwiches from which the crusts have been trimmed and which consist of only three things: thinly sliced wholewheat bread, butter, and one filling, such as thin slices of cucumber, salmon, finely chopped boiled egg, or watercress.

If all this seems too delicate for words, perhaps it is simply a reflection on the attitude to life in different cultures. British travellers in America often lament that, come four o'clock, there is no place to retire for a proper cup of tea, much less a tea-time repast, just as Americans in Britain often exclaim at the plethora of tea rooms in villages, towns, and cities all over the islands. Britain may no longer stop for tea, but it certainly slows down to savor its traditional afternoon meal. Nothing can better highlight or sum up a festival of the British Isles than tea.

Consider stopping the festival once a day with a breathing space for tea. Organize morning cooking demonstrations with students, either in the library or in classrooms, and serve scones, soda bread, honey cake, or oatmeal cookies with tea in the afternoon. Individual classes can have their own tea parties, reserving one great British tea for everyone on the final day of the festival. It all depends upon time, space, and energy.

English Scones

(Recipe makes 8–12 scones)

2 1/3 cups sifted cake flour	6 tbsp softened shortening
2 1/2 tsp baking powder	5 tbsp milk
1/2 tsp salt	2 eggs
1 tsp sugar	(1/2 cup raisins, optional)
	1 greased cookie sheet

Heat the oven to 450 degrees Fahrenheit (230 C). Sift the first four ingredients together into a mixing bowl. Blend the shortening (butter, margarine, or Crisco) into the dry ingredients, either with a pastry blender, two knives, or fingers, until it reaches the consistency of coarse cornmeal. (Add the optional raisins at this point.) Add the milk and stir. Beat the eggs and fold into the dough, saving one tablespoon to brush on the scones just before they go into the oven. (For lighter scones, beat the egg whites separately.)

Turn the dough onto a floured surface. Roll it no less than 3/4 inch thick. Thinner dough will limit rising ability of the scones, resulting in a crisper, flatter product. Use a round biscuit cutter to shape scones. Arrange them on a greased cookie sheet, apart.

Brush scones with reserved egg. Bake 10–15 minutes, or until lightly browned. Serve hot or at room temperature, either in a basket covered by a tea towel, or from a porcelain plate.

Scones are traditionally eaten sliced, spread with butter and strawberry jam followed by a dollop of unsweetened whipped cream or clotted cream (available from some import shops in the U.S.). Scones may be sliced and toasted under a grill ("broiler" in U.S.) for breakfast.

Welsh Honey Cake (Teisen Fel)

(One cake serves 6–8)

2 cups sifted all-purpose flour	1/2 cup warm, runny honey
1 generous tsp ground cinnamon	1 tbsp warm honey
1/2 tsp baking soda	2 tbsp confectioners' sugar
1/2 cup softened butter	2 tbsp milk (optional)
1/2 cup soft brown sugar	Electric mixer
3 eggs, separated	1 × 9-inch cake pan

Heat oven to 400 degrees Fahrenheit (200 C). Sift the first three ingredients into a bowl and set aside. Beat together the butter and brown sugar until creamy. Beat two of the egg yolks and blend them into the creamed mixture. Give the other egg yolk to the cat. Then beat in the honey, poured in slowly, and stir continuously.

Stir in the flour mixture. If the resulting blend seems too stiff, add the optional milk.

Beat one of the egg whites until stiff and fold it gently into the mixture. Pour the cake batter into a greased 9-inch cake pan. Bake for 20–25 minutes.

Remove the cake from the oven, and let it cool for two minutes. Turn the cake from the pan and cool thoroughly on a wire rack.

Beat the remaining egg whites with the confectioners' sugar until a stiff meringue is formed. Brush the one tbsp of honey onto the top of the cooled cake. Then spoon on the meringue, and raise it into peaks with the back of the spoon. Bake in a 325 degree Fahrenheit oven for 10–12 minutes, or until the meringue is golden brown.

When the cake is cool, slice it, and serve. Welsh honey cake is often served with rummed whipped cream: whipped cream flavored with ample amounts of Jamaican rum. It is up to the festival organizer whether or not this tradition is honored.

Scots Oatmeal Cookies

(Recipe makes 3–4 dozen cookies)

3/4 cup sifted all-purpose flour	1/2 tsp vanilla
1/2 tsp baking soda	1/4 tsp water
1/2 tsp salt	1 egg
1/2 cup butter, softened	1 cup uncooked rolled oats
6 tbsp sugar	1 six ounce package
6 tbsp brown sugar	semi-sweet chocolate
1 greased cookie sheet	morsels

Heat oven to 375 degrees Fahrenheit (190 C). Sift the first three ingredients together into a mixing bowl and set aside.

Cream the butter, white and brown sugars, vanilla, and water.

Beat the egg into the butter mixture.

Blend the flour mixture into the butter mixture, stirring well. Add the oats and chocolate morsels and blend.

Drop rounded teaspoons of batter onto a greased cookie sheet and bake for 10–12 minutes. More cookies can be made by dropping smaller amounts of batter.

Irish Soda Bread

(One round loaf makes 10–15 slices)

4 cups sifted all-purpose flour	1/4 cup softened butter
(or 3 cups all-purpose, and	2 cups raisins (optional)
1 cup wholewheat flour)	1 1/3 cups buttermilk
1 tsp salt	1 egg plus 1 egg yolk
1 tsp baking powder	1 tsp baking soda
1 two quart casserole dish	

Heat oven to 375 degrees Fahrenheit (190 C). Sift the first three ingredients together. With pastry blender or two knives, cut in the butter until pastry is like coarse cornmeal.

(Optionally, stir in the raisins, to which may be added candied cherries or other candied fruit, dates, or preserved citrus peel, up to a total amount of 3 1/4 cups.)

Blend together the buttermilk, egg, and baking soda. Let this mixture foam slightly and stir it into the pastry.

Knead the dough on a floured surface until it is smooth. Shape it into a ball. Place the dough in a 2–quart, greased casserole dish. With a sharp knife, make a cross 1/4 inch deep in the top of the dough. Brush the top with the single egg yolk. Bake for 70 minutes and cool thoroughly in the casserole dish before turning out, slicing, and serving with butter and jam.

Traditional Trifle, Common to all Parts of Britain

(Recipe will serve 12 people)

3 egg yolks	Raspberry jam
2 1/3 cup heavy cream	1/3 cup sherry
1 tbsp sugar	8 ounces frozen raspberries
1 tsp cornstarch	2 small bananas, peeled and sliced
Day-old sponge cake	thinly
4 tbsp flaked almonds, lightly toasted	

Break the sponge cake into pieces and spread a little raspberry jam on each piece. Put them in a mixing bowl with the raspberries and pour sherry over them. Stir well.

To make a custard blend the egg yolks, sugar, and cornstarch together in a bowl. Heat half the heavy cream in a saucepan, and when it is hot, pour it into the egg mixture, stirring constantly to keep it from curdling. Return this blend to the saucepan, and stir over a very low heat until it thickens. Remove from heat and allow to cool.

Sprinkle the sliced bananas over the sponge cake and raspberry mixture and top with the cool custard. Transfer to a glass serving bowl. Whip the remaining half of the heavy cream, and spread it over the top of everything. Sprinkle the almonds over the top. Cover the plastic wrap and refrigerate for a few hours before serving.

Making a Proper Pot of Tea

Making tea is actually very simple. (First boil sufficient water and heat the teapot with some of it.) Pour out the water from the teapot and add one teaspoon of tea per person, plus one for the pot. (This rule applies for standard size teapots. Vary amounts for larger pots.)

Tea bags are perfectly suitable, too. For about eight cups of tea, place three tea bags into a standard pot and fill with freshly boiled water. Allow the tea to brew for about five minutes, covering the pot with a tea cozy if you wish, and serve. Some tea drinkers prefer to have leaves in their cups. To avoid this, pour loose tea through a strainer.

In Britain, several types of tea are available for varying tastes and times. Lapsang Souchang, for instance, is a smokey tea, preferred with Indian food. Earl Grey is an aromatically flavored tea, normally served with lemon. China teas are drunk without any additives. English breakfast, Ceylon, Kandy, and Indian teas come in varying grades and strengths, and most people drink them with milk. Fruit flavored and herbal teas, especially camomile and mint, are also popular but have never replaced standard Indian or Ceylonese tea.

Sources of Inspiration

Trying to select a *few* books about Great Britain is worse than having to decide which of thirty-eight ice cream flavors one will have. Given the vast amount of reading material about, and emanating from Britain, the following represent a personal choice that should give a library a fairly wide coverage, with great scope for growth. Since Britain has produced so many great writers, I have not attempted to provide even a "top forty." Another book will have to be published to cope with even that many. For help in selecting British writers for your collection, consult "The Queen's English" listing below.

A General Overview

Cecil, David. *Max, A Biography.* London: Constable, 1983.
    Like Dr. Johnson and Oscar Wilde, Max Beerbohm is famous as an artist and public personality. He was England's supreme parodist and cartoonist, a leading wit and an Edwardian dandy. This book is not only a picture of the man but of his age.

Coones, Paul. *The Penguin Guide to the Landscape of England and Wales.* Harmondsworth, Middlesex: Penguin, 1986.
    Learn about the sub-tropical gardens of the Scilly Isles of Cornwall, the peaks of Derbyshire, the Moors of Yorkshire, the hills and mountains of Wales and the Lake District, the glacial plains of East Anglia, and every other geographical feature of England and Wales.

Cowie, Leonard. *Plague and Fire: London 1665–66.* London: Wayland, 1979.
    In two successive years in the 17th century, London suffered two terrible disasters—bubonic plague and a raging fire. This is the story of these disasters, taken from extracts of the diaries of Samuel Pepys and John Evelyn.

Davies, Hunter, and Frank Herrmann. *Great Britain: A Celebration.* London: Hamish Hamilton, 1982.
    Nineteen gloriously illustrated chapters capture the dignity and frivolity, tidiness and eccentricity of Britain and her people, from Blackpool's seaside tattiness to the majesty of Durham cathedral, from the Wembley soccer Cup Final to the Sale Room at Sotheby's.

Digby, Ian. *Scotland: A Year of the Land.* London: Colour Library, 1983.
    This giant collection of stunning photographs and accompanying captions reveals the magical landscape of Scotland, from loch and brae to castle, fen, croft, and craig.

Dobson, Julia. *Children of the Tower.* London: Heinemann, 1978.
    Julia Dobson has the rare gift of writing history in a way that children find palatable, even exciting. Here she weaves tales of murdered princes, of children who have witnessed the imprisonment and executions of their parents, and of children of officials who have lived in the Tower from its earliest days to the present.

Greene, Carol. *England.* Chicago: Childrens Press, 1982.
    England's varied terrain, rich history, ancient tradition, and unique life-styles have been fostered on a cluster of islands a part of, yet separate from, Europe. This is their abbreviated story.

Halliday, F. E. *An Illustrated Cultural History of England.* London: Thames and Hudson, 1981.
    Illustrated with a wealth of material, from neolitic carvings to the artistic achievements of today, the book is an odyssey of English history, art, politics, economics, and social life.

Halsey, Margaret. *With Malice Toward Some.* New York: Simon and Schuster, 1959.
    This is the freshest, wittiest, most readable introduction to the English people one can find, even though it has aged fifty years since Halsey (an American) experienced England and wrote these memoirs.

Handpicked Tours in Britain. London: Automobile Association, 1977.
    Over four hundred illustrated pages of driving tours, with scenic and historic sites within easy reach, are planned for motorists who can base themselves in a historic city or town. This book is essential not just for vacationers but also for armchair tourists.

Illustrated Guide to Britain. Basingstoke, Hampshire: Drive Publications, 1975.
    Arranged by short motor journeys for sightseers, this Automobile Association book is worth its weight in gold for its tips on history, architecture, and countryside and includes information on local horse-racing, angling, and other sports, maps, walks, and places to see.

Ingrams, Richard, comp. *England, An Anthology.* London: Collins, 1989.
    This book of Quintessential England, from suburbia to churchbell-ringing, from dappled terraces to running of the hounds, reveals to non-Britons the soul and heartbeat of this country, with superb wood-engravings by John O'Connor.

Jenkins, Alan. *London's City.* London: Heinemann, 1973.
    Stand on 2000 years of human history when you enter this financial heart of Britain: The City. This book helps armchair travellers enjoy The City's churches, Guildhall, Barbican, Cathedral (St. Paul's), and ancient monuments, including the Tower, St. Katherine's Dock, and the grave of the real Mother Goose in the graveyard of St. Olave's Church.

London. New York: Time-Life, 1976.
    A book in the Great Cities Series, *London* provides a photographic tour of what has been called "the most civilized city on earth."

McCormick, Donald. *Islands of Scotland.* Reading, England: Osprey Press, 1974.

This guide to 247 Scottish islands reveals a hint of the Celtic majesty of those mountains, wed to the western sea, where life continues much as it has for centuries.

McKenney, Ruth, and Richard Bransten. *Here's England—A Highly Informal Guide,* 3rd ed. New York: Harper and Row, 1971.

This is a witty tourist's manual, from the American point of view, including most of England and pointing out differences, similarities, and peculiarities in the two cultures but maintaining a reverence for the ancient history of the Mother Country and her European ways.

Morris, Jan. *Wales.* New York: Oxford University Press, 1982.

In this book, Welshmen down the ages speak of their tiny nation's struggle to preserve its identity, language, and customs against the odds of history.

Nicolson, Nigel. *The National Trust Atlas.* London: George Philip and Son, 1984.

This is an illustrated guide to over 500 miles of unspoiled coastline; 550,000 acres of land; and country houses on a majestic scale all owned and protected by the National Trust and open to the public. Comprehensive maps of England and Wales help motorists locate the properties easily.

Norrie, Ian, and Dorothy Bohm. *A Celebration of London: Walks Around the Capital.* London: Andre Deutsch, 1984.

A tourist's photographic guide to the capital of the United Kingdom shows where to find the unusual, the unexpected, and the breathtaking in city squares, public buildings, churches, tea rooms, parks and pubs.

Osborne, John. *The Silent Revolution: The Industrial Revolution in England as a Source of Cultural Change.* New York: Scribner's, 1970.

This is a discussion of the beneficial cultural changes in artistic taste, moral values, education, and the structure of law which attended the onslaught of industrialism, which had its beginnings in northern England.

Parker, Rowland. *The Common Stream.* London: Collins, 1975.

This is the story, the evocation, of English village life, based on Parker's years of detailed research, telling how people lived, what they ate and wore, the hardship they endured, and the artifacts they have left. Above all, it is a story of continuity.

Smith, Lesley, ed. *The Making of Britain: The Middle Ages.* New York: Schocken Books, 1985.

Look at the history of Britain from the Norman Conquest to the defeat of Richard III. Learn how villages developed and about the life there, the manor system, the Magna Carta, the King's Court, and the Age of Discovery and Exploration.

Snodin, David. *A Mighty Ferment: Britain in the Age of Revolution, 1750–1850.* San Francisco: Seabury, 1978.
Explore the politics, culture, and social changes in Britain during a turbulent century.

Sutherland, Dorothy. *Scotland.* Chicago: Childrens Press, 1985.
This is a well-written introduction to Scotland, its people, customs, kilts, bagpipes, harps, mountains, and way of life.

Veber, May. *Ireland Observed.* New York: Oxford University Press, 1980.
Ireland is a land of ancient magic, ambiguous behind its mists and married to the sea. Veber tours the country, talks to the people, walks in castles and galleries, drinks Guiness in its pubs, and finds Ireland to be a generally marvellous place.

Walmsley, Jane. *Brit-Think, Ameri-Think, A Transatlantic Survival Guide.* London: Harrap, 1987.
Two countries divided by a common language? So near and yet so far? Find out the humorous side of the common bonds which unite England and the United States.

Whines, Nicholas. *A Children's History of London.* London: British Broadcasting Corporation, 1988.
Paintings and engravings by artists over the centuries, along with panoramic and aerial photographs, illustrate a lively text and activity book which gives young readers a glimpse of the rich life and history of London.

Williamson, Jan. *The Children's Book of Britain.* London: Usborne, 1980.
Without condescending to children, Williamson gives a kid's-eye view of things to do and see.

Winks, Robin W. *An American Guide to Britain.* New York: Scribner's, 1977.
How to adapt to British customs, currency, cars, and manners; what to buy, read, and look for; what foods to try, which beers to drink: learn it all by taking eleven circular motor tours based on important British cities, from Cambridge to Oxford, Bath, and other well-known cathedral towns.

A Passion for Gardens and Wildlife

Coats, Peter. *Great Gardens of Britain.* New York: Spring Books, 1970.
The diversity and quality of British gardens clearly shown in photos and texts about Nymans, Exbury, Pylewell, Kinross, Luton Hoo, Blenheim, and other stately homes from Cornwall in the southwest to Montgomeryshire in Wales to Country Down in Ireland and Logan in Scotland.

Dudgeon, Piers, ed. *The English Vicarage Garden.* London: Michael Joseph, 1988.
Thirty Anglican priests, bishops, and laypeople write about noteworthy rectory gardens of roses, herbs, and other plants that thrive in England's Gulf Stream

climate. There are excellent full color photos of gardens set against centuries old churches, walls, and houses.

Fitter, Richard, ed. *The British Book of Birds.* London: Drive Publications, 1986.
The most complete illustrated guide to Britain's bird-life available, featuring over 300 species in full color with a wealth of information about each, including song, habitat, behavior, nesting habits and distinguishing features.

Grigson, Geoffrey. *The Englishman's Flora.* St. Albans, Hertfordshire: Paladin, 1975.
Both rare and common flowers and plants of field, hedgerow, and garden that have been of significance to generations of British people in daily life; ceremonies of spring, summer, and winter; magic and medicine, providing food for thought and body; are examined in detail.

Smith, Roland. *Wildest Britain: A Visitor's Guide to the National Parks.* Poole, Dorset: Blandford Press, 1983.
This richly illustrated book shows Britain's ten national parks—wild, full of scenic majesty, and teeming with flora, fauna, and geological variety, from seashore to mountain peak.

The Queen's English

Amis, Kingsley. *The Amis Anthology: A Personal Choice of English Verse.* London: Hutchinson, 1988.
These poems, chosen from the 1400's to the present day by novelist Amis because of the "special illusions" they have created, reflect a broad spectrum of interest, appeal, and writers, from John Lyndgate (1370–1450) to George Szirtes.

Blue, Lionel, Rabbi. *Bright Blue: Rabbi Lionel Blue's Thoughts for the Day.* London: British Broadcasting Corporation, 1985.
Rabbi Blue's humor and common sense make his pithy essays into the nature of humanity among the wisest, and most entertaining, writing in Britain today.

Brett, Simon, ed. *The Faber Book of Useful Verse.* Boston: Faber and Faber, 1981.
Here are poems for "use" by weather forecasters, farmers, lovers (male and female), children, aspiring poets, mathematicians, advertisers—poems for everyone with a particular need, beginning with work from the eighth century BC, and concluding with the 1980's, from Hesiod and Virgil to Robert Louis Stevenson and Tom Lehrer.

Coward, Noël. *Blithe Spirit. Private Lives. and Hay Fever.* London: Pan, 1960.
Noël Coward's sparkling mood can be seen nowhere better than in these three glittering plays, written between 1930 and 1942.

―――. *The Lyrics.* London: Methuen, 1983.
Two hundred and seventy-six lyrics, in chronological order, make up the most complete collection in print of Noël Coward's songs, from "Mad Dogs and

Englishmen," "Don't Put Your Daughter on the Stage, Mrs. Worthington," to "A Room With a View" and "The Girl Who Came to Supper."

——. *The Diaries.* Edited by Graham Payne and Sheridan Morley. London: Macmillan, 1982.
Called a "goldmine of gossip" by *The Guardian,* the diaries of the British playwright, actor, and songwriter reveal the thoughts of one of the most colorful characters to stride the stage and one of this century's wittiest English writers.

Fenster, Robert. *Shakespeare Games.* New York: Harmony Books, 1982.
Thirty-six games, puzzles, anagrams, puns, matches, fill-ins, and mazes, plus a scoring system, delight the erudite, stump the smart, and excite a festival organizer looking for spicy events.

Fry, Christopher. *Selected Plays.* New York: Oxford University Press, 1986.
Five of Fry's most popular plays are here, including *The Boy with a Cart, A Sleep of Prisoners,* and *The Lady's not for Burning:* dramas rooted in Anglo-French history and religion.

Gardner, Helen, ed. *The New Oxford Book of English Verse.* New York: Oxford University Press, 1975.
This anthology attempts to represent the range of poetry written over seven centuries, including British, American, and Commonwealth poets.

Grigson, Geoffrey. *The Oxford Book of Satirical Verse.* New York: Oxford University Press, 1980.
Few forms of satire are more wickedly enjoyable, writes Grigson in his introduction to these 232 poems form the 1500's to the 1970's.

Howard, Philip. *The State of the Language: English Observed.* London: Hamish Hamilton, 1984.
Howard asks if the English language is deteriorating, or if its richness of variety, from Dublin to Chicago to Brisbane to New Delhi, is enhancing the most widely-spoken tongue in the international community.

Kavanagh, P. J. *The Oxford Book of Short Poems.* New York: Oxford University Press, 1987.
The editor has chosen 650 of the best English language poems of less than fourteen lines, from medieval times to the present, including work by Chaucer, Shakespeare, Milton, Brontë, Cowper, and Blake, plus poems by lesser-known writers.

Lambert, J. W., and Michael Ratcliffe. *The Bodley Head, 1887–1987.* London: The Bodley Head, 1987.
Thorough research and good sense of period are seen in this history of a major British publisher, whose authors include Maurice Sendak, Betsy Byars, Susan Cooper, C. S. Lewis, Rosemary Sutcliff, Oscar Wilde, and other great names in English language writing.

Larkin, Philip. *Collected Poems.* Boston: Faber and Faber, 1988.

All of Larkin's published poetry, besides some previously unknown, written from his middle teenage years in the 1930's up to his death in 1985, reveal the heart of a great contemporary British writer.

Lathan, Robert, ed. *The Illustrated Pepys.* London: Bell and Hyman, 1978.

Pepys, the perfect diarist for the general reader, had an unquenchable joy in the curiosity of life in the 1660's, which included the Restoration, the Plague, and the Great Fire of London. The extracts in this edition, one-twelfth of the original, capture the full flavor of the famous diary and are enhanced by contemporary prints, paintings, and maps.

Miles, Bernard. *Favorite Tales from Shakespeare.* New York: Hamlyn, 1976.

Beautifully illustrated storybook style, this book takes five of Shakespeare's plays and turns them into exciting tales for children. Included are *Macbeth, Midsummer Night's Dream, Romeo and Juliet, Twelfth Night,* and *Hamlet.*

Morley, Frank. *Literary Britain: A Reader's Guide to Its Writers and Landmarks.* New York: Harper and Row, 1980.

Organized along the major pre-motorway highways of Britain so that a traveller could take in as much as possible en route, this book takes the visitor to *hundreds* of literary locations whose associations will be savored by English language students wherever they may be.

Townsend, John Rowe. *Written for Children: An Outline of English Language Children's Literature.* New York: Penguin, 1977.

An imminently readable history of children's books in Britain, the Commonwealth, and America, including poetry and picture books, this challenging appraisal of the genre is one of the most concise, entertaining, and lucid of its type.

Wright, Peter. *Cockney Dialect and Slang.* London: Batsford, 1981.

"Nahthen! Gisalook atha kitchen cook!" To the initiated that means "Now then! Give us a look at that book!" Use this book to learn about Cockney rhyme and slang from London's East End. It tells how the dialect developed, how to pronounce it, and how to invent it, for new rhymes are made up daily.

Royalty

Fraser, Antonia, ed. *The Lives of the Kings and Queens of England.* London: Weidenfeld and Nicolson, 1975.

Lady Antonia Fraser presents the pageant of almost a thousand years of England's history through the lives and deeds of her sovereigns—some merry, some cruel, sinister or perverse—spanning ten dynasties from the invading Normans of 1066 to the House of Windsor today.

Litchfield, Patrick. *A Royal Album.* London: Elm Tree Books, 1982.

This is a collection of photographs of the Royal Family by the man who took the official wedding portraits of the Prince and Princess of Wales in 1981, including formal and informal pictures of the Family as they are both in official regalia and at home.

Millar, Oliver. *The Queen's Pictures.* London: Chancellor Press, 1984.
Of all the great European royal art collections, that of the British Royal Family is the only one not to have been absorbed into a national collection. This is the first record of a collection which spans centuries and possesses some of the world's greatest artworks.

Morris, James. *Pax Britannica.* New York: Penguin, 1979.
This description of the British Empire at its climax at the Diamond Jubilee of Queen Victoria in 1897 reveals what the Empire encompassed, and how Britain ruled over half the globe.

Buildings: Churches, Castles, Ancient Monuments

Brabbs, Derry. *English Country Churches.* London: Weidenfeld and Nicolson, 1985.
Evocative photographs of some of the best of England's medieval parish churches along with brief histories provide an education in architecture and social culture.

Burke, John. *English Villages.* London: Batsford, 1975.
Through text and photos, the author examines the particular qualities— architectural, historical, and social—of villages in each geographical division of England from seaboard to mountain, looking at local crafts, industries, and building materials.

Burman, Peter. *St. Paul's Cathedral.* London: Bell and Hyman, 1987.
Seven carefully researched and well illustrated chapters explore Christopher Wren's architectural masterpiece, the cathedral of the diocese of London, which was made even more famous the world over during the televised wedding of the Prince and Princess of Wales.

Chambers, James. *The English House.* London: Methuen, 1985.
For sheer diversity, English houses are unrivalled in Europe. This book examines domestic dwellings from grand country residences to humble farm cottages, Georgian villas, modern high-rise flats, Victorian row houses, and Regency Squares.

Cook, Olive. *The English Country House.* London: Thames and Hudson, 1974.
England's great stately homes owe their existence to the five hundred years of internal peace which fostered unity and tradition after the middle ages. This book treats these houses as works of art, relating them to the changing manners and habits of mind from which they evolved.

Goodall, John. *The Story of an English Village.* London: Methuen, 1978.
This picture book shows the growth of an English village from medieval clearing to present day urban congestion, seen from the same viewpoint every

hundred years or so, in exquisite watercolor and pen and ink by a prominent children's artist and illustrator.

Hibbert, Christopher. *Tower of London.* New York: Newsweek, 1980.

Vast, gloomy, and aloof from the bustle of modern London, the Tower still echoes with beheadings, tortures, treasons, and battles of yore. Here are the Crown Jewels, rare manuscripts, tons of medieval armor, and the very much alive Yeomen of the Guard in a living museum of British history. This large-format book captures the history and the beauty of this royal fortress in illustrations, charts, and fully documented text.

Johnson, Paul. *British Cathedrals.* London: Weidenfeld and Nicolson, 1980.

This book delves into the history and art of British cathedrals, not so much individually as by period, from the earliest buildings of Canterbury, Norwich, and Durham, through Norman, Gothic, Decorated, Perpendicular, Renaissance, and Modern. It is illustrated with interesting photos and floorplans and contains a chapter on how these magnificent piles of stone and glass were built. (See below.)

Plumb, J. H. *Royal Heritage: The Story of Britain's Royal Builders.* London: British Broadcasting Corporation, 1977.

By night, the majesty of St. Paul's Cathedral in London is emphasized by shadows in spotlights. Wren's masterpiece is visited by many tourists from America who enjoy the world-famous boychoir. The choir school is housed in a building behind the small medieval tower in the foreground.

Royal building—from the Tower of London through great medieval churches and castles, the Banqueting House, Chelsea Hospital, the Brighton Pavilion—and collecting—from paintings and statuary to glass, jewelry, stamps, books, and furniture—are revealed as a celebration of royal patronage and taste.

Rowse, A. L. *Windsor Castle in the History of the Nation.* London: Weidenfeld and Nicolson, 1973.

In this age of air travel, most visitors arriving at Heathrow are familiar with the towers, parapets, and terraces of Windsor Castle, residence of the sovereign and visible embodiment of Church and State. This well-illustrated book tells the Windsor story, from its Norman foundation to the second Elizabethan age.

The English at Prayer

The Book of Common Prayer. London: Society for the Promotion of Christian Knowledge, 1928.

Using the flowing English of Archbishop Thomas Cranmer, the Anglican prayerbook is based on the ancient texts of the western church and was considered by Shakespeare the most formative book in his literary development. It was carried throughout the world by the expanding colonial development and forms the basis of current worship in the Church of England.

The English Hymnal. London: Oxford University Press, 1960.

One of the two great collections of Christian verse used in services of the Anglican Church, this hymnal represents work from earliest times to the 1930's when the book was compiled, with music ranging from plainsong and Gregorian chant to Bach, Handel, the Wesleys, and Vaughan Williams.

The English Missal. London: Knott, 1930.

This complete *Book of Common Prayer* for the Church of England incorporates prayers, rites, and ceremonies for the Christian year and reflects the work of the Oxford Movement in restoring the ancient heritage of Anglican Catholicism.

Frere, Walter Howard. *A New History of the Book of Common Prayer.* London: Macmillan, 1950.

First published in 1855, this history of the book which, along with the Authorized Version of the Bible, has been ranked as the foremost work in the English language has gone through various editions and includes thorough documentation of controversy, Reformation and Roman theology, and continuing developments.

Hymns Ancient and Modern. London: William Clowes and Sons, 1950.

This is one of the two prominent hymnbooks of the Church of England. It covers a broad spectrum of music and verse for the Christian year, including the work of many British poets from Blake and Tennyson to Isaac Watts and Augustus Toplady.

A Taste of Britain

Althaus, Catherine, and Peter ffrench-Hodges. *Cook Now, Dine Later*. London: Faber and Faber, 1976.
    This collection of English recipes for dishes to be cooked the day before serving includes soups, salads, meats, vegetables, and desserts, chiefly for the working family and for those who want to enjoy entertaining more.

Ayrton, Elisabeth. *The Cookery of England*. London: Andre Deutsch, 1975.
    An astonishing variety of over 400 recipes from the 15th century onwards, translated into modern terms to serve from four to eight people, are accompanied by historical notes: this book helps prepare all items simply, from fresh ingredients.

Canter, David. *The Cranks Recipe Book*. London: J. M. Dent, 1982.
    Over 300 British vegetarian recipes, some of which are available daily at Cranks Restaurant near Carnaby Street in central London, show the scope and variety of texture and taste to expect from a balanced, non-carnivore diet.

Driver, Christopher, and Michelle Berriedale-Johnson. *Pepys at Table: Seventeenth Century Recipes for the Modern Cook*. London: Bell and Hyman, 1984.
    Recipes which diarist Samual Pepys enjoyed and wrote about have been adapted for today's cook, giving opportunity for a Pepys Feast with green pea tarte, capon and colliflowers, stewed venison, syllabub, and codlin tart—with music to accompany it.

Fitzgibbon, Theodora. *A Taste of Wales*. London: Pan Books, 1971.
    As pleasurable to read for its historic photographs and anecdotes as it is to use as a source for traditional Welsh food preparation, *A Taste of Wales* is an asset to any kitchen.

Grigson, Jane. *The Observer Guide to British Cookery*. London: Michael Joseph, 1984.
    Arranged by region so that readers may expect haggis from Scotland, roast beef from Yorkshire, and stew from Ireland, this useful and informative collection of recipes includes food lore and anecdotes from farmers, fishermen, and chefs.

Hemphill, Rosemay. *The Penguin Book of Herbs and Spices*. London: Penguin, 1975.
    Hemphill gives a detailed discussion of forty-eight herbs and aromatic seeds, from allspice to vanilla pod, along with herbal history and traditions; how to plant, harvest, and dry herbs; and how to make a herb lawn.

Keen, Liane. *Make a Meal of It: Recipes for When You Haven't a Thing in the Fridge*. London: Robin Clark, 1979.
    Judicious use of leftovers and a basically-stocked cupboard work culinary miracles for the author of this handy British collection.

Norwak, Mary, ed. *A Book of Norfolk Recipes.* Norwich: Norfolk Federation of Women's Institutes, 1984.

Spiced gooseberries, poached carp, beckaye, plaice flan, Stewkie blue cockle pie: these recipes from East Anglia reflect the region's seafaring traditions as well as its reputation as the cereal belt of England.

Ray, Elizabeth, ed. *The Best of Eliza Acton.* Baltimore: Penguin, 1974.

Recreate the dishes that graced the tables of Jane Austen, Lord Byron, and Tobias Smollett in this new edition of a 19th-century collection, the notes and explanations of which enable a modern cook to achieve bygone taste and elegance.

Recipes from the Country Kitchen. London: Reader's Digest Association, 1980.

One of the glories of this large and attractive collection of British recipes is its "compleat map" showing traditional foods from each country and (in England) each county. Readers can make Irish colcannon, baked tanrogans from the Isle of Man, and Jersey Wonders from the Channel Islands as well as over 500 other items. There is an illustrated history of rural cookery from medieval times to the present.

Sass, Lorna. *To the Queen's Taste: Elizabethan Feasts and Recipes.* London: John Murray, 1977.

Most of these recipes came from books published in the reign of Elizabeth I, whose flamboyant delight in food finds a sympathetic echo today. Through these recipes turn mundane spinach into a fruity side dish, poach salmon in ale, and bake a blackbird pie.

Simply Divine: Recipes from the Cooking Canon and Rabbi Blue. London: British Broadcasting Corporation, 1986.

Exotic chapter headings, such as "Fancy Religious," "What the Actress Fed the Bishop," "Exodus Eating," "Teddy Bears' Picnics," and others show the humor with which these two English clergymen, one Jewish, one Anglican, share their passion for cooking.

Smith, Delia. *Delia Smith's Complete Cookery Course.* London: British Broadcasting Corporation, 1983.

This omnibus of English cookery by a television chef offers lessons in preparing roasts, casseroles, pastry, cakes, and vegetarian dishes, emphasizing fresh ingredients in the best English tradition.

British Sporting Life

Doban, E. F., Jr. *Starting Soccer: A Handbook for Boys and Girls.* New York: Harper and Row, 1976.

Action photos make this entertainingly-written instruction book an excellent tool for youngsters to use on their own or with an adult coach.

Duckham, David. *Rugby Union: Backplay*. London; Pelham, 1981.
   The techniques and skills of rugby football, at which the British excel, are revealed by an international player.

Farmer, Bob. *How to Play Cricket*. London: Hamlyn, 1979.
   It may look like baseball from a distance, but the resemblance stops there. After reading this book, you may want to organize a team at your school.

Rosenthal, Gary. *Everybody's Soccer Book*. New York: Charles Scribner's Sons, 1981.
   Besides explaining kicks, passes, and ball control, this book gives a history of the sport and shows how soccer has spread around the world.

Westacott, H. D. *The Walker's Handbook*. New York: Penguin, 1978.
   Maps, tents, clothes, rights of way, hostels, farmers, shoes, safety—all a walker in Britain needs to know in order to walk happily and safely.

British Periodicals: A Selection

A La Carte: The Food and Wine Magazine
IPC Magazines
King's Reach Tower
Stamford Street
London SE1 9LS
   Published ten times a year, this glossy magazine is composed of articles on all aspects of dining, from recipes to out-of-the-way restaurants, from cheese production in rural farms to society wining and dining in the best London hotels.

British Heritage
2245 Kohn Road
POB 8200
Harrisburg, Pennsylvania 17105
   Six issues a year look at the historic sites of Great Britain, from abbeys and castles to battlegrounds, villages, and coalmines, with sojourns into craft, food, books, and cultural events.

House and Garden
Vogue House
Hanover Square
London W1
   A monthly magazine, *House and Garden* shows the latest decorating trends and gardening updates for the upwardly mobile.

In Britain
Box 1238 Allwood
Clifton, New Jersey 07012
   In Britain gives readers a colorful monthly visit to the best historic, scenic, and culinary spots in the Isles, with a calendar of events, helpful ads for hotels and car rentals, and excursions to unique traditional events in out-of-the-way spots.

Interiors
Pharos Publications
234 King's Road
London SW3 5UA

    Published eleven times a year, *Interiors* is probably the most fashionable British magazine, reflecting the lives of the tasteful rich in their beautifully appointed houses.

For Further Information

Contact the information bureau at the British Embassy, requesting brochures, posters, leaflets, and other sources of information about the United Kingdom:

The British Embassy
3100 Massachusetts Avenue, N.W.
Washington, D.C. 20008

Chapter Four

Una Festa d'Italia:
A Festival of Italy

Can any other country boast as many superlatives as Italy? Just think of a few: great collections of art from antiquity, from the middle ages, and the Renaissance; world-renowned design in modern automobiles, fashion, and architecture; a rich cuisine that reflects its Mediterranean climate and geography; literature ranging from early Latin poets to doctors of the church to Renaissance scholars; sacred and liturgical music designed to reverberate from gallery to gallery in the majestic cathedrals of Venice, Rome, Milan, Florence, and nearly every other major city and town from the Alps to Calabria; grand opera and grand houses in which to perform it; varied landscapes that encompass Tuscan hillsides, the southern Alps, large natural lakes, miles of seaside, hot natural springs, volcanoes, and sunbaked vineyards.

Italians are among the world's foremost contributors to the arts. From Leonardo da Vinci, Andrea Della Robbia, Michelangelo Buonarotti, and Giovanni Bellini to Monteverdi, Palestrina, Guiseppi Verdi, and Rossini, Italians have excelled in painting, sculpture, ar-

119   Italian Bookmark

If the Eiffel Tower is the international symbol of France, the Statue of Liberty the symbol of the United Sates, and Big Ben the symbol of Britain, then the Leaning Tower of Pisa must be an instantly recognizable symbol of Italy. Until 1991, students were allowed to climb the circular staircase inside the campanile from which they could enjoy bird's eye views of the cathedral and surrounding city. Built almost entirely of marble, these medieval structures illustrate the magnificent creative energy of the Italian people.

chitecture, and music. Modern artists include filmmaker Frederico Fellini, actress Sophia Loren, painter Modigliani, and architect Renzo Piano. Italian potters produce terracotta and ceramic ornaments and culinary utensils, just as their ancestors have done for thousands of years. Artisans on the island of Murano produce exquisite glass in the method developed by their Venetian forebears in the Middle Ages.

From their peninsular country, Italians have spread throughout the Western world. Large colonies of Italian immigrants have carried their culture to Australia, Britain, Canada, South America, and the United States. American teenagers pay homage to Italian cuisine every time they phone an order for a pizza. Gastronomes sing the praises of Italian wines, from vino nobile de Montepulciano to pinot to amarone. Most kitchen cupboards stock parmagiano cheese and tomato sauce or puree to enliven spaghetti, ravioli, and the many other pastas that derive from Italian cooking. Italian communities celebrate saints' days with street fairs, dancing, singing, cooking and eating, bringing Mediterranean sunshine to all the parts of the globe in which they have settled.

Venice is one of the world's most magic places. Here, at the Ponte Rialto, the Grand Canal winds its way from the Lagoon to the Venice Basin. Una Festa d'Italia can involve students in learning about cities like Venice, Rome, Florence, Naples, Sienna, and Milan, each of them centers of art, history, and excellent cuisine. Are there Italian place names in your area? As a research project, compare the Venice, Parma, or Verona in your state with the original.

"Una Festa d'Italia" can include many varied activities, based upon the Italian love of beauty in all its forms:

1. Music and Musicians
2. Art and Artists
3. Literature and Writers
4. Food
5. Religion

An Italian festival could be planned for a saint's day, such as that of Francis of Assisi (October 4) or Antony of Padua (June 13); during the autumn for a harvest festival; in the spring when sunshine warms the earth; or as part of a cycle of cultural and geographical celebration at any time of the year.

From the earliest days of the church Roman Catholic Christianity is closely linked with Italian art, history, and music. Non-Catholics can learn much about Italian culture and artistic symbolism without diluting their own beliefs through study of Italy; indeed, such a study is essential for a deeper appreciation of artistic expression of the Middle Ages and Renaissance. The church was the mother of art, and through art sought to spread Christianity to an unlettered populace. In an age which no longer expresses itself through ancient Christian symbolism yet still appreciates the fine art of the great Christian eras, a historical study of the development of Roman Catholicism will lead to deeper understandings. Una Festa d'Italia can incorporate seminars, lectures, and research opportunities to broaden knowledge about these epochs of history, the development of the Italian city-states, and the influence of religion and politics on all forms of the arts.

This is an excellent school-wide festival for an energetic teaching librarian to organize, turning the media center into a piazza of art, music, food, and literature. Cooperation of art, music, and language teachers, along with involvement of students, will provide a lively and profitable **Settimana in Italia.**

Una Mostra del Marmo Falso: Fake It!

A Faux Marble Display

To honor the great Italian art of the past and to capture something of the elegance and ambience of the Italian peninsula, build a marble portico using a flat wall (figure 26) and simple cardboard shapes painted to look like marble.

What You Need:

Cardboard:
    Empty cardboard tubes from a carpet store
    Empty large appliance box
    Grocery boxes
    Two flat pizza boxes
Artist's craft knife
Drawing materials
Ruler
Paint:
    Household latex paints (colors to achieve faux marble)
    Tempera
Brushes:
    Household brushes for large project
    Artists' brushes for fine marbling details
Sponges (torn into fragments for texturing marble)
Roller brush trays (for each access to paint)
Glue
Staples and stapler
Masking Tape
Old newspapers (to protect floor and work surface)
Rubber gloves (optional, to keep paint off hands)

To begin, take a good look at the best place for the design. This could be against a flat wall, around an existing doorway or window, or on a free-standing chalkboard or easel. Get an idea of the size available and make sketches, looking in a few books about Italian architecture as you go. Try to find a chapter on Palladio, Brunelleschi, or Alberti, three great Renaissance architects. Look at a picture of the facade of San Giorgio Maggiore in Venice, or at eighteenth-century British and American efforts at reproducing the Italian style, which recall the heritage of ancient Greece and Rome. Before we let

Set a dramatic stage for an Italian festival by faking a classical doorway made from cardboard. Make it 3-D with boxes and tubes, or flat with shadows painted on. To make fake marble: ① sponge the cardboard white or off white. Don't aim for total coverage; ② sponge on another color of your choice, letting first coat show through; ③ Paint on dark, squiggly lines, diagonal and intersecting, with an artist's brush; ④ Paint on light lines, delicately. Make a renaissance notice board, cut from flat cardboard and marbleized. Pin daily or weekly festival events there, along with book notes, clippings, free recipes or photos.

(Figure 26) A Faux Marble Display

our heads get caught in the clouds, however, remember that this display must be simple and that the basic effect is one of geometric balance and artistic trickery.

This is an excellent project for student involvement! The adult in charge should do most of the cutting, but a student team can help with measuring and painting. Steps 5a and 5b (pages 126–127) require no special skills, and young students enjoy sponging on the paint. Older students will have the patience to apply the paint in step 5c (page 127).

Having decided where to put the display, gather your materials:

For the columns you will need either two large cardboard tubes of the sort used by carpet manufacturers or large sheets of cardboard from a refrigerator box.

For the base of the columns you will need two cardboard boxes. Two flat pizza boxes can be turned into the capitals.

For the faux marble, you will need several colors of latex paint and tempera, a selection of small artists' brushes in varying sizes, a household sponge or two, and some paint trays.

You will need a large staple gun, glue, and masking tape to hold the columns and pediment sections together.

Rubber gloves will protect your hands, and copious spreading of newspapers will protect the work area. Wear old clothes.

What to do

1. Measure the display area. Decide how tall the columns will be. Make a careful sketch and write down the dimensions as you go.

2. If you are lucky enough to find cardboard carpet rolls, measure them and cut off the excess. To turn flat cardboard into round columns, trim the board to the correct height. Then slowly and carefully fold the sheet of cardboard in upon itself. Two or three people can do this fairly easily. You may find that it helps to roll the cardboard onto a small wastepaper basket or paint can. When the cardboard is pliable enough to form a relatively round column, cut off the excess, leaving enough for a slight overlap. Staple, glue, and tape the column together. Repeat to form the other column.

(Alternative I: If you like creative painting, this is probably easier: cut out a flat column in silhouette, letting paint create the effect of three-dimensions. Sponge on "shadows" with dark-tinted paint along one side of column and highlight the brightest light on the front of the column with a narrow line of very light tint. Include the capital, the column, and the base in the cutout.)

(Alternative II: Instead of trying to make a round column, make a square one by dividing the sheet of cardboard top to bottom into quarters, carefully measuring so that each segment is the same size. Using a ruler and pencil, mark off the four dividing lines. Score with the craft knife. Bend the segments open until you have a four-sided column.)

3. Choose two grocery boxes to become the pedestals, or bases, of the three dimensional columns. If the columns are going to rest flat against the wall, you will probably need to adjust the width of the boxes so they don't project too far and throw the columns off center. Adjust the width with ruler and craft knife.

(Alternative I: For cutout, one-dimensional columns, make cutout, one-dimensional bases as part of the column or cut out a separate cardboard square on which to rest each column)

(Alternative II: Use pizza boxes instead. This will give less height, and be less architecturally impressive, but certainly involves less painting later on.)

4. The pediment, or top of the door frame, is really just a triangle. Measure the space to be covered between the columns, allowing for an overhanging eave on each side. You may be able to make the pediment from one large refrigerator box, cut open to reveal a large plane of flat cardboard. Failing access to one of these, assemble the pediment from several flat pieces of cardboard taped together.

(Alternative I: Measure and draw the pediment on a roll of butcher paper or artroom paper. After painting it, pin it to the wall above the columns.)

(Alternative II: Vary the style of the pediment by making a semi-circular top instead of a triangle, or make it simpler yet: cut out a rectangle of cardboard, long enough to stretch across both columns with an overhang on each side.)

5. Paint to achieve the effect of marble.

a. First, give each cardboard column and the pediment a coat of white latex paint with a sponge. Apply the paint liberally, but it does not matter if some of the cardboard shows through. Turn the sponge in your hand to avoid repeating the same pattern over and over.

Sponging should give a cloudlike appearance, allowing bubbles and the texture of the sponge to show. Allow this coat to become tacky, but not thoroughly dry.

(Hint: Instead of buying paint for this project, ask colleagues and students to look through home storage units for half-used cans. If white paint is not available, sponge on a base coat of *light* paint, such as magnolia, tan, buttermilk, yellow, or even light green. Marble isn't always white.)

b. Next, use the sponge to apply a coat of another color of your choice—gray, light blue, light yellow. Look at real marble or photographs to see the many varieties of color in nature. It is not necessary to completely cover the white with this second coat. In fact, you may at the end of this step have three colors visible: cardboard tan, white, and your own color choice.

c. Now the creative fun begins. Select a dark color to complement your second coat. If you have sponged on gray, then black, dark gray, or deep gray-purple is good. For yellow, choose a rich red, orange, or purple. With a fine artist's brush dipped in this dark color, spread wavy lines of paint diagonally along the cardboard. Repeat this frequently, stopping occasionally to daub the paint with the sponge, in effect, diluting it into your second coat.

If you wish, dip the sponge back into your second coat color as you do this to help blend in the effect of the marble stripe. Continue this diagonal "striping" until the entire surface of the columns and pediment is treated. Then proceed diagonally in the opposite direction, repeating all the above. It is not necessary to allow these lines to dry before beginning work in the opposite direction.

d. Using a much finer brush dipped into a complementary lighter color, paint light, delicate lines parallel with and crossing over the dark lines which you sponged in. White paint is ideal, but light yellow and pastel shades of red are also good, depending upon your color theme.

e. To create shadows along the sides of flat columns or on the pediment, dip the sponge in a darker shade of your overall second coat. Achieve this darker shade by adding small bits of black or brown to your second coat color. Start experimenting with very small amounts of black or brown, since a little will go a long way. Tempera or poster paints mix perfectly well with household latex paints.

On flat columns, sponge on a light coat of darker color along the sides, top to bottom, trying to blend the color in gradually toward the center, so that by the time you have reached one-quarter of the way into the column, no paint is being spread. In other words, dark to the outside, light to the inside.

To add shadows to the pediment, lightly pencil in lines parallel to the gable "roof." These lines should stop when they reach the top of the pediment. In effect, you will draw a triangle inside the pediment. Apply masking tape to the lines to achieve a fine, clean finish. With dark paint on your sponge, carefully apply "shadow" along the underside of one of the parallel lines. Apply a much thinner line of darker paint along the other lines.

f. Wash out the sponge and brushes thoroughly in warm, soapy water. By the time you've finished, the cardboard forms may be dry enough to position onto the display area. The marble effect is best observed at a distance, but if you have used a delicate approach, your work may look real up close, too.

(This technique of faux marbling works well on cardboard fireplaces for Christmas displays. Using oil-based paints, and working slightly slower, the same technique can be used to refinish old furniture, library check-out desks, plant pots, and garden benches.)

6. What goes between the columns? In effect they are only rather ornate picture frames. If placed around a doorway, put the name of the festival within the pediment and add two terracotta pots with bay trees on either side: the festival theme is set. If the Italian facade is placed against a wall, organize the students to paint a mural of a Tuscan hillside town, a grape arbor, or a sun-filled sky with the hills and sea beneath. Use reference books and books about Italy to inspire creativity.

To letter the title of the display, look at some book jackets or study a few books on calligraphy and typesetting. Visit a local cemetery or stone mason's yard to see what lettering looks like in real granite or marble. Copy designs there and try to duplicate it on the faux marble.

L'attivite delle Feste: Festive Italian Activities

Make a Renaissance Mosaic

Since earliest days of Italian civilization, artists and architects have used mosaics to create splendidly patterned floors, walls, and representational artwork. A mosaic project can help students create a beautiful object while learning something of the ancient history of this craft. While permanent mosaics would be made of stone or glass, we will use paper to achieve the effect without the expense or the training needed to duplicate real Italian mosaics.

What You Need:

Graph Paper for mosaic design
Color construction paper and/or gift wrap
Plain white or color paper for base sheets
Glue stick
Pencils and erasers
Rulers
Scissors

a. Study the designs (figure 27) taken from life sketches in the Basilica of San Marco in Venice. Look at reference books for further ideas. Notice that stone mosaics have several similarities with that particularly American art form, the patchwork quilt. Both are based on simple interconnecting geometric shapes. Photocopy figure 27 so that students may refer to it.

b. First, have students draw simple geometric shapes, such as squares or rectangles, on the graph paper. Subsequent shapes should be identical to and connect with the others.

Ask them to create a *counterpoint motif* that cuts through each geometric shape, adding interest and possibility of greater use of color. This counterpoint motif may be a triangle in each corner of the square or rectangle. It may be as simple as dissecting each geometric pattern with a cross.

The instructor may ask them to repeat the motif in each of the original geometric shapes, or they may move on to the next step after drawing the counterpoint in only one of the shapes.

c. To make the mosaic in color, students will need to make templates which they will trace onto color paper. To make a template, cut out one of the original geometric shapes on the graph paper. Cut out each of the segments formed by the counterpoint motif.

To achieve a harmonious effect, the same colors should be repeated in each square. In part two of figure 27, the squares have been halved

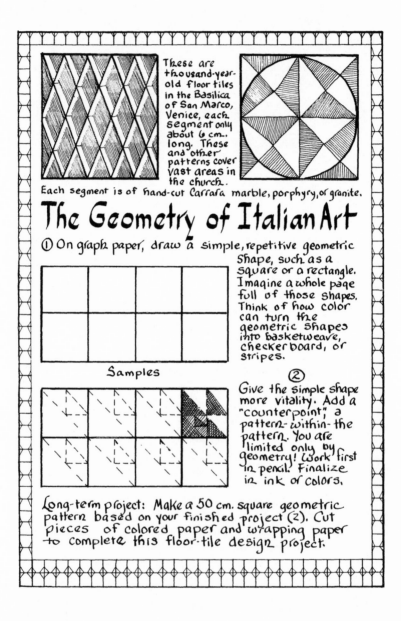

These are thousand-year-old floor tiles in the Basilica of San Marco, Venice, each segment only about 6 cm. long. These and other patterns cover vast areas in the church.

Each segment is of hand-cut Carrara marble, porphyry, or granite.

The Geometry of Italian Art

① On graph paper, draw a simple, repetitive geometric shape, such as a square or a rectangle. Imagine a whole page full of those shapes. Think of how color can turn the geometric shapes into basketweave, checkerboard, or stripes.

Samples

② Give the simple shape more vitality. Add a "counterpoint," a pattern-within-the pattern. You are limited only by geometry! Work first in pencil. Finalize in ink or colors.

Long-term project: Make a 50 cm. square geometric pattern based on your finished project (2). Cut pieces of colored paper and wrapping paper to complete this floor-tile design project.

Figure 27

by a diagonal line, creating triangles. To create an authentic mosaic, for instance, each of the bottom triangles should be cut from one color, rather than using random colors. To make it easier, students could number or label each separate cut-out. All number one's could be blue, all number two's red, and so on.

When they have assembled several cut pieces, students should glue them to their base sheet. The base sheet can be made an integral part of the design when gluing the mosaics into position. Instead of positioning them contiguously, as in the original design, space them so that the base shows through, creating an even border between each piece of "patchwork." (figure 28)

d. These mosaic patterns can be turned into borders around the base sheets, or if time permits, they can fill the entire plane. The instructor could mention that designs of this sort were drawn by

(Figure 28) American patchwork quilts, like this one from 1840's Tennessee, are another form of geometric art with which students should be familiar. Using books in the "Sources of Inspiration" at the end of this chapter, compare American patchwork quilts with *all' antica* floor and wall mosaics from the Mediterranean. How do they differ? In what ways are they alike?

architects and masons for each mosaic pattern or picture before each piece was cut from stone by artisans. A short discussion of the tools and time involved in these large projects would give the students a greater appreciation for this simpler paper mosaic activity.

e. Display the finished products around the school, on top of low-level library shelving or on desks and study carrels. The mosaics could be protected with clear vinyl book wrap. They may then be used as place mats during the festival Italian meal or they could be converted into book jakets.

Become a Michelangelo

What You Need:

A garden ornament or statue
Paper
Drawing tools
Felt-tip pens
Coloring media (optional)
Light box (if available)

Italians love beautiful gardens, oases of dark green against the summer sunshine, usually with a fountain and always with a sculpture. Such sculpture gardens became the teaching academies of Renaissance Florence. There, in the Medici garden, the young Michelangelo first learned to carve. Take students to a local garden center to sketch garden ornaments, which could vary from terracotta urns (typically Italian) to poured concrete cherubs and dolphins. Look at books of Italian art and landscape to see pictures of authentic statuary and copy that. Go to a local museum to sketch antiquarian sculpture or replicas of Greek or Roman statues. Easiest of all, bring a garden statue to school and use it as a model for drawing. Explain that this is the way young Italian Renaissance artists, such as Donatello, Montegna, and Michelangelo, began their careers.

Back at school, help the students select their best drawing. They can then (a) do a felt-tip line tracing, using a light box; (b) add shadows, background, and other details; (c) make a color version using oil pastels, felt-tips, crayons, acrylics, or other media at the discretion and advice of the group leader.

Display the work prominently near the faux marble portico.

Discuss and Research Venice in Peril

Venice is one of the most remarkable cities on earth, set on the light-refracting waters of a lagoon off the north Adriatic Sea. Its art treasures and historic buildings are unique in the world. For nearly 1500 years Venice has exerted a magic spell over those who live and visit there, yet it is sinking into the sea.

A research project could release interesting facts: what are the foundations for the buildings of Venice? When did the medieval campanile of San Marco fall down and how many people were killed? Where did the famous horses of San Marco come from? How many islands are there in the city? What is the "main street" of Venice called? What is "the ghetto"? What is a vaporetto? How long do bodies stay buried on the island of San Michele? Which island is famous for glass blowing? What is polenta? Why is Venice sinking into the sea?

Another project is to find cities in America that are named after Italian cities, towns, or regions. The starting point is the index of an atlas. Is there a Venice, a Florence, a Naples, or a Milan in your state? Draw an outline map of your state or of the United States. On another sheet of paper, draw an outline map of Italy. Tape the two sheets of paper together. Place a dot on each map for shared place names and draw a connecting line. You could also include civic and commercial statistics, such as population, industries, and climate.

A geography lesson or an exploration of an interesting corner of the world, the results of the research could be presented in written form, in drawings, and in *conversazione* (learned social gatherings) that could also explore other cities and regions of Italy.

Saints Alive! Artistic Symbols

Study the artistic symbolism of the religious painters of the early Christian era up to the Renaissance. Consult a reference work to find lists of saints, saints' days, and saints in art. Explain that symbols evolved to teach the illiterate masses about their religion. Combine a study of symbolism in artistic expression with slides and other reproductions of Italian art from the Middle Ages and the Renaissance.

Knowledge of paintings, sculptures, and those who made them and paid for their execution and knowledge of symbolism are paramount. Watch a group of untutored students wandering through a museum or gallery and compare them with students who have, through assigned tasks, learned what to look for. One group will be easily bored, distracted, and noisy; the other will be interested, involved, and perhaps noisy, but for a different reason.

Provide a list of Christian religious symbolism in art, based on the following pattern:

The Saints: Their Symbols in Art

Agnes: a lamb
Francis of Assisi: birds, animals, the stigmata
Jerome: a lion
John the Baptist: skin of an animal, lamb
Joseph: carpenter's square
Lawrence: gridiron (on which he was grilled alive)
Nicholas: anchor, boys in a boat, three purses
Patrick: shamrock, harp, serpent
Peter: keys, cock, boat
Mary: stars, lily

Refer to *Hall's Dictionary of Subjects and Symbols and Art* (see page 149) for further examples.

a. As an art project, have students design a symbol for themselves, as if they had been canonized. Would the symbol represent their hobbies, their grades in school, their afterschool jobs, or a special talent?

b. In the Middle Ages, good church members would have believed in a host of saintly mediators and protectors. There would have been saints for their birthdays, saints for their parish church, their town, their profession, their country, and saints for special illnesses and adventures. Provide a special task sheet (figure 29) to help students understand the concept. Reference books (see page 148) will provide the necessary lists.

c. Ask students to look for artistic symbols in their school, such as an animal mascot; in places of worship, such as a star, a cross, a crescent moon, an open book, lilies, crowns, or symbols studied in Italian painting; in newspapers and magazines, such as an American flag, a baseball; in interstate highway signs, such as stylized gas pumps, motel rooms, or cross cutlery.

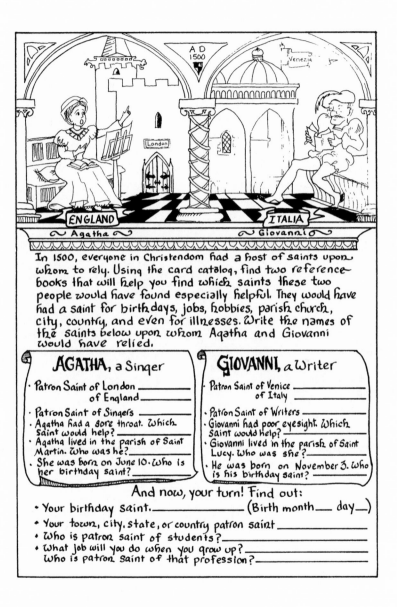

In 1500, everyone in Christendom had a host of saints upon whom to rely. Using the card catalog, find two reference books that will help you find which saints these two people would have found especially helpful. They would have had a saint for birthdays, jobs, hobbies, parish church, city, country, and even for illnesses. Write the names of the saints below upon whom Agatha and Giovanni would have relied.

AGATHA, a Singer

· Patron Saint of London _____ of England _____
· Patron Saint of Singers _____
· Agatha had a sore throat. Which Saint would help? _____
· Agatha lived in the parish of Saint Martin. Who was he? _____
· She was born on June 10. Who is her birthday saint? _____

GIOVANNI, a Writer

· Patron Saint of Venice _____ of Italy _____
· Patron Saint of Writers _____
· Giovanni had poor eyesight. Which Saint would help? _____
· Giovanni lived in the parish of Saint Lucy. Who was she? _____
· He was born on November 3. Who is his birthday saint? _____

And now, your turn! Find out:

· Your birthday saint. _____ (Birth month___ day___)
· Your town, city, state, or country patron saint _____
· Who is patron saint of students? _____
· What job will you do when you grow up? _____ Who is patron saint of that profession? _____

(Figure 29) Artistic Symbolism and Saints Task Sheet

What do these symbols say to people today? Why do literate people need symbols?

Discover Italian Americans

Make bulletin board space available to display magazine photos and newspaper articles about Italian Americans. They will range from movie stars to musicians to politicians to people in all walks of life.

Include local residents of Italian descent, too. Social studies students could interview Italian families to find out about immigration, assimilation, and preservation of Italian identity through customs, foods, and religion.

Oratori: Guest Speakers

1. If there is an Italian community nearby, ask a **Cook,** an **Artist,** or a **Language Teacher** to speak about an aspect of Italian immigrant life. Ask a **grocery owner** or **wine importer** to discuss Italian foods and cuisine.

2. Invite an **opera enthusiast** to talk about that finely developed Italian art form. If there is no opera near you, inquire at the music department of a neighboring university or college. Show slides, listen to recordings, or rent a video of a popular opera such as "La Boheme" or "Madame Butterfly" by Puccini or "The Barber of Seville" by Rossini.

3. Ask an **art historian** or school **art teacher** to speak about one aspect of Italian painting or sculpture, perhaps limiting the talk to one artist (Leonardo, Michelangelo, Donatello, Bellini), one city (Florence, Venice, Rome, Padua, Milan, Naples), or one epoch (Roman antiquity, Middle Ages, Renaissance, Twentieth Century). Prior to the talk, work with history or art teachers to provide student research assignments within the topic.

Topics for research and discussion could include:

Comparisons of Renaissance art in Northern Europe with that in Italy.
The master/apprentice system in Medieval and Renaissance Italian art workshops.
Social and political upheavals in Renaissance Italy: the plague, the Medici, Savanarola.

The effect of Columbus's historic trip to the New World on Italian art and cuisine.

4. Invite someone to discuss one aspect of **Italian literature,** which could range from Dante's *Inferno* or Vasari's *Lives of the Artists* to the recently popular novel by Umberto Ecco, *The Name of the Rose.* Italian American writers, such as Mario Puzo, could form the bases for class discussions and seminars.

5. If you live in a wine-producing area, invite a **wine-maker** to tell how wine is made, from grape harvest to crushing to fermentation and bottling.

Viaggi: Trips to Take

1. **Visit a Museum of Art** to see Italian painting. This is easy to do in metropolitan areas but more of a problem in small towns, where reproductions of artwork in books or frameable prints may be the only alternative. Before visiting a museum or gallery, or studying reproductions in detail, assign each student a particular artist to research, so that during the course of the visit, they themselves may tell others about the artist's life, work, and reputation. Actively involve the students to help them learn and remember.

2. **Visit a Winery** to see how grapes are turned into wine. Many areas of America, from California to the East Coast, pride themselves on their vineyards and offer educational tours.

3. **Visit "Little Italy" or another Italian community** in your area and, if possible, shop in an Italian grocery store and eat in an authentic Italian trattoria.

4. **Save money for a trip to Italy** for there is nothing like the real thing. The country is too large to cover in a short time, so pick a destination, such as the artistic capitals of Florence and Venice, and spend two weeks immersed in paintings, sculptures, gelati, and fine food.

Musica Italiana per la Festa

1. With the school music department, plan some recitals of Italian keyboard music. Students may be familiar with the work of Scarlatti, whose music ranges from relatively easy to difficult. They

can play the instrumental versions of some of the works of Palestrina, Monteverdi, or Verdi, or they could learn the overtures to some Italian operas. Work with the music teachers to plan an event with an Italian flavor that could include beginning students as well as those with more proficiency.

Include school choral groups, too, who could perform some Italian madrigals, a chorus from an opera, or a liturgical piece.

2. To set the mood for an Italian meal of pizza or zucchini toscano, play some recordings of Luciano Pavarotti quietly in the background. If there is an accordian player, hire him or her to play some romantic ballads from time to time, either during a foodfest or simply as a lunchtime entertainment in the manner of the Venetian gondoliers.

Who Broke Michelangelo's Nose?
(Drama and Storytelling)

Tell or read the story of Pinocchio from one of its many forms and editions. Encourage younger students to create scenes from the story during pauses in the telling. With the drama teacher and older students, work on an improvisation of Pinocchio that could lead into a scripted performance.

Renaissance artists were not without their intrigues and misfortunes. Read Vasari's *Lives of the Artists* (page 150) to find out who broke Michelangelo's nose. Or find out why Pope Julius II threatened to throw Michaelangelo off a 65-foot scaffold. Read about the self-assured artist Andrea Mantegna who married against his stepfather's wishes. Tell the story and act it out with a friend.

Become familiar with the lives of some Italian saints and tell their stories. The life of St. Francis, lover of animals and friend of the poor, is a good place to begin. Ask students to enact scenes from his life. Many saints met gruesome ends. Appeal to youngsters' fascination with gore and horror by telling them the story of St. Peter Martyr who met his death at the hands of zealous swordsmen. Link the story with reproductions of paintings of this saint, represented in art by a sword in the head.

Parla Italiano: Vocabulary and Drama

By the end of the festival, everyone should be able to say "Buon giorno," "Ciao," and "arrivederci!" with confidence. Ask the language department or an Italian speaker in the community to serve as "conversationalist in residence" during the festival. While few children would be turned on by a lecture on Italian phrases, they might pick up a few words if the process were turned into a game.

a. Place a new **Italian word of the day** in prominent places throughout the library and school. Announce it over the public address system at the start of school. Print it in the daily bulletin. Begin every conversation with a hearty "Buon giorno" and teach students to say "per favore" when they wish to check out a book or ask a question. When someone does you a favor or when a boisterous child responds favorably to your plea for silence, give him a grateful "grazie."

b. Encourage creative drama in small groups by handing out sheets of some common, useful Italian words and phrases (pages 140–143). Go over pronunciation, if necessary, with the help of a linguistic friend, and ask students to act out daily scenes speaking only Italian. Suggest scenes such as:

Going out for a pizza
Shopping for vegetables
Asking for directions to the post office
Meeting an acquaintance in the street
Counting out change from a purchase

Since Italians are famous for generous gestures and use of the hands, eyes, arms, and body in verbal communication, turn this drama activity in a lively session by "side-coaching" commands such as, "use your arms," "raise your hands," or "lift your eyebrows." Remember, too, that Europeans in general are much more polite in everyday speech than Americans are and that they use those charming words "please" and "thank you" much more than Americans do.

Remind students that all syllables of Italian words are pronounced and that all consonants are emphasized sharply, quite in contrast to the rather slouchy way we pronounce English. Vowels are always pronounced the same. There is no such thing as a short "a" or a long "a." Refer to an Italian grammar or tourist guide for guidance in pronunciation.

A helpful list of Italian words and phrases

Basic Italian Expressions

1. Yes	1. Sì
2. No	2. No
3. Please	3. Per favore
4. Thank you.	4. Grazie.
5. Thanks very much.	5. Mille grazie.
6. Good morning.	6. Buon giorno.
7. Good evening.	7. Buona sera.
8. My name is . . .	8. Mi chiamo . . .
9. What is your name?	9. Come si chiama?
10. Goodbye.	10. Arrivederci/Ciao
11. See you later.	11. A piu tardi.
12. How are you?	12. Come sta?
13. Very well, thanks.	13. Molto bene, grazie.
14. And you?	14. E lei?
15. Excuse me.	15. Mi scusi.
16. You're welcome.	16. Prego.
17. Do you speak English?	17. Parla inglese?
18. Do you understand?	18. Capisce?
19. I don't understand.	19. Non capisco.
20. I'd like . . .	20. Vorrei . . .
21. Do you like . . .?	21. Le piace . . .?
22. I like . . .	22. Mi piace . . .
23. I don't know.	23. Non so.
24. Where are the toilets?	24. Dove sono i gabinetti?
25. I'm looking for . . .	25. Cerco . . .
26. It is closed.	26. E chiuso/E chiusa.
27. It is open.	27. E aperto/E aperta.

Some Useful Questions

28. Where is . . .?	28. Dov'é . . .
29. How . . .?	29. Come . . .?
30. When . . .?	30. Cuando . . .?
31. Why . . .?	31. Perche . . . ?
32. May I . . .?	32. Posso . . . ?
Can I . . .?	
33. Who?	33. Chi?

34. What?	34. What?
35. Do you have . . .?	35. Avete . . .?
36. At what time . . .?	36. A che ora . . . ?
37. How much does it cost?	37. Quanto costa?

Some Directions

38. Straight ahead	38. Dirrito
39. Traffic lights	39. Semaforo
40. Turn left	40. Giri a sinistra.
41. Turn right	41. Giri a destra.
42. It is on the left.	42. E a sinistra.
43. Opposite	43. Di fronte
44. Next to	44. Vicino a
45. Behind	45. Dietro
46. At the next	46. Al prossimo

Some Words to Play With

47. Post office	47. L'ufficio postale
48. Post Card	48. Cartolina
49. A stamp	49. Un Francobollo
50. Mail box	50. Cassetta delle lettere
51. I want to send	51. Desidero inviare
52. United States of America	52. Stati Uniti
53. Pizzaria	53. Pizzeria
54. Restaurant	54. Ristorante, Trattoria
55. The cheese	55. Il formaggio
56. The milk	56. Il latte
57. The salad	57. L'insalata
58. The soup	58. La zuppa, La minestra
59. The bread	59. Il pane
60. Vegetables	60. I legumi
61. Pizza	61. Pizza
62. Spaghetti	62. Spaghetti
63. Seafood sauce	63. Vongole
64. Tomato sauce	64. Salsa pomodoro
65. Sausage	65. Salsiccia
66. Ice cream	66. Gelato
67. I'm just looking.	67. Sto solo guardando.
68. I'll take it.	68. Io prendo.

The Days of the Week

69. Monday	69. Lunedi
70. Tuesday	70. Martedi
71. Wednesday	71. Mercoledi
72. Thursday	72. Giovedi
73. Friday	73. Vernerdi
74. Saturday	74. Sabato
75. Sunday	75. Domenica
76. Today	76. Oggi
77. Tomorrow	77. Domani
78. Yesterday	78. Ieri
79. The morning	79. La mattina
80. The afternoon	80. Il pomeriggio
81. The night	81. La notte

Counting

1. One	1. Uno
2. Two	2. Due
3. Three	3. Tre
4. Four	4. Quattro
5. Five	5. Cinque
6. Six	6. Sei
7. Seven	7. Sette
8. Eight	8. Otto
9. Nine	9. Nove
10. Ten	10. Dieci
11. Eleven	11. Undici
12. Twelve	12. Dodici
13. Thirteen	13. Tredici
14. Fourteen	14. Quattordici
15. Fifteen	15. Quindici
16. Sixteen	16. Sedici
17. Seventeen	17. Diciasette
18. Eighteen	18. Diciotto
19. Nineteen	19. Dicianove
20. Twenty	20. Venti
21. Twenty-one	21. Ventuno
22. Twenty-two	22. Ventidue
30. Thirty	30. Trenta
40. Forty	40. Quaranta
50. Fifty	50. Cinquanta

60.	Sixty	60.	Sessanta
70.	Seventy	70.	Settanta
80.	Eighty	80.	Ottanta
90.	Ninety	90.	Novanta
100.	One hundred	100.	Cento
1000.	One thousand	1000.	Mille

Cibi Italiani: Festival Foods to Make

Italy's vast and highly sophisticated cuisine contains robust peasant cooking as well as elegant, subtle foods from the sea, the rocky hillsides, and fertile, sunny flatlands. In addition to the world-famous pastas and pizzas, Italy offers tasty vegetables, seafoods, meats, and cheeses. For the festival, thumb through an Italian cookbook and choose a cake, an ice cream, or cookies. The following vegetable treat, however, is fun to prepare, is ideal for an Italian cooking demonstration, and uses materials readily available in most places. The cooking aromas alone will draw passerby into the festival area. Why not try making:

Zucchini Toscano

Ingredients:

Six to ten medium zucchini
Six to ten cloves of garlic
2 Tbsp dried mixed herbs
One large onion (or more)
1/4 cup (or more) sliced olives
1 green or red pepper, thinly sliced
One cup olive oil (do not use any other cooking oil)
Boiling water to cover zucchinis in frying pan
Salt and pepper to taste
One cup (or More) dried bread crumbs
1/2 cup (or more) freshly grated parmesan cheese (or substitute sharp cheddar)

Utensils:

Sharp kitchen knife
Cheese grater
Two frying pans (or wise use of one)
Large slotted kitchen spoon

Mixing bowls to contain separate ingredients
Serving plate

Slice each zucchini once lengthwise and saute the halves lightly in a frying pan of salted water to which has been added one crushed garlic clove (or more) and a large pinch of herbs. When the zucchini have cooked for about five minutes, remove them to a board or plate to drain.

Heat the olive oil gently in a frying pan. Add the sliced onion, sliced olives, and as many crushed or sliced garlic cloves as you wish. After about five minutes, add some of the zucchini slices. Sprinkle more herbs on each zucchini. Scoot the other vegetables to one side or pile them on top of the zucchini, which should cook until they are just tender. Turn the zucchini over once to ensure that they cook in the oil on each side. When they are tender, place them on a serving platter.

If the onions and other vegetables are browning too quickly, lower the frying pan temperature or remove them to a side plate.

When all the zucchini are cooked, arrange them in rows on the serving plate and sprinkle them generously with grated bread crumbs, herbs, parmesan cheese, and the cooked onions, olives, and garlic cloves. They may be eaten warm, but this dish is best when it has been allowed to cool thoroughly and to marinate in its own juices for two to four hours at room temperature.

Zucchini Toscano is best eaten with white Italian bread, a crisp green salad, and a glass or two of Vino Nobile de Montepulciano. It may be served as a main course or as an accompaniment to roast lamb, chicken, or veal. Like many peasant recipes, Zucchini Toscano may be adapted by using more of some things, less of others. Do not, however, use any oil other than olive. Quantities may be enlarged or decreased as deemed appropriate for the festival. The zucchini may be sliced into bite-sized portions for toothpick tastings. Zucchini Toscano is a classic spring and summer dish throughout Tuscany and Umbria and embodies the sun and ambience of northern Italy.

Bitsa Pizza

One of Italy's most famous exports is, of course, the well-loved pizza. Celebrate Italy with a pizza party, either catered from a local pizzeria or made at school with cooperation of the cafeteria. Ask students to nominate their favorite ingredients. Who can come up with the tastiest combinations? Who can invent the most novel, yet edible, pizza? Is the pizza merely a good way of using up left-overs? Visit the kitchens of a local pizzeria and find out how the crust is made. Send a research party to several Italian ristoranti to analyze ingredients and compare methods.

Un Giornale: Publish!

At the conclusion of the festival, gather sketchpads and drawings, reports on the lives of painters and sculptors, journalistic articles about guest speakers and concerts, recipes from Italian cooks, and stories about other aspects of the celebrations, not forgetting a list of reading materials that could extend the fun. Choose the best of everything submitted and publish it as a free handout. Send copies of the journal to everyone who helped with the festival, from speakers and demonstrators to guides in museums and parents of especially active students.

Give it an Italian name, of course. A newspaper is called "un giornale" and a magazine is "una revista," while news is simply "notizie."

Sources of Inspiration

Town and Country

Gault, Henri. *The Best of Italy.* New York: Crown, 1984.
This book for travellers provides over 1500 "candid, opinionated and refreshingly irreverent ratings" of Italian restaurants, hotels, and shops.

Hoffman, Paul. *Cento Citta: A Guide to the "Hundred Cities and Towns" of Italy.* New York: Henry Holt, 1988.
This tourist's view of Italian small cities and towns provides hotel lists, food and transport recommendations, and historical and art details.

Honour, Hugh. *The Companion Guide to Venice.* London: Collins, 1977.
This companion provides intimate knowledge of museums, streets, shops, parks, stations, and other places through text, maps, and pictures in what amounts to a room by room, wall by wall look at the treasures of this most wonderful of cities.

Lawrence, D. H. *Twilight in Italy.* New York: Viking, 1958.
Lawrence's Italy is not just a country of ruins and art galleries, but a living landscape filled with lively people who he describes with intuitive understanding.

Lear, Edward. *Edward Lear in Southern Italy.* Introduction by Peter Quennell. London: William Kimber, 1964.
Known largely for his limericks and nonsense verse, Lear was also a highly skilled artist in oils and watercolors, which he put to use in recording his extensive travels in southern Italy. He wrote as fluently as he drew. The combination of his drawing and journal entries brings 19th-Century Italy vividly to life.

Mariella, Cinzia. *Passport to Italy.* New York: Franklin Watts, 1982.
This handy reference book provides essential information about the country, its major cities and art treasures, customs, and foods.

Money, James. *Capri, Island of Pleasure.* London: Hamish Hamilton, 1986.
This social history of literary associations on the romantic island on the edge of the bay of Naples includes names from Emperor Tiberius in AD 26 to Somerset Maugham, Oscar Wilde, Compton MacKenzie, and Noël Coward.

Niero, Antonio. *The Basilica of Torcello and Santa Fosca's.* Venice: Edizione d'Arte, 1989.
This guidebook to the original cathedral of Venice, consecrated in 639 and rebuilt in 1008, illustrates the magnificent mosaics on the floors and walls of the ancient building and would be an ideal resource for an art project.

Sabino, Catherine. *Italian Country Living.* London: Thames and Hudson, 1988.
Take a colorful tour to celebrate the beauty of Italy's seashore, mountains, and countryside and savor the Italian passion for artful living—in golden vineyards, Alpine ridges, luxurious villas on Lago Maggiore, Sardinia, Capri, or the Amalfi coast.

Sardo, Douglas M. *The Riddles of Venice: A Book of Six Treasure Hunts in Venice.* New York: Save Venice Inc., 1989.
This colorful paperback provides maps of the city and pleasant treasure hunts (preferably done in the city itself), solvable with a Venice guidebook, that lead to famous poems or works of art.

Stein, Conrad. *Italy.* Chicago: Childrens Press, 1984.
Explore Italy's history, geography, people, culture, and major attractions through this young person's guide.

Thompson, Kenneth. *Skills in Research: About Italy.* New York: Cassell (Macmillan), 1979.
Learning how to do research—fact finding, recording, consolidation of information, presenting acceptable results—while learning about Italy in detail is the scope of this book for middle school students.

Vantaggi, Rosella. *Sienna: Town of Art.* Sienna: Plufigraf, 1985.
From the magnificent marble cathedral to the grand piazza, Sienna is a city that owes its beauty to 14th-century architects and town-planning. This book illustrates much of Sienna's artwork, architecture, and history.

Italian Art

Baxandall, Michael. *Painting and Experience in Fifteenth Century Italy.* New York: Oxford University Press, 1991.
For students of Renaissance painting, this book sharpens the powers of observation, widens outlooks, and stimulates curiosity.

Berenson, Bernhard. *The Italian Painters of the Renaissance.* Ithaca: Cornell University Press, 1980.
Read about the life, times, and work of Carpaccio, Titian, and a host of fellow creative geniuses.

Bernard, Bruce. *The Queen of Heaven.* London: MacDonald Orbis, 1987.
This is a huge visual anthology of narrative and devotional paintings on the theme of the Virgin Mary, including works by the greatest Italian masters (Fra Angelico, Titian, Giovanni Bellini, Giotto) as well as artists from other parts of Byzantium and Renaissance Europe.

Brown, Partricia Fortini. *Venetian Narrative Painting in the Age of Carpaccio.* New Haven: Yale University Press, 1988.
Drawing upon her knowledge of the primary sources in the Grand Scuoli of Venice, Fortini traces the exciting history of story painting in 15th- and 16th-

century Venice in this lavishly illustrated, readable book, focusing on the Bellinis, Carpaccio, Bastiani, Mansuetti, and other artists.

Burckhardt, Jacob. *The Altarpiece in Renaissance Italy.* Oxford: Phaidon, 1988.
This is a sumptuous visual reference to much of the great painting and sculpture of Italy, from Raphael, Giotto, and Cimabue to Michelangelo, Mategna, and Veronese, as well as lesser figures such as Grancia and Ferrari.

Dogo, Guiliano. *Guide to Artistic Italy.* Venice: Electa, 1981.
Arranged alphabetically by village and town, this illustrated guide provides thumbnail sketches of artworks all over Italy, in town squares, fountains, churches, and galleries.

Farmer, David Hugh. *The Oxford Dictionary of Saints.* New York: Oxford University Press, 1984.
This is an alphabetical listing of saints in the Roman, Anglican, and Sarum calendars, including artistic symbols by which they are represented in art.

Ferguson, George. *Signs and Symbols in Christian Art.* New York: Oxford University Press, 1961.
Divided into fourteen chapters, text and illustrations reveal the symbolism inherent in representations of religious personages, Earth and Sky, animals, birds, insects, flowers, and Old Testament characters.

Hall, James. *Hall's Dictionary of Subjects and Symbols in Art,* rev. ed. London: John Murray, 1992.
Valuable for understanding the hidden symbols in Italian art and sculpture— symbols that would have been fairly obvious to contemporaries of the artists.

Honour, Hugh, and John Fleming. *A World History of Art.* London: Macmillan, 1982.
Nearly 1000 illustrations, maps, and plans provide an up-to-date history of the visual arts from the Ice Age to the present, covering world religions, secular art, antiquity, and the twentieth century—including, of course, Italian painters and sculptors.

Labella, Vicenzo. *A Season of Giants: Michelangelo, Leonardo, and Raphael.* London: Little, Brown, and Co., 1990.
Superbly photographed paintings, drawings, and statues of these three giants of Renaissance Italy accompany a finely written account of quattrocento politics and social conditions.

Levey, Michael. *Early Renaissance* and *High Renaissance.* New York: Penguin Books, 1991.
In these two illustrated volumes, the author provides a social and artistic history of nearly two centuries of Italy, foremost among other European nations of the Renaissance.

Murray, Peter and Linda. *The Art of the Renaissance.* New York: Thames and Hudson, 1989.
Covering artists as diverse as Jan Van Eyck, Pierro della Francesca, Mantegna, and Bellini, the book closes with the advent of the artistic giants Leonardo, Michelangeo and Raphael.

Olson, Robert J. M. *Italian Renaissance Sculpture.* London: Thames and Hudson, 1992.
This well-illustrated book surveys the extraordinary Italian artistic achievements from about 1260 to 1600 and could provide grand ideas for displays and art projects.

Steadman, Ralph. *I Leonardo.* London: Jonathan Cape, 1983.
British artist Steadman's obsession with Leonardo led him to trace the life of the great Italian Renaissance man from his ordinary beginnings in Vinci, outside Pisa, to his triumphs in art and science. Steadman's humor and drawings combine with his own wit to create biographical enlargements upon Leonardo's life and inventions.

Vasari, Giorgio. *Lives of the Artists,* 2 vol, trans. George Bull. New York: Penguin, 1987.
This 16th-century collection of artists' biographies provides contemporary insights into their lives through Vasari's shrewd judgements and his precise pinpointing of emotion.

A Little History

Burkhardt, Jacob. *The Civilization of the Renaissance in Italy,* 2 vol. New York: Harper and Row, 1958.
This scholarly study of emergent Renaissance culture in Italy presents a history of its democratic government.

Cateura, Linda Brandi. *Growing Up Italian.* New York: Morrow, 1987.
Being brought up as an Italian American shaped the lives, characters, and careers of twenty-four prominent people, including Mario Cuomo, Tony Bennett, Geraldine Ferraro, and Francis Ford Coppola.

De Sanctis, Francesco. *History of Italian Literature,* 2 vol, trans. John Redfern. New York: Basic Books, 1959.
Scholarly, yet interestingly translated by John Redfern, this provides the best overview of the subject available.

Ets, Marie Hall. *Rosa: The Life of an Italian Immigrant.* Minneapolis: University of Minnesota Press, 1970.
In 1884, with the jostling European multitudes immigrating to America, a sturdy young Italian woman, named Rosa, arrives in New York. This is the story of her survival and triumph in the New World, told to Marie Hall Ets by Rosa herself.

Plumb, J. H. *The Italian Renaissance: A Concise Survey of Its History and Culture.* New York: Harper and Row, 1965.

Plumb paints a concise picture of the growth of art, learning, and science in Florence, Milan, Rome, and Venice, featuring the contributions of great people.

Learn to Speak Italian

Duff, Charles. *Italian for Adults.* London: English Universities Press, 1965.

A clearly arranged and interesting approach to the language, as well as an initiation in Italian life-styles and culture, this book is not devoid of wit and humor.

Hughes, Charles A. *Italian Phrase Book and Dictionary.* New York: Grosset and Dunlap, 1971.

This convenient, pocket-sized book offers a pronunciation guide, helpful tips on securing accommodations, meals and clothing, and suggestions for travelling in Italy for the first time, followed by an English/Italian dictionary.

Italian at Your Fingertips. New York: Routledge and Kegan Paul, 1987.

Providing very practical help in constructing sentences on the spot, this book has comprehensive English and Italian cross-reference sections to make shopping and basic conversation easier.

Messora, N. *Mastering Italian.* London: Macmillan, 1989.

A complete, self-contained course for individual study or classroom use, with sound tapes and practical conversational exercises.

Fiction and Literature

Benson, E. F. *Mapp and Lucia.* London: Black Swan, 1984.

A little learning is a dangerous thing, as Lucia finds out when she tries to make fellow townspeople think she speaks Italian in this 1920's novel of rich one-upmanship.

Bentley, Eric. *The Genius of Italian Theatre.* New York: New American Library, 1964.

Spanning 400 years of Italian drama, these seven plays include Tasso's "Amyntas," "Turrandot" by Gozzi, and "The Deceived" (which may have inspired Shakespeare to write "Twelfth Night") by an unknown writer.

Boccaccio, Giovani. *The Decameron: A Selection.* Wolfesboro, New Hampshire: Longwood, 1984.

Like the tales of the Arabian nights, which go on and on, these bawdy tales provide nights and nights of reading pleasure.

Crichton, Robert. *The Secret of Santa Vittoria.* London: Hodder and Stoughton, 1967.
   A very comic World War II novel about the rescue of one million bottles of wine from the German invaders as the people of the Italian hill town of Santa Vittoria rally behind Bombolini, the clownish wine merchant.

Eco, Umberto. *The Name of the Rose.* New York: Warner Books, 1984.
   This medieval murder mystery, involving a wonderful monastic library, interestingly reveals much of what cultural life must have been like before the Age of Enlightenment.

Fante, John. *1933 Was a Bad Year.* Santa Barbara: Black Sparrow Press, 1985.
   The Great Depression grips America, and a 17-year-old Italian American boy has to forget his own dreams to help out the failing family business in a small, poverty-ridden town.

Gallico, Paul. *The Snow Goose.* New York: Knopf, 1941.
   Gallico, born in 1897 of Italian Austrian parents, produced a jewel in *The Snow Goose,* a classic story of the rescue of Allied soldiers from Dunkirk in World War II.

Guareschi, Giovanni. *The House that Nino Built.* New York: Penguin, 1967.
   A chaotic, uproarious family does everything wrong in an amusing story of eccentric behavior.

Holland, Isabelle. *Of Love, Death, and Other Journeys.* New York: Dell, 1975.
   After living with her mother and stepfather in various parts of Europe, a 15-year-old girl meets her real father for the first time.

Kay, George R. comp. *The Penguin Book of Italian Verse.* New York: Penguin, 1966.
   Printed in the original Italian with English translations beneath: here are poems by St. Francis of Assisi, Michelangelo Buonarotti, Boccaccio, Dante, and other great poets.

Michelangelo. *The Sonnets of Michelangelo.* Trans. by Elizabeth Jennings. Manchester, U.K.: Carcanet, 1988.
   Ranging from formal thanks to passionate arguments, addressing patrons, lovers, and God, Michelangelo's sonnets reflect on his art and his physical and metaphysical struggles, dominated by vehement energy mastered by a longing for order.

Moravia, Alberto. *The Wayward Wife and Other Stories.* London: Penguin, 1964.
   Moravia writes of the tensions of human relationships in these eight stories of love, brutality, and victimization.

Pasinetti, P. M., ed. *Great Italian Short Stories.* New York: Dell, 1962.
   Thirty stories, from Boccaccio to Pirandello, span centuries of Italian writing, and include the tales that inspired Shakespeare to write "Romeo and Juliet" and "Othello."

Pirandello, Luigi. *Six Characters in Search of an Author.* London: Methuen, 1979.
    An intriguing dramatic variation on the theme of life versus art where actors
and a director in the midst of rehearsals are interrupted by six mysterious figures
who demand to be put into a play.

Stone, Irving. *The Agony and the Ecstasy: A Novel of Michelangelo.* Garden City, New
    Jersey: Doubleday, 1961.
    Set in the days of the Borgias, the warring popes, and the Medicis, this novel
of the great artist, writer, and composer Michelangelo crackles with intrigue and
the pursuit of beauty.

West, Morris. *Daughter of Time.* New York: Dell, 1963.
    San Stefano, a small town in Italy, seethes with corruption and violence in this
novel that probes the story of the murder of the mayor by a madonna-faced young
woman.

Italian Food

David, Elizabeth. *Italian Food.* London: Penguin, 1984.
    This exciting book demonstrates the enormous and colorful variety of Italy's
regional cooking, listing over 400 dishes and the herbs and spices required to
make them, with useful chapters on Italian wines and cheeses.

Howe, Robin. *Regional Italian Cookery.* London: David and Charles, 1972.
    Sample the exuberance, sun, tomatoes, olive oil, and garlic; taste the difference
between foods of the North and the South; savor the wines, cheeses, and gelati;
and trace your culinary journey on the handy food map on page ten.

Ross, Janet, and Michael Waterfield. *Leaves From Our Tuscan Kitchen.* London:
    Penguin, 1979.
    First published in 1899, this revised edition of a vegetable cookery classic
provides exquisite insight into the variety of Italian cuisine.

Santin, Gino. *La Cucina Veneziana: The Food and Cooking of Venice.* London: Ebury
    Press, 1988.
    This culinary journey into one of the world's best loved and most artistic of
cities gives an insider's appreciation of the food and cooking of the region of
Venice, with beautifully photographed visits to markets, shops, vineyards, and
canal-side cafes, and recipes of early 100 time-honored foods, from tiramisu to
carciofi santini.

Wasserman, Sheldon and Pauline. *Italy's Noble Red Wines.* New York: Sterling,
    1987.
    Written by an American couple who continue to visit the vineyards of Italy,
this is a complete, authoritative, and candid discussion of Italian red wines, from
Valpolicella and Sangiovese to Chianti, Vino Nobile de Montepulciano, and
Cabernet, beautifully illustrated with photographs and drawings.

For Further Information

Contact the Italian Embassy information office for posters, pamphlets, and brochures about travel, culture, food, and government:

> Embassy of Italy
> 1601 Fuller Street, N.W.
> Washington, D.C. 20009

Chapter Five

Beauty in Simplicity:
A Festival of Japan

Japan is a country that evokes many images today—powerful industrial giant in the Western Pacific. Tiny island chain with overcrowded, skyscrapered cities. Bullet trains. Sushi bars. Exquisite porcelain and many-tiered pagodas. Kimonos and Shoguns and oriental martial arts. Japan is certainly a mixture of many things, but in this festival, we will focus on some of the gentle aspects of an ancient island culture, replicating traditional scrolls and garden temples, folding origami, and cooking a vegetable stir-fry.

In Japan, a symbiotic blend of two religions, Shinto and Buddhism, helps people to live in harmony with themselves and nature. Long before Buddhism arrived in Japan in 6th century A.D., the old folk religion of Shinto, "the way of the kami," had led Japanese people to make the best of life, to live in rapport with nature, and to honor the gods, or kami ("superior ones"), with offerings of food, wine, and money. In Shinto temples, there were rarely statues but symbols, such as swords or mirrors, to represent the gods, chief of which was the Sun Goddess, from whom, it was believed, the

FESTIVAL OF JAPAN

Japanese Bookmark

Emperor descended. A strong sense of "pollution," or uncleanliness, developed in Shinto, and only correct ceremonial actions, not repentance, could purify contamination with untouchable items. Correct rites also honored the kami in order to get the desired results of more rain, an abundant harvest, or a healthy baby. Shinto festivals grew up around the agricultural year, celebrating harvests and plantings, the coming of spring and autumn, with offerings of produce, money, and entertaining parades and parties at the local shrines. In Shinto grew up the belief in the deity of one's ancestors, who are honored today with graveside gifts of food and wine, much as graves in the west are decorated with flowers.

When Buddhism was brought to Japan, the upper, educated classes readily took to it, and it gradually became the state religion, though it never totally replaced Shinto. Buddhism, which developed in India, is gentle, peaceable, and tolerant, looking upon life as transitory, impermanent, and often painful. This religion, though innocent of traditional beliefs in a deity, was able to incorporate the beliefs of Shinto so that today most Japanese celebrate holidays that combine tenets of both systems.

This is primarily a festival of Japan. It incorporates several events and activities which trace their origins to ancient times, such as construction of a tokonoma, or celebration of Tanabata. It offers the chance to make some simple Japanese foods, to make giant paper fish, and to experiment with origami. During the festival, or as a preparation for it, students can learn about Shinto, Buddhism, and the geography, history, and celebrations of Japan.

Create a Corner of Beauty: Tokonomo Display

What You Need:

Roll of art room paper or butcher paper
Artist's brush
Black ink or watery black tempera paint
Reference source showing Japanese scrolls
Ornament:
    Vase,
    Small statue
    Garden sculpture
    Japanese Temple Light (see figure 38, page 175)

Incense cones (optional)
Low coffee table or carpet

Build a *Tokonoma,* or "corner of beauty," suspending a *Kakemono,* or hanging scroll, from the display board (figure 30, below). Place a table in front of the board to hold a vase with one flower, a small temple ornament (available from most garden centers), or a statue of the Buddha.

The scroll can be made of butcher paper. Using a large, soft artist's brush, paint a design on the lower left-hand side of the paper. Copy a painting in a book about Japan, or paint an outline of a temple, a vase of flowers, or a branch of cherry blossoms. In the upper right-hand side of the paper, paint the title of the festival, imitating Japanese characters as much as possible, examples of which may be found in books at the end of this chapter.

From an oriental shop, purchase a box of small Japanese incense cones. Burn cones from time to time on a small fireproof dish in front of the kakemono to create a sweet-smelling ambience.

Paint a cherry branch in blossom with India ink and a drinking straw.

Place a large drop of ink in the center of the paper. Chase the ink by blowing it through the straw. The force of breath turns the ink into intricate, treelike patterns.

Paint one or two pink blossoms on the branch with 3 movements of a brush.

(Figure 30) A Display

Speakers and Visits: Martial Arts and Ikebana

1. Invite a **Japanese citizen** or an American of Japanese descent to visit the festival and to talk about some aspect of Japan: schools and children, holidays, art, religion, economics, or food.

2. Invite **someone who has travelled in Japan,** or who has Japanese procelain or lacquerwork, Japanese dolls, fans, or kimonos, to speak about life and art there.

3. Ask a **Buddhist** to talk about that religion, meditation, and philosophy.

4. Arrange for a **martial arts instructor** or studio to demonstrate karate or another form of this physical and mental art. Find out if any students are proficient in the oriental martial arts and ask them to demonstrate their skills.

5. Find out if a local flower club can demonstrate **ikebana,** the traditional Japanese art of symbolic flower arranging.

6. Demonstrate how to make a **Kakemono** in public with two or three student artists. The teacher prepares one or two scrolls in advance, and talks about how to make them while the student artists illustrate the lecture before an audience.

Make Kakemono: Hanging Scrolls

What You Need:

Butcher paper, or roll of white art room paper
Watery black tempera paint
Large artists' brushes (oriental, if possible)
Weights to hold down paper while painting:
    Pebbles, Paint Cans, Books
Ribbon
Cardboard box, painted with gloss black laquer outside, gloss red laquer inside
Thumbtacks or pins for wall display

Having made one hanging scroll for the festival display, teach the children to make one too, using butcher paper, black tempera, and, where possible, large Japanese or Chinese bamboo brushes (or use large artist's brushes with a fine tip).

Give each child a length of paper. To keep it from rolling up, place weights (pebbles, paint cans, books) on each end. Mix the tempera in

(Figure 31) Box to display student's Kakemono

a small container with water until it is creamy in consistency. Dip the tip of the brush in the paint, and with large, swift strokes, paint a simple outline figure—of a tree, a house, or a single cherry branch.

When the paintings are dry, roll them up and tie a ribbon around each one. Artists may paint their names on the back of the scrolls for easy identification. Store the kakemono on their sides in a cardboard box painted shiny black (figure 31).

To display the scrolls, hang them on a bright red background, red being a traditional Japanese color. Attach them to the wall with thumbtacks about two inches below the top of the scroll and two inches from the bottom so the paper will curl slightly into the picture. Hang the kakemono artistically, with equal space between each. Instead of hanging them all, make a rotating display of only a few at a time or put them up in various locations around the school.

Variations

1. Set up a still life of a vase with one branch from a tree or some artificial flowers, a Japanese-style garden ornament from a garden center, a Japanese doll, kimono, fan, or mask. Use these as ideas for painting a scroll.

2. Divide the art students into teams of five to ten people each. Ask each person to paint one scene from a folktale or story, each one depicting a different event. Traditionally, kakemono told stories in series of scroll pictures, so this fits in perfectly with time-honored practice.

3. Use kakemono to mount drawings in the Hokusai project which follows.

In Each Room a Center of Peace: Build Tokonoma and *Bonkei*

What You Need:

Refer to ingredients above for Tokonoma construction

For *Bonkei:*

Small cardboard boxes or tin cookie boxes
Sand
Scissors or craft knives
Small decorative objects
   Stones, Potted Plants, Statues
Kitchen fork

Each classroom, library, office, or hallway can have a tokonoma, or "corner or beauty" (figure 32), using one of the kakemono above a table or desk that holds a spray of flowers, a piece of statuary, an arrangement of stones, or a *bonkei,* a small miniature landscape which students can make in cardboard boxes, cut down to make trays.

To make a *bonkei,* cut most of the sides from a cardboard box and fill the remaining tray with sand. Place a stone, a little statue, or a potted plant on the sand. Smooth the sand and trace even, flowing patterns in it with a fork.

Three Japanese Fans: An Art Project

What You Need to Make All Three Fans:

Pencils
Rulers
Scissors
Color construction paper (Fan 1)
Ribbon or Yarn (Fan 1)
Stapler (Fan 1)
Heavy card (Fans 2 and 3)
Round or oval shape for tracing around:
   Plate, Wasterpaper Basket (Fan 2)

A CORNER OF BEAUTY

Make a quiet
tokonoma with
a kakemono, or
scroll, and a
bonkei, or miniature
landscape in a
box of sand.
Rake the sand with
a fork to make
a pattern
around the
plant and
stone.

Figure 32

Tempera paints (Fans 2 and 3)
Small artists' brushes (Fans 2 and 3)
Glue (Fans 1 and 2)
Color tape or contact paper (Fan 2)
Paper brad (butterfly clip) (Fan 3)
Color felt-tip pens or crayons (Fan 3)

Fans are used in Japanese drama, in traditional dress as an accessory, and for keeping cool. There are several types of fans to make.

1. **Folded fans** can be made from construction paper. You will need three or four sheets of color construction paper, about 10 by 8 inches long (figure 33). Fold each sheet, accordion style, and staple or brad them together at the bottom. At the top, staple adjoining sheets together.

To decorate the fan with a Japanese landscape, paint the paper, and let it dry, before folding.

2. **Flat fans** can be cut from cardboard. These fans may be oval or round. Trace around a small wastepaper basket or plate or use a compass. Leave a handle on one end, which should be reinforced with another piece of cardboard glued onto both sides, slightly overlapping onto the fan itself to keep it from bending.

Paint a landscape or a simple Japanese-style tree branch on both sides of the fan. Wrap the handle with color tape, plastic ribbon, or contact paper.

3. There is another type of fan used in Japan that is similar to those still found in the Southern United States. These fans can be made of cardboard or stiff card and fastened at the bottom with a paper brad or butterfly clip. To make one of these **sliding fans**, cut out three identical shapes, rather like the profile of a light bulb. Decorate each piece with collage, paint, crayon, or felt-tip. See if you can make the decoration "join up" when the fan is opened. In Japan, these fans are often used to serve delicate cakes and sweetmeats.

Hokusai: Study a Japanese Art Master

The woodcuts of Hokusai (1760–1849) became very popular in the West during his lifetime. His is famous for his many views of Mount Fuji, his scenes of daily life among workers and farmers, and

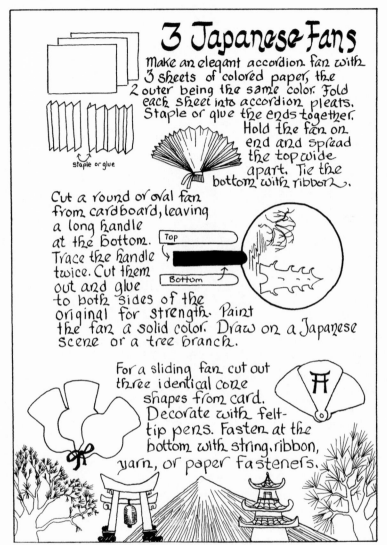

3 Japanese Fans

Make an elegant accordion fan with 3 sheets of colored paper, the 2 outer being the same color. Fold each sheet into accordion pleats. Staple or glue the ends together. Hold the fan on end and spread the top wide apart. Tie the bottom with ribbon.

staple or glue

Cut a round or oval fan from cardboard, leaving a long handle at the bottom. Trace the handle twice. Cut them out and glue to both sides of the original for strength. Paint the fan a solid color. Draw on a Japanese scene or a tree branch.

Top

Bottom

For a sliding fan cut out three identical cone shapes from card. Decorate with felt-tip pens. Fasten at the bottom with string, ribbon, yarn, or paper fasteners.

Figure 33

especially for his stormy seascapes composed of fierce waves ripped into foamy birdshapes by the wind. While all students can appreciate this art (refer to "Sources of Inspiration" at the conclusion of this chapter), artists from grade five and up can try their hands at copying Hokusai's distinctive style themselves.

What You Need:

Books or prints of Hokusai's paintings and woodcuts
Paper
Pencils
Brushes
Watercolors
Still life, such as *bonkei* (see page 160)

First, discuss Hokusai's style. Is it realistic or interpretive? Lead students' observations so that they can describe his graceful depiction of people and landscape. Second, ask them to look at the *bonkei,* the relationship of container to sand to plant or pebble. Finally, ask them to draw the *bonkei* in the style of Hokusai or give them a Hokusai print or seascape to copy. For mature artists, the project could take several art periods.

Display the finished projects to create an oriental ambience during the Japan festival. Mount the drawings on kakemono scrolls in red or other brilliant colors for added drama.

Celebrate a Japanese Festival

Like traditional festivals in other cultures, Japanese holiday celebrations are tied to specific times of the year. Schools can celebrate these festivals out of season, of course, by adapting the ideas of the celebrations. The New Year's Day and Children's Day events can be held at any time of the school year to fit into the Beauty in Simplicity Festival.

Shogatsu: New Year's Day Celebrations

On January 1 (Ganjitsu), all Japanese celebrate their birthdays. In some cities, boys and girls tie paper fortunes to the bare branches of trees to bring luck in the coming year. Children wear new kimonos, eat rice cakes, and fly kites. At midnight on December 31, evil is chased away by the ringing of bells, so everyone has a good time until January 15 when Shogatsu closes with the burning of a new year decoration made of pine, bamboo, and plum branches.

What You Need:

Students' ideas for celebrating a birthday party
Strips of paper, about 3 × 5 inches (8 × 13 cm)
String or yarn
Scissors
Pencils or pens
Felt
Double-sided cellophane tape

What to do

1. Celebrate everyone's birthday with a Ganjitsu party. Serve something good to eat. Play games, such as Fukiware (number 4, page 166). Dance to records. Set up a talent show. Have special treats for classmates and teachers whose birthdays occur during school vacations. To get student input, as them what they'd like to do to celebrate a plenary birthday.

Decorate a Fortune Tree

2. Decorate a bare tree branch, indoors or out, with fortune papers. Give everyone three long strips of paper. Ask children to think of some good things they would like to see happen, such as getting a new bike, having world peace, or stopping pollution. Ask them to write these wishes in the form of a prediction, or fortune, on the strips of paper.
   "This year we will stop littering the highways."
   "This year you will get A's in French."
   "This year you will visit a faraway city."
Put all the fortunes in a box and mix them up. Students will each draw one fortune and tie it onto the Fortune Tree. A clean-up committee (or everyone who made the fortune tree) should be prepared to safeguard against littering the environment. When the fortunes have been on the tree for a specified amount of time, especially if the fortune tree is outdoors, they should be removed.

Play "Name That Fortune"

3. With the remaining fortunes in the box, play a drama game, "Name That Fortune." Ask students to select a strip of paper. They

will then act out the fortune for the others who may hold up their hands when they think they know what the fortune says. This is really a form of charades, except there are no teams.

As a variation, form teams of two or three people. Each team selects one fortune which they must act out together after a minute's planning.

Play "Fuki Wari"

4. **Fuki Wari** is similar to pin the tail on the donkey but with more moving parts! Draw a head with no facial features on a large sheet of paper. Hang this on a wall. From other paper, cut out eyes, eyebrows, eyelashes, a smiling mouth, and a nose. Either blindfolded or with their eyes firmly shut, children try to place the features on the face. Double sided tape or rolled-up tape will make them stick. Make the head from felt, glue it to a board, and it will be reusable year after year.

Build a Bonfire

5. If you celebrate Shogatsu on New Year's Day, or immediately after resuming school after the winter holiday, gather old Christmas trees, wreaths made of natural objects, and pine boughs for an outdoor bonfire, making certain that all safety precautions are followed. Turn this into an early spring cleaning by ceremonially doing away with Christmas. Where possible, and with permission, scatter the cool ashes in a woodland as a natural fertilizer or place them on a garden compost heap, to welcome the certain approach of spring.

Kodomo-no-Hi: Children Have Their Day (May 5)

Parents honor their children by flying paper carp, one for each of their children, from a bamboo pole in front of their house on May 5. Carp are strong, long-lived fish, relatives of aquarium goldfish. They symbolize the parents' wish that their children grow up to be strong and to have long, healthy lives.

Make a Carp: An Art Project

What You Need:

Paper: butcher roll, brown grocery bags, construction paper, typing paper
Pencils
Coloring media: tempera, watercolor, felt-tips, crayons

Glue
Scissors
String
Cellophane tape

Make paper carp to hang in the library, classrooms, and hallways. Carp can be any size, depending upon the paper available. They can be made from brown grocery bags, construction, butcher, or art paper. They can even be cut from newspaper.

Ask children to draw a fish with a big open mouth on their paper, making it as long as they can. Cut it out and trace around it to make another just like it. Give the fish scales, fins, and eyes with paint, felt-tips, or crayons (figure 34). The adult can provide a template, of

Make a Fishy Festoon for Children's Day

make a carp and cut it from paper. Use it as a template to make another just like it. Glue it together around the edges but leave the mouth open. Put small wads of newspaper in the fish to give it body. Thread a string through its mouth and hang it where it will catch a breeze.

Figure 34

course, but students can develop their own creativity by drawing freehand.

Glue the two halves together around the edges, except for the mouth which should remain open. Tie a string on the top and bottom of the mouth and hang the carp from a pole, a bookshelf, or the ceiling. To keep the string from tearing a hole through the paper, reinforce the hole on both sides with tape. Hang a line across the room and suspend the fish from that. Children should write their names on the tails to avoid mix-ups when it comes time to take their carp home.

Carp can also be made from one piece of paper, and decorated on both sides. Some students may want to make other fish, from salmon to sharks, to symbolize the strength they wish to achieve.

Visit a Fish: A Themed Trip

If there is a large aquarium nearby, take a group visit to study the fish, plants, and other aquatic life there. Take along sketch pads and draw pictures of interesting specimens. Talk to a curator about diets, water requirements, and how long fish live in captivity.

Visit a fish hatchery. Find out if a local pet shop sells the expensive Japanese Koi, beautifully marked ornamental fish that can run into hundreds of dollars. If a field trip is out of the question, set up a small aquarium or fishbowl in school to study fish movement. Make sketches of goldfish, guppies, snails, and water plants. Write haiku verse about fish. (see "Tanabata: Festival of the Stars," page 173).

Do the Crab Walk: A Game to Play

Children may have done "the crab walk" in physical education classes. They can also do it here, for this is a traditional Japanese game. It is appropriately played on Kodomo-no-Hi when artistic aquatic creatures are hanging about on poles or on festoons around the school.

To stage a crab race, form two relay teams. Players get into a crab position by leaning backwards and moving along on all fours. They move to a pre-determined goal line and back, when another member of the team takes over, and so forth, until one team has won.

Hina-Matsuri: Dolls in March

On March 3, Japanese girls remove their collection of ceremonial dolls from their lacquer storage boxes and arrange them for display.

Many of the dolls may have belonged to their great-grandparents, for they are passed down from generation to generation. The dolls are dressed in traditional robes, and represent the Emperor, the Empress, and other important figures. Families hold tea parties so that children may go from house to house to see the dolls, after which they are put away in their boxes until next year.

What to Do

1. **Arrange a display of dolls** of all types. Someone may have a collection of dolls in national costumes that they would be willing to exhibit in the library. There may be a collection of antique dolls which someone would share. Expand the limits of the display by asking students to bring a favorite toy to school for display or show-and-tell.

2. **Study examples of traditional Japanese costumes** in books and use them as bases for drawings. Cut out the drawings, glue them to construction paper or mounting board, and display them.

3. **Visit a toy museum** to see what children played with in days gone by. Ask a toy collector if a few careful children could visit. Invite an expert on old toys to speak during the festival, showing slides or bringing along examples.

4. Have a party, and **serve Citrus Baskets, a traditional Japanese treat.**

What You Need:

Oranges and grapefruit
Kitchen knives
Bowls
Chopped apples, grapes, pears, and other fruits or berries
Set citrus-flavor gelatin, cut into cubes

Cut oranges or grapefruits into basket shapes (figure 35), leaving a handle at the top. Use a very sharp kitchen knife to cut away slightly less than a quarter of the fruit on either side of a handle. Carefully scoop out the fruit. Fill the basket with chopped mixed fruit and

(Figure 35) Turn a citrus fruit into a basket by carefully cutting away the top half, leaving a handle in the middle. Scoop out the fruit and replace it with grapes, orange segments, and small cubes of fruit-flavored gelatin.

citrus gelatin. Children can make their own baskets with adult supervision.

Origami: Two Easy Paper Sculptures

Make some origami creations (figures 36 and 37). The Japanese are experts in this art of folding paper to make animals, airplanes, flowers, and buildings. By experimenting with a few basic folds, children can come up with inventions of their own.

What You Need:

Origami paper (from specialty shop) or
Ordinary typing paper or craft paper
Drawing and painting media

    a. Make a house by folding a piece of ordinary typing paper in half. Then fold this into quarters and unfold again. Fold the top right and top left corners down to make triangles and unfold again. Bring the right and left sides to the middle, opening them out flat to make one large triangle (gable). With a felt-tip pen draw in windows and doors.

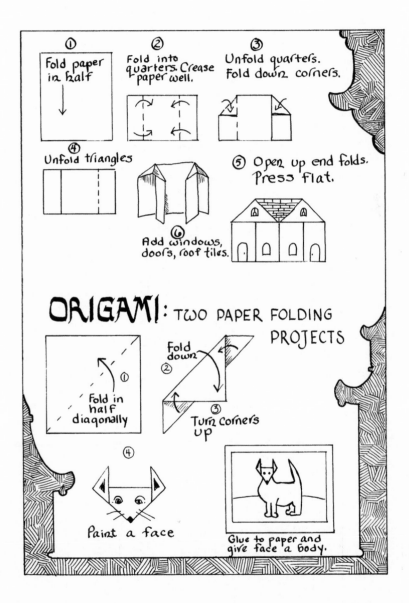

① Fold paper in half

② Fold into quarters. Crease paper well.

③ Unfold quarters. Fold down corners.

④ Unfold triangles

⑤ Open up end folds. Press flat.

⑥ Add windows, doors, roof tiles.

ORIGAMI: TWO PAPER FOLDING PROJECTS

① Fold in half diagonally

② Fold down

③ Turn corners up

④ Paint a face

Glue to paper and give face a body.

Figure 36

This PUPPET can be ready in less than ten minutes

① Fold a rectangle of paper in thirds, lengthwise.

② Fold in half.

③ Fold each half in half again, into the center.

④ Reverse the last fold so that openings of this envelope are on the outside.

⑤ Insert fingers and thumb into openings. This puppet can talk!

⑥ Decorate with eyes, ears, hair, teeth, nose — anything to give character.

Figure 37

b. Make an animal face by first folding a paper square in half to make a triangle. Then fold the top corner down so that it extends past the bottom of the triangle. Finally turn up the corners to make ears. Give the animal definite character by adding eyes, nose, stripes, whiskers, spots, or other features with paint, crayons, felt-tips, or collage.

Tanabata: Festival of the Stars

This festival is a time of lanterns and poetry that occurs on "the seventh day of the seventh moon" when the boys' star and the girls' star meet in the Milky Way. Paper lanterns are hung from trees and poles, and children write poems on rice paper which they tie to tree branches.

Make a Temple Light: A Craft Project

Cardboard grocery boxes (three per lantern)
Pencil
Craft knife
Tempera or latex Paint:
    Black
    White
    Red
    Gray
    Brown
    Yellow
    Green
Large art-room brushes
Sponge
Votive candles and glass containers
Low-wattage electric or battery-powered lamp (optional)
Crepe paper or color acetate (optional)
Glue
Masking tape

What to do

To make a lantern from a cardboard box (figure 38), cut out most of the surface area of each of four sides of the box, leaving enough to make the framework. Paint the remaining lantern shape with black tempera. Glue crepe paper or color acetate inside the lantern openings. Illuminate the lantern with votive lights inside their glass containers. Take proper safety precautions, making certain that the candles will not come into contact with paper. (A low-wattage electric lamp can also be placed inside the lantern, but it must not be allowed to burn for long periods nor left burning when no one is present.)

Turn the lantern into a temple light with a roof cut from another box (figure 38). Cut four triangles of equal dimension, making certain that the bottom of the triangles is some inches wider than the top of the original lantern. Tape the triangles together and rest them on top of the lantern. Make a base for the temple light from another cardboard box larger than the lantern. The base should be about half as tall as the lantern. Cut away some cardboard from each side, leaving "legs" at each corner. Experiment with leg designs by scribbling on paper before cutting. Paint the entire temple light with a sponge dipped in an unmixed blob of white (5 parts), black (1 part), and red (1 part) tempera to make it look like stone. Adjust the color with more or less of certain colors (including green, yellow, and brown) until it looks like a garden-weathered stone lantern.

Haiku: Write Poetry

Study Japanese *haiku* poetry. A haiku verse has seventeen syllables and three lines:
    First line: five syllables to tell the setting
    Second line: seven syllables to tell the action
    Third line: five syllables to conclude

> The bird's nest was cold
> Slowly the robin snuggled
> Snow fell in spirals
>
> October sunshine
> Yellow leaves are blowing free
> Fleeing bare branches

Spend time creating and playing with words and feelings to capture the gentle lilt and lift of haiku verse. Ask the children to write good copies of their best haiku and display them—hang them from a large tree branch inside the library. Or make a flat tree branch from paper and hang both it and the verse on a wall. Another option is to letter the haiku onto kakemono (figures 30 and 32).

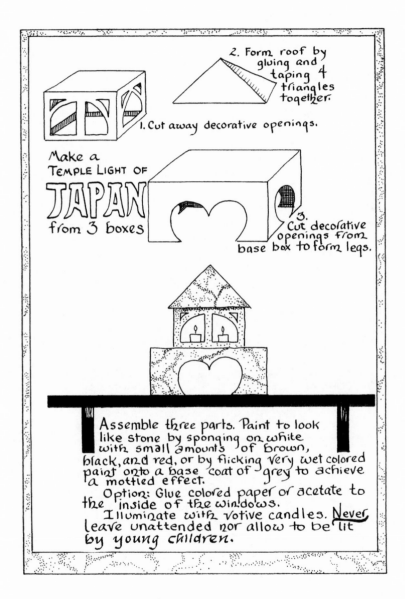

2. Form roof by gluing and taping 4 triangles together.

1. Cut away decorative openings.

Make a TEMPLE LIGHT OF JAPAN from 3 boxes

3. Cut decorative openings from base box to form legs.

Assemble three parts. Paint to look like stone by sponging on white with small amounts of brown, black, and red, or by flicking very wet colored paint onto a base coat of grey to achieve a mottled effect.

Option: Glue colored paper or acetate to the inside of the windows.

Illuminate with votive candles. Never leave unattended nor allow to be lit by young children.

Figure 38

Make a Haiku Book: A Craft Project

What You Need:

Corrugated cardboard, cut into booksize squares or rectangles
Fabric remnants or gift wrap or color paper
Glue
Construction paper
Felt-tip pens

Cover two squares of cardboard of any size with fabric remnants or color paper (figure 39). Glue the cover sheet to the cardboard securely with white glue. Fold the ends over the edges, and glue them down on the inside of the cardboard. To make the pages of the book, fold construction paper into accordion pleats. Glue the beginning pleat to one of the cardboard covers and the ending pleat to the other cover. When the book is dry, open it out and write a haiku verse on it. Paint a Japanese scene beneath or around the haiku. These books make wonderful displays on a bookshelf or tabletop.

Karuta: Play the Poetry Game

What You Need:

Poetry books
Note cards
Glue
Photocopy machine
Scissors

Students may select their favorite poems, anything from Shel Silverstein to Ogden Nash to Jack Prelutsky. Photocopy each poem and glue it to a piece of thin card, cutting away any extra margins so that only the poem remains. Then cut the poem in half, dividing it horizontally between lines. Put all the half-poems into a box and dump them onto the floor, mixing them thoroughly. Players have to match the pieces. The winner is the one with the most complete poems at the end of a set time period. (If you cut all the poems to the same size and use the same color backing paper, it is more difficult to make matches, and therefore prolongs the enjoyment.)

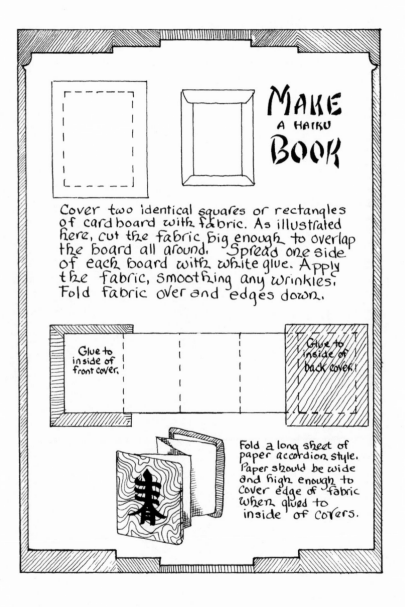

MAKE
A HAIKU
BOOK

Cover two identical squares or rectangles of cardboard with fabric. As illustrated here, cut the fabric big enough to overlap the board all around. Spread one side of each board with white glue. Apply the fabric, smoothing any wrinkles. Fold fabric over and edges down.

Glue to inside of front cover.

Glue to inside of back cover.

Fold a long sheet of paper accordion style. Paper should be wide and high enough to cover edge of fabric when glued to inside of covers.

Figure 39

Noh Plays: Creative Drama

Noh plays are very ancient traditions in Japan. They use symbolic movements, dance, masks, and music to tell stories. Students can experiment with these devices to tell folktales with which they are familiar, not necessarily Japanese ones.

1. Make masks from paper plates.

What You Need:

A folktale
Paper plates
Drawing media: pencils, felt-tips
Cardboard for handles (optional)
Scissors or craft knives

Decide on the folk tale. This can be anything from *Cinderella* to a tale from Africa, China, or Japan. Read the tale and pick out the different emotions involved in the plot and story—anger, love, sadness, happiness. Draw pictures of human faces to represent these emotions on the back of paper plates (figure 40). Japanese masks would be held in front of the face by a handle. You may hold the paper plates in your hand or attach a handle of cardboard, similar to the ones made for the flat fans, above.

Figure 40

Try to let a few simple actions depict the action of the story. For instance, a few large steps in place could represent a journey. A large shoulder shrug could represent going to sleep, defeat in battle, or death. Several large shrugs could show crying.

Ask one or two good readers to tell the story while others act it out, using masks and gestures to animate the plot and characters. Participants will need to analyze the story carefully, so that each character has a separate mask for each emotion to be portrayed. A tape or compact disc player could provide background music. Traditional Noh plays also include percussion and stringed instruments, so there is scope for lots of noise. No stage or props are required, but if there is a display of haiku, painted Japanese costumes, lanterns, fortune trees, or a Tokonoma, that will be a perfect background.

2. **Make an origami puppet play** (refer to page 172).

What You Need:

Construction paper
Scissors
Glue
Pencils

Fold a large sheet of construction paper into thirds, lengthwise. Then fold the length in half. Fold each half in half again, dividing the paper into quarters, the ends meeting in the middle. Fold the paper in half again, this time with openings on the outside. Insert fingers and thumb into the slots and the puppet will "talk." Cut features (teeth, beard, hair, tongue, eyes, horns, ears, nose, warts) from paper and glue them onto the puppet.

Filial Piety: Research Your Ancestors

In ancient times, followers of Confucius, while not believing in an afterlife, condoned the people's veneration of their ancestors because it helped stabilize society through demonstrations of filial piety. In Japan today, Taoists, Buddhists, and Shintoists honor their ancestors with reverence, prayer, and gifts, just as in other religions those who have lived and died are remembered with ceremonies, flowers, candles, and affection. There are some Festival projects which can open understandings on these practices.

1. **Find old photographs of members of your family.** Ask older family members to help identify the people in the pictures. Are you related to these people? Can you find out what kind of life they lived by what they are wearing? Does your family have a "tree" that lists your ancestors? Based on one of these old photographs, write a short story about life as it may have been before you were born.

2. **Visit a cemetery,** especially one with a long history, to examine gravestones, landscape, and atmosphere. Do any of the graves have flowers? Who placed them there? Read inscriptions on grave markers: write down quotations from poetry, the Bible, or proverbs that you see on some stones. Take along some thin paper and crayons to make a rubbing of designs on some grave stones. What is the earliest date you can find on a grave marker in this cemetery?

Cemeteries are not necessarily morbid places. They can be oases of quiet, with landscaped gardens, wildlife, and fine examples of funerary art. Provide time in this visit for the children just to be quiet, to sit and listen to the sounds around them. This might be a good time to write haiku verse, inspired by this atmosphere of mystery and beauty.

Many rural cemeteries, especially in the Southern United States, have traditional "decoration days" when families gather there for reunions, picnics or "dinners on the ground," and church services. They come primarily to decorate the graves of their ancestors with flowers. Visit a decoration day, if possible, and take part in the proceedings. Some children may do this as part of their family life. Ask them to tell others about what happens—whom do they meet, what kinds of flowers are there, who makes music, are they allowed to play games?

In Mexico, and in parts of the United States along the Mexican border, people celebrate the Day of the Dead on the first two days and nights of November. Families visit the tombs of their ancestors to distribute flowers and candles, to clean the cemetery, and to feast and play music. Children have special sugary sweets in the shape of skulls and skeletons. Find out how this relates to the oriental customs of revering ancestors. Are any ceremonies similar?

3. If appropriate, **discuss the fact of death:** death comes to all living things. Philosophies in different cultures and religions offer

many opinions about living, death, and afterlife. Students can research funerary customs in ancient Egypt or China, pre-colonial America, or any other culture, reporting on beliefs and practices. Students can discuss their own opinions or those of their religion. They can discuss the Hindu, Buddhist, and Shinto theories of reincarnation, the Buddhist and Roman Catholic beliefs in purgatory, or theories that life stops totally at the death of the body. Of course, the group leader (librarian or teacher) will have to be sensitive to local taboos, prejudices, or sentiments in organizing a project about, or even a discussion on, death and dying.

A Major Festival Cooking Experience: A Japanese-inspired Stir Fry

Chinese restaurants have long been a feature of life in cities throughout the world, and nowhere more than in America where most small towns boast at least one Chinese eatery. Japanese restaurants are flourishing now, as well, offering customers elegantly served meals, often cooked at the table over hibachi grills, with sake warmed in bowls of hot water.

What You Need:

Hotplate or stove
Wok or frying pan (or Electric wok or frying pan)
Kitchen knives
Bowls
Chopping surface
Wooden stirring spoons
Paper plates
Chopsticks or plastic forks
Garbage bags and clean-up cloths
Vegetables (see below)
Vegetable or nut oil for frying
Seasonings and other additions (see below)
Rice
Rice cooking pan
Water for boiling rice
Salt

A festival can feature a simple vegetarian version of a Japanese meal, enlisting many hands in washing, chopping, and serving.

Depending upon the size of the participating group, the leader will need one or two (or more) hot plates, a frying pan, wok, or an electric wok; sharp kitchen knives; chopping boards and containers for vegetables; wooden stirring spoons; and paper plates.

Cheap chopsticks (*haishi*) are available in many housewares or department stores to lend authenticity (and fun) to the eating of the meal. Plastic forks, of course, can be made available for the less adventurous. Clean-up crews should include student "mess sergeants" equipped with garbage bags, wiping cloths, and soapy water.

The group leader should organize a group of parent volunteers to oversee the vegetable preparation and to supervise or do the stir frying, either following a demonstration of the procedure, or as a main festival cooking event. Delegate various responsibilities by asking students to bring in one or two raw vegetables each for the meal, either potluck style or from a list similar to this one, organized by length of cooking time:

Group A	Group B	Group C
(longer cooking time)	(medium cooking time)	(short cooking time)
Asparagus (tough)	Asparagus (young)	Bean sprouts
Broccoli	Mushrooms	Scallions
Cabbage	Peppers	Spinach
Carrots	Squash	Tomatoes
Cauliflower	Zucchini	
Celery	Turnips (young)	
Eggplant		
Potato		
Pumpkin		

Onions and garlic come in a category of their own. They should be added to the work **first**, and cooked until they are soft so that their particular tastes can disperse throughout the remaining vegetable mixture. If you are averse to garlic, leave it out, or use it sparingly.

Tasty Additions:

To add texture, taste, and nourishment, cooks may add any or all of the following during the final seconds of cooking:

Noodles (precooked and stirred in vegetable oil to keep from sticking together)

Nuts (cashews, peanuts, walnuts, or others), chopped

Seeds (sunflower, pumpkin, sesame)
Tofu (broken into small pieces)
Water chestnuts (chopped or sliced)

For seasonings, try adding any of these in moderation, but not all at once:

Grated fresh ginger
Honey
Mirin (Japanese seasoned vinegar)
Orange Juice
Sesame or Walnut Oil
Soy Sauce
Tabasco
Tamari sauce
Thinly diced fresh hot peppers
Wine (red, white, sherry)

Seven Golden Rules

1. Practice slicing uniformly so that like vegetables will cook at the same rate.

2. Have containers of vegetables, arranged in cooking groups, within arm's reach of the wok or frying pan.

3. Cook on very high temperature.

4. Do not leave the frying pan or wok once you have started cooking.

5. Stir constantly.

6. Remove vegetables to the side of the wok if they are cooking too quickly. When cooking with a frying pan, it may be necessary to remove vegetables from the heat totally, so have containers ready.

7. Serve as quickly as possible when vegetables are done.

Rice: What to do

One team of cooks should be in charge of the rice. Since cooking times vary, according to the amount being prepared, follow the instructions on the package.

1. Read cooking instructions on the package of rice you have chosen.

2. Wash the rice, if necessary, in cold, running water.

3. Bring sufficient salted water to a boil, add the rice, and return to boil. Cover the container and cook on lowered temperature an additional 12 minutes (or according to instructions on package). Stir occasionally to prevent sticking.

4. Some cooks like to add a drop or two of cooking oil to the boiling water to prevent sticking and to prevent the rice from boiling over the edge of the pan.

Stir-Fried Vegetables: What to do

1. Students wash and, if necessary, scrub the vegetables under running water, at the same time washing their hands.

2. Under supervision and instruction, students chop and slice the vegetables **thinly**, placing those in Group A (which need longer cooking time), Group B, and Group C (which need little cooking time) in separate containers.

3. Leaders heat frying pans or woks on high temperature and when they are hot, add vegetable or nut oil, moving it all over the cooking surface with a wooden spoon.

4. Leaders and supervised student cooks first add thinly sliced onions and garlic cloves, stirring them constantly. After about thirty seconds, move them to the side of the pan or to other containers.

5. Next, in order of Group Divisions (A, B, C), add mixtures of vegetables. First stir fry all the A vegetables until they are not quite done, then add the B vegetables, and finally, anything from the C group. **STIR CONSTANTLY**. If any vegetable appears to be browning too quickly, move it to the side with the onions and garlic.

6. Serve the stir-fried vegetables on a bed of fluffy white rice on paper plates. Organize a cafeteria-style line for efficient, quick service.

Konnichiwa: Speak Japanese

It would take many years to master the writing of the Japanese alphabet. Students can learn to greet one another, however, so that by the end of the festival they can say a few pleasant words.

Good Morning	Ohayo
Hello	Konnichiwa
Thank You	Arigato
Good-Bye	Sayonara
Good-Night	Oyasuminasai

To be very polite to one another and to their teachers, students can add **san** to the ends of names when they say hello. To greet their teacher in the morning they might say:

Konnichiwa, Mr. Smith-san.

An adult would greet fellow adults similarly, but to say hello to a child, he would add **chan** to the end of the name:

Ohayo, Carol-chan.

Festival Publications: Make a Book

Before the festival begins, publish a brochure of events to include every activity, from arts and crafts, to speakers, to trips, to cooking events. Reproduce the festival bookmark to give away.

Besides publishing a list of available books and other materials about Japanese culture and religion, collect students' haiku, a recipe or two from a Japanese-style cook, and some black and white paintings or drawings and put them together for a "Japan Week" magazine. Make your school's voice enhance international relations: send a copy to the Japanese Embassy in Washington, D.C. (2520 Massachusetts Avenue, NW, 20008) or to your nearest Japanese consulate.

Sources of Inspiration

A Selection of Books About Japan

Benedict, Ruth. *The Chrysanthemum and the Sword.* New York: New American Library, 1985.
   This anthropological study of Japanese society, ethics, and customs is designed to provide insight into a culture far different from that of the United States.

Condon, John C. *With Respect to the Japanese: A Guide for Americans.* Yarmouth, Maine: Intercultural Press, 1984.
   Americans visiting Japan, or wanting to learn how to blend into Japanese culture without sticking out or making faux pas, will benefit from this collection of insights.

Davidson, Judith. *Japan: When East Meets West.* Minneapolis: Dillon, 1983.
   This book looks at Japan's traditional yet modern society—customs, stories, festivals, and a typical Japanese child's life-style.

Earhart, H. Byron. *Religions in Japan: Many Traditions Within One Sacred Way.* New York: Harper and Row, 1984.
   Japan's melding of several religious traditions (Shinto, Buddhist, Taoist, and Confucianist) lead to ceremonies, customs, and particular views of itself and its relation to the world.

Earle, Joe, ed. *Japanese Art and Design: The Toshiba Gallery.* London: Victoria and Albert Museum, 1986.
   Japanese art, grounded in ancient religion and belief in the essential unity of man and nature, is well illustrated in this collection of paintings, scrolls, ceramics, and ivory carvings.

Greene, Carol. *Japan.* Chicago: Childrens Press, 1983.
   This book for young readers surveys the charm, culture, geography, and society of Japan today.

Hearn, Lafcadio. *Writings From Japan.* New York: Penguin, 1984.
   In 1890, Lafcadio Hearn visited Japan and liked it so much he never left. He describes in vignettes of Japanese life exquisite gardens, Samurai legends, and pet insects that live out their lives in miniature cages.

Hillier, Jack. *Art of Hokusai in Book Illustration.* New York: Sotheby Parke Bernet, 1980.
   Hokusai, who lived and worked in the 19th century, is one of the most famous Japanese artists of all time. This is a survey of his graphic woodcuts.

Leicht, Hermann. *History of the World's Art.* London: Spring Books, 1965.
   The chapter on Japanese art gives a concise history from pre-historic times to the early twentieth century, with emphasis on the woodcuts of Hokusai, temple statuary, and porcelain.

Logan, Bill, ed. *All Japan—The Catalog of Everything Japanese.* New York: Quarto, Ltd., 1984.

   This vast collection of information includes locations of cultural centers, shops, design artists, potters and calligraphers, educational institutions, bonsai growers, and literally hundreds of other organizations and individuals that represent Japanese culture in the United States.

Strange, E. F. *Hokusai, the Old Man Gone Mad with Painting.* New York: Folcroft Library Editions, 1977.

   Famous for his dramatic paintings and woodcuts of the views of Mount Fuji, Hokusai is also known for his stormy seas and wave patterns, all illustrated beautifully here.

Sugimoto, Etsu Inagaki. *A Daughter of the Samurai.* Garden City, New York: Doubleday, 1934.

   This touching, revealing story tells how a daughter of feudal Japan, where an eternal flame burned before her family shrine, became an American in one generation.

Sullivan, Michael. *Chinese and Japanese Art.* New York: Grolier, 1965.

   Looking into the distant centuries first, Sullivan traces the evolution of porcelain, scroll painting, calligraphy, and statuary in China and Japan.

Tsuchiya, Yoshio. Juliet W. Carpenter, translator. *A Feast for the Eyes: The Japanese Art of Food Arrangement.* New York: Kodansha International, Ltd., 1985.

   A sumptuously-illustrated book to engage the senses in the harmonious pleasures to be derived from the Japanese culinary experience.

Wilson, Robert. *East to America: A History of the Japanese in the U.S.A.* New York: Morrow, 1980.

   Three generations of Japanese Americans tell their story through oral history and memorabilia, telling how they overcame prejudices and hardships in the new world.

Japanese Poetry

Atwood, Ann. *Haiku: The Mood of the Earth.* New York: Scribner's, 1971.

   Haiku and color photographs show young people the relationship of human beings and nature.

Behn, Harry, comp. *Cricket Songs: Japanese Haiku.* Trans. by Harry Behn. New York: Harcourt, Brace and World, 1964.

   Catch the sparkle and beauty of the 17-syllable non-rhyming verses in this beautifully printed book.

Buchanan, Daniel C., comp. and trans. *One Hundred Famous Haiku.* Tokyo: Japan Publications, 1975.

Covering many emotions and moods, these poems inspire meditation and reflection upon the many meanings of life.

Japan in Fiction

Buck, Pearl. *The Big Wave.* New York: Scholastic Book Services, 1968.
Volcanic eruptions under the sea send a tidal wave to destroy a Japanese village by the coast. Jiya tries to warn his father, but is too late.

Coatsworth, Elizabeth. *The Cat Who Went to Heaven.* Illus. by Lynd Ward. New York: Macmillan, 1958.
A pet cat wants to be included in a picture of the animals paying homage to Buddha.

Copeland, Helen. *Meet Miki Takino.* Illus. by Kurt Werth. New York: Lothrop, Lee and Shepard, 1965.
Miki is a little Japanese-American boy who has a host of things to be proud of at his first grade party.

Friedman, Ina. *How My Parents Learned to Eat.* Boston: Houghton Mifflin, 1984.
A young girl tells how her Japanese mother and American father met in Yokohama in this picture book.

Garrigue, Sheila. *The Eternal Spring of Mr. Ito.* New York: Bradbury Press, 1985.
Despite religious and cultural differences, Sara shares a special friendship with Mr. Ito and delivers a bonsai to his family held in a Canadian prisoner of War camp during World War II.

Godden, Rumer. *Little Plum.* London: Macmillan, 1971.
This is the affectionate story of two little girls and their dolls, one of whom is a little Japanese doll named Little Plum.

————. *Miss Happiness and Miss Flower.* Harmondsworth: Penguin, 1966.
Two Japanese dolls find themselves in the home of a lonely British girl who, through books, finds out how to build them a little Japanese house and garden.

Kawabata, Yasunari. *Snow Country.* New York: Berkeley Publications, 1960.
In this novel of mature love, the dark winter of Japan's west coast brings together a young man and a geisha.

Klass, David. *The Atami Dragon.* New York: Scribner's 1984.
Jerry and his sister go to Japan with their dad after their mother's death, and Jerry joins a Japanese baseball team.

————. *Breakaway Run.* New York: Lodestar, 1987.
Seventeen-year-old Tony escapes his own American home difficulties by living as an exchange student with the Maeda family in Japan, where he learns endurance, how to deal with loss, and how to love.

Leithauser, Brad. *Equal Distance.* New York: Knopf, 1985.
A young law student goes to Japan to learn how to grow up but continues to cavort with new found friends.

McAlpine, Helen and William. *Japanese Tales and Legends.* London: Oxford University Press, 1968.
From the creation of Japan, peopled by gods, to the epic of Heike, the noble warrior race, these tales follow the lives of woodcutters, fishermen, fairy children, princesses, and other adventuresome characters.

Namioka, Lensey. *Village of the Vampire Cat.* New York: Delacorte, 1981.
Two young Samurai rid a village of an extortionist Vampire Cat.

Oe, Kanzaburo, ed. *The Crazy Iris and Other Stories of the Atomic Aftermath.* New York: Grove Press, 1985.
These stories of Japan after the atomic bomb show the impact of destruction on peasants, artists, and children.

Paterson, Katherine. *Of Nightingales that Weep.* New York: Avon, 1980.
In this picture book, a beautiful daughter of a samurai warrior is caught in a fight between two warring clans.

————. *The Master Puppeteer.* New York: Crowell, 1975.
A young puppeteer apprentice in 18th-century Japan uncovers thievery in the underworld connections of his trainer, a master puppeteer in Japanese theatre.

Speak Japanese

Dunn, C. J. *Teach Yourself Japanese.* London: English Universities Press, 1958.
Three hundred pages of exercises and a pronunciation guide can lead the persistent and serious student into a working knowledge of Japanese conversation.

Hepburn, James Curtis. *A Japanese and English Dictionary, with English and Japanese Index.* Rutland, Vermont: Charles E. Tuttle, 1983.
This useful compendium of words and expressions will enable the ardent student to expand vocabulary and build confidence.

For Further Information

The Japanese Embassy
2520 Massachusetts Avenue, N.W.
Washington, D.C. 20008
Telephone 202-234-2266

The Japanese Culture Center
1275 Space Park Drive
Houston, Texas 77058
    Specialists in translations, ikebana flower arranging, and tea ceremonies.

Japanese American Association
7 W. 44th Street
New York, New York 10036
    Specialists in Japanese cooking instruction, ikebana, and the tea ceremony.

Consulate General of Japan
400 Colony Square
1201 Peachtree Street, N.E.
Atlanta, Georgia 30361
Telephone 404-892-2700
    There are consulates in several other major regional U.S. cities. Check the telephone directory.

Asia Society
3414 Milam
Houston, Texas 77002
Telephone 713-520-7771

Garden Valley Japanese Cultural Institute
16215 S. Gramercy Place
Gardena, California 90247
Telephone 213-324-6611

U.S.–Japanese Cross-Culture Center
244 San Pedro Street
Los Angeles, California 90122
Telephone 213-617-2039

Japan Design Center
40 E. 49th Street
New York, New York 10017
Telephone 212-838-6803

Chapter Six

¡Viva Los Niños d'España!
A Hispanic Festival

Unlike the Anglo-American majority, the sons and daughters of Hispania come from sun-drenched lands. Their culture reflects a colorful past, deeply rooted not only in geography and climate, but religion, love of family, and the languages of the Iberian peninsula: Catalan, Basque, Portuguese, and Spanish. Hispanics today are rapidly becoming the largest ethnic minority in the United States. Though there are over twenty-five million African Americans in the United States, estimates give Hispanics from sixteen to thirty millions. Latin Americans are making Spanish the second tongue in the States. Historians think that by the year 2000 fifty percent of Americans will be able to converse well in Spanish.

It is wrong to think of Hispanics as solely Mexican, though Chicanos (or Mexican Americans) form the largest Hispanic sub-group located mostly in Texas and California. Puerto Ricans, in New York and New Jersey, and Cubans, in Florida, are also well represented, with lesser numbers from other Latin American countries. While grounded in a common tongue and religion, their cultures

193   Hispanic Bookmark

are different. A festival organizer may want to celebrate Cinco de Maya, a favorite Mexican holiday. That's great, but don't expect it to have deep meaning for people from Colombia or Dominica. Several Hispanic countries celebrate El Dia de la Raza, however, to commemorate Columbus Day. While a grand fiesta for Cinco de Maya will offer opportunities for recitations, dramatic readings, music, and parades, festival organizers may want to celebrate a more inclusive holiday. Cubans pride themselves on high standards of education and living, while the goals of many Mexican Americans differ from those of either Puerto Ricans or Cubans. Regardless of their origin, however, Hispanics are famous for their legendary Latin temperament which makes them ready for a fiesta at the drop of a hat. Teachers will do well to bone up on a few Mexican, Texan, South American, Spanish, or Caribbean festivals for ideas on what to do. Kids can make *piñatas,* carry *los barcos* in *processiones,* dress up in *charros* and other costumes, and make music with gourd *maracas.* They can celebrate national holidays, saints' day, heroes' birthdays, or changes in the seasons while learning about a culture that is rich in pageantry and folklore.

A Latin American or Hispanic festival will stimulate discussion and understanding of immigration. Even young students can find out about the great migrations of people to the United States in the late nineteenth century and the continuing immigrations from Europe, Asia, and the rest of the world, including Latin America. They will discover that some people come to the States for political freedom, as refugees from tyranny, or for better economic opportunities. They can learn that some foreign nationals, such as legally entered Mexicans, can cross freely back and forth to their native lands, while others, such as Cubans, can never hope to return as long as Castro is in power. Students can discuss the effects of police states, such as Cuba, former "people's republics" in Eastern Europe, Asia, and Africa, and countries founded on principles that severely limit individual rights and freedoms. They can find out how refugees or immigrants are treated when they begin their lives in America. They can discuss the effects of prejudice, both on those at whom it is aimed, and on those who feel it. While learning about Hispanic settlement patterns in the United States, some students can talk about their own families' roots, perhaps bringing artifacts, family trees, or photographs from the old world to school. On the Great Seal of the United States is the motto "E pluribus unum," or "out of many, one." This clearly shows that the United Sates is a nation formed by people from many countries. Many traditions coexist in America without fear of reprisal, imprisonment, or abolition.

One fear voiced by many Hispanics is that their culture is being diluted by mainstream American influences; that native foods are being displaced by hamburgers and French fries; and that salsa or mariachi music is being eroded by disco. A school or library emphasis on things Hispanic can give Latinos a moment to recapture something of their heritage while showing Anglos and people of other races and groups some of the important aspects of Spanish-American life.

The Flags of Spanish America: A Festival Display

Latin American countries have many colorful traditions, holidays, and emblems. Capture the sunny atmosphere with a display of Hispanic national flags made by students. Hang the flags from the ceiling near a bulletin board which itself can be made of flags. Detailed explanations for making these flags as a class project follow.

What You Need:

Construction Paper
   Red, White, and Blue for United States American Flag
   Green, Yellow, and others for Latin American flags
Pictures of Latin American flags
   (See sources at end of the chapter)
Drawing media: pencils, felt-tips
Thumb tacks or pins

Show that the United States has incorporated Spanish-speaking people into its culture by making a large stylized Stars and Stripes from paper (figure 41). To the white stripes, add the national flags of various Latin American countries, along with the names of those countries in letters.

If the focus of the festival is on one particular country or holiday, use only the national flag of that country. Consult an encyclopedia article to find drawings of the flag and other national emblems, such as Mexico's Eagle and Cactus. Encourage students to interpret these national symbols in original works of art for display. Mexico is

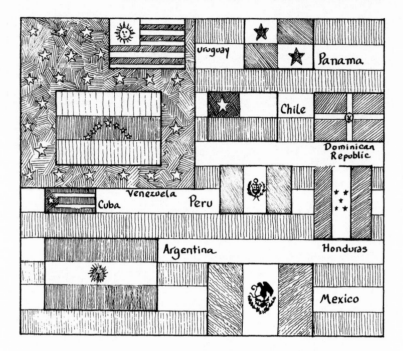

(Figure 41) Spanish American Festival Display

particularly rich in symbols. Most children are familiar with *piñatas*, a form of which may be made as a festival project. They may be less aware of the pottery and candy figures of the saints or the skull masks and sugar skeleton figures given during the festival of the dead in November. Research in encyclopedias and other sources will reveal other crafts and typical products that may be used as national symbols.

Special Holidays to Celebrate

Look at a list of national, religious, and other holidays in each Latin-American country to see if some of these special fiestas will provide a convenient hook on which to hang a celebration. Mexicans, in particular, are always ready to hold a fiesta. Every profession in Mexico has an annual special day to honor its work in the nation. When **El Dia de los Profesores** rolls around, school children bring a gift to their teachers. When mail carriers celebrate their day, householders provide them with food and drink on their rounds. Or, instead of finding a festal day, let students brainstorm to invent their own fiesta—No Homework Day, Automatic A-on-Every-Test Day, El Dia de los Estudiantes, Great School Food Day, or Football Day.

January 6, **El Dia de los Tres Reys.** In Puerto Rico, children expect gifts from the Three Kings on this festival that brings Christmas to a close.

March 2 (1836), **Texas Independence Day.** While Santa Ana was besieging the Alamo, Texas declared its independence from Mexico. This was followed by the battle of San Jacinto on April 21 at which Sam Houston defeated General Santa Ana. The United States recognized the Republic of Texas on March 2, 1837, with Sam Houston as its president.

March 22 (1873), **Abolition of Slavery Day.** Puerto Ricans celebrate the freedom of all men and women on this important day.

April 21 (1837), **San Jacinto Day.** This is an official Texas state holiday in honor of Mexican recognition of Texan independence. To Texans this is as great a holiday as July 4.

May 5 (1862), **Cinco de Maya.** This major Mexican holiday is celebrated by lengthy parades, parties, and feasts. It commemorates the defeat of 6000 French soldiers by 2000 Mexicans, commanded by General Ignacio Zaragoza, at the Battle of Guadalupe near Puebla de los Angeles. The reason for this altercation? The French had enthroned Maximillian as emperor of Mexico, but his "subjects" did not want him. On this fiesta day in Mexico, the President reviews the troops, streets are decorated with flags and banners of Mexico's red, white and green, and there is ample opportunity for eating frijoles, drinking cervesa, and dancing to mariachi bands.

June 14, **Casals Festival.** In San Juan, Puerto Rico, a huge music festival takes place around the middle of June for several days in which orchestras, choirs, and soloists from many nations take part. The festival is named in honor of Puerto Rican cellist Pablo Casals.

June 24, **La Festa de San Juan Battista.** Puerto Ricans enthusiastically celebrate their patron saint's day with parties, carnivals, music, and dancing. The night before, many families camp out all night on the beaches, singing and telling tales around bonfires and wading into the surf at dawn as a symbol of good luck for the coming year. As in all Roman Catholic countries, Puerto Rico celebrates many local saints' days with parades, processions, and music.

August 2, **La Fiesta de la Señora de los Angeles.** In Cartago, Costa Rica, the black stone statue of the Virgin Mary, called **La Negrita,** is carried in procession throughout the city, accompanied by pilgrims from all over Central America and Mexico.

September 15–16 (1810), **El Grito de Delores.** This Mexican **Fiestas Patrias,** the anniversary of independence from Spain, honors Father Miguel Hidalgo y Costilla, the hero priest, whose speech incited the Mexicans to strive for self-determination. At the beginning of the celebration, a mayor or senior official begins the **gritto** (cry, greeting) with the words of the original speech: "Mejicanos, viva nuestros heroes," or "Mexicans, long live our heroes!" Everyone responds with a loud "viva!" The celebrations are sometimes called simply **Diez y Seis,** Spanish for 16.

Central American countries also celebrate their independence days on September 15 with parades led by torch bearers. Before regional conflict prevented it, relay racers carried a lighted torch from Guatemala to Panama on September 15 and 16 commemorating the simultaneous independence finally won from Spain in 1821.

September 29, **La Fiesta de San Miguel.** In the beautiful Mexican town of San Miguel de Allende people converge on the plaza to "wake up" St Michael at 4:00 AM with mariachi bands, fireworks, and church bells. Later in the morning, several frisky bulls are released into the streets where brave young men (and a few women) try to become matadors for a few hours. In the cool of the afternoon, a parade of horsemen (**charros**) and horsewomen (**charras**) winds through the streets with marching mariachi bands and floats depicting St. Michael's eternal battle with evil. In the evening, dancing and fireworks displays last until 4:00 AM the next day.

October 12 (1492), **Dia de la Raza.** Mexicans call Columbus Day "Day of the Race," meaning that the Mexican people were founded on the day of his discovery of the New World.

In Costa Rica, Columbus Day is a time for parades and night-long parties similar to those of Mardi Gras.

November 2, **Dia de los Muertos.** All Souls' Day is celebrated in Mexico with a profusion of marigolds, the pre-Columbian flower of death, when families decorate ancestral graves not only with marigolds and other flowers, but also with candles and food.

November 19 (1493), **Discovery Day.** On this day, Christopher Columbus, or Cristobal Colon, sailed to Puerto Rico.

December 10 (1898), **American Annexation of Puerto Rico.** On this day, Spain surrendered Puerto Rico by treaty to the United States.

December 12, **Nuestra Señora de Guadalupe.** From all over Mexico and central America, rich and poor alike converge on a chapel where tradition says that the Virgin Mary appeared to a boy named Juan Diego.

December 1–31, **La Navidad, or Fiesta Navidena.** Christmas festivities in Spanish-speaking countries are very important times, not only for religious exercises, but also for the secular trappings that make them such lively occasions. Here the religious life blends into colorful dance, song, and story-telling, with piñatas, ritual street drama of **Las Posadas** when Mexicans re-enact the **Santa Familia**'s search for a place in Bethlehem, and parties. In New Mexico, the exteriors of houses, churches, and entire communities may be lit with **luminarias,** candles in paper sacks filled with sand.

Fly a Flag: Research and Art Project

The flags of Latin American countries and Puerto Rico make interesting art projects. Students can learn about symbolism through color and design. They can learn more Spanish words when they interpret countries' mottoes. Young artists can put their measuring skills to practice by making large flags out of color paper.

What You Need:

Art-room paper
Reference books for pictures of flags
Drawing and coloring instruments
    Pencils, Felt-tips, Tempera, Brushes
Color construction paper
Glue
Scissors
Fabric, Needles, Thread (optional)

Help students recognize Latin American flags by providing an activity sheet (figure 42) with outline drawings which should be colored in. Suspend large paper flags from the ceiling as a festival display. Using reference books or the outlines on the activity sheet,

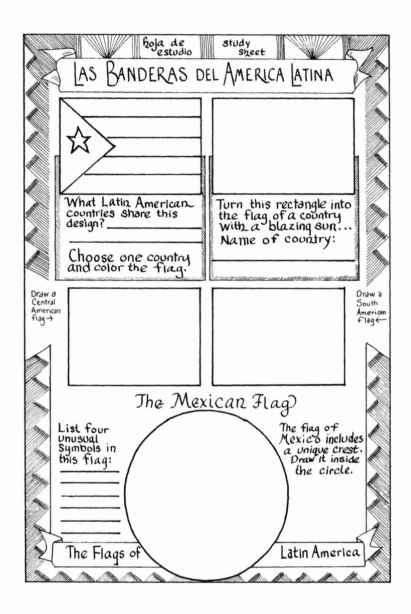

(Figure 42) Spanish American Arts & Crafts—Fly a Flag

students can enlarge the flag of Mexico, Dominica, El Salvador, or other Hispanic states on plain artist's paper. They can either paint in the color with tempera, or cut the colors from construction paper and apply it to the base with glue. For display purposes, both sides of the design should be filled in.

Students well-versed in needle and thread can make flags from fabric. The Columbian, Cuban, and Puerto Rican flags use simple geometric shapes that would not be too difficult. The state insignia of Mexico, the Dominican Republic, and Peru would require embroidery or use of fabric paint, although the geometric patterns of the flags do not present special difficulties.

Paint a Mexican-Style Mural: A Research and Art Project

What You Need:

Reference books, geography books
Art paper rolls or butcher paper
Cellophane tape or masking tape
Pencils
Erasers
Measuring sticks
Tempera or watercolor paint
Felt-tip pens
Polyurethane varnish
Brown enamel
Brushes
Thumbtacks or pins

Mexican artists are among the most creative and enthusiastic muralists in the art world. Native Aztecs were excellent sculptors on a grand scale, whose work, including bas relief murals, may be seen today in museums and on ancient ruins in Mexico. Early inhabitants of colonial Mexico decorated mission churches with exquisite combinations of native Indian and Spanish mural ornamentation. Subsequent generations have made murals from precious stones, mosaic tiles, and paint.

Students can paint a mural along Mexican themes by studying some examples in books (Stein's *Mexico*, the Insight Guide *Mexico* by Apa Productions, Catalano's *The Mexican Americans,* and others in "Sources of Inspiration" at the end of this chapter). Taking these and

Figure 43

other sources as their guides, students can sketch things that seem typically Mexican: adobe houses, donkeys and horses, cattle, charros, chili peppers, old-fashioned Spanish costumes, Catholic missionary brothers, rugged terrain, sea coasts, or sombreros (figure 43). The best murals are not just pretty combinations of pictures, however, but thematically grouped characters that tell a story, much like stained glass windows in medieval European cathedrals. For Cinco de Maya, students can tell the story of Zaragoza's defeat of Maximillian's forces. For Columbus Day, or Dia de la Raza, tell the story of European discovery, exploration, and colonization of the New World, with drawings of ships, native inhabitants, colonial buildings, military engagements, and geographical scenes.

On a large sheet of butcher paper, or on butcher paper sheets laid side by side and taped together to make a wider mural, student planning committees can pencil in the rough idea of the mural before painting it with tempera, acrylics, felt-tip pens, or watercolors. For ease, the mural may be painted while the butcher paper lies on the floor or after it is hung on a wall. A mural can also incorporate collage. After it is finished, give the mural an antique appearance with one or more coats of polyurethane varnish tinted with several well-stirred-in brushfuls of brown enamel.

Build a Costa Rican Ox Cart: A Craft Project

What You Need:

The book *Costa Rica in Pictures* (or similar)
Cardboard boxes
Sketch paper
Pencils and erasers
Compasses
Scissors
Craft knives
Wooden dowel rods
Handsaw to cut dowels to size
Sandpaper to smooth dowel ends
Round template (wastepaper basket, plate)
Strips of cloth or old leather belts (optional)
Paints (tempera, acrylic)

Costa Rica's once plentiful decorated ox carts are passing into history, although a few craftspeople still make them, mostly for tourists. Students can build miniature ox carts like the originals with cardboard (figures 44 and 45). First, find a photograph of one of these carts in *Costa Rica in Pictures* (see "Sources of Inspiration," page 227). Notice the intricate geometric and floral patterns painted on the wheels and sides of the carts. Direct students in transferring similar designs onto sketch paper with pencil. Other patterns are also acceptable, from Aztec, Inca, Mexican, and other Hispanic murals and paintings. Students can use compasses to make perfect geometric designs on the wheels. American patchwork quilt patterns or Italian mosaic designs (see pages 128–131) can also be used here.

To make the ox cart, each student needs a box from the grocery store. The teacher will need to supply other boxes to provide materials for the wheels, which can be drawn around the top of a round wastepaper basket and cut out. Another way to draw round wheels is to tie one length of string to a thumb tack, the other end around a pencil. Press the tack into the middle of the cardboard, and run the pencil around in the circle created by pulling the string taut.

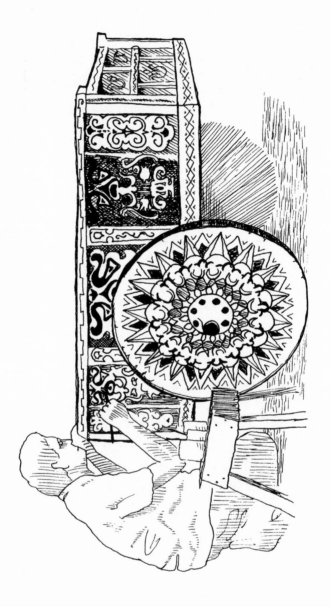

Figure 44

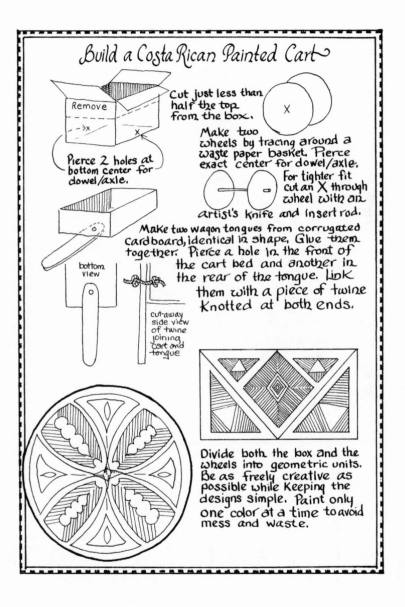

Build a Costa Rican Painted Cart

Remove

Pierce 2 holes at bottom center for dowel/axle.

Cut just less than half the top from the box.

Make two wheels by tracing around a waste paper basket. Pierce exact center for dowel/axle. For tighter fit cut an X through wheel with an artist's knife and insert rod.

Make two wagon tongues from corrugated cardboard, identical in shape. Glue them together. Pierce a hole in the front of the cart bed and another in the rear of the tongue. Link them with a piece of twine knotted at both ends.

bottom view

cutaway side view of twine joining cart and tongue

Divide both the box and the wheels into geometric units. Be as freely creative as possible while keeping the designs simple. Paint only one color at a time to avoid mess and waste.

Figure 45

Scraps of cardboard from wheel-making can be put to use as tongues for the cart.

Each student will need a piece of straight dowel for the wheel axle. The dowel may be placed directly through the center of the sides of the box, just above the bottom, or students can make cradles for the dowel from sturdy cloth or leather, such as an old belt. These cradles can be looped through holes in the bottom of the cart and tied securely.

Making the cart itself is relatively straightforward. The top flaps should be cut off with an artist's knife or with sharp scissors. The axle holes must be pierced at precisely the mid-center of the sides of the cart. The holes should be just as large as the dowel. Friction in use will make them run smoothly.

The wheels should also be pierced exactly in the center. With an artist's knife, the teacher can crisscross a centrally positioned pencil dot three times. This will admit the axle in a tight fit and may be glued in position after the painting has been completed.

The tongue can be cut as long as the box or longer. It will be sturdier if it is made of two identically-cut sections of corrugated cardboard, then glued together. Make the cart tongue pivot for steering by securing it to the center-front of the bottom of the cart with a piece of twine or rope, knotted at either end. The rope will pass through the floor of the cart and through a hole in the tongue. Large paper fasteners may also work if the cardboard is not too thick.

Before applying tempera paints, sketch in the design. Use a ruler to keep the designs symmetrical and balanced. Try to avoid random splotches of color. A carefully measured and drawn design will provide the most satisfying effect, though younger artists may find pursuit of accuracy too tedious. Designs may be executed with a baroque flourish or they may be painted in simple imitation of nature, with leaves and flowers and trees. The wheels can look like sunbursts radiating from the axle, or they may be painted to look like feathered headdresses, arrowheads, plants or concentric circles. Write in the colors which you plan to use. When the design is pencilled in, **paint with one color at a time only.** When that has dried, go on to another color. This will build up the colors without unnecessary messiness, and the result will be sharp definition.

The carts may be used to display fruits and pine cones, books for a festival, or other artifacts. Students can take them home to dress up their rooms and to hold pencils and school supplies.

One Adobe House or an Entire Pueblo: A Research and Craft Project

What You Need:

Pictures of adobe buildings
Cardboard grocery boxes
Stiff card boxes (from cereals and other kitchen products)
Match boxes
Twigs and small branches from trees
Handsaw to trim twigs
Craft knives
Scissors
Sketch paper
Pencils
Glue
Masking tape
Paint (tempera, latex, or acrylic)
Brushes
Sponges
Old newspapers to cover work surface when painting
Modelling clay or self-hardening craft clay (optional)

Create a single adobe-style house from one cardboard box or put together an entire village when a whole class gets involved. First assemble the boxes—photocopy paper boxes or boxes used to transport canned foods. Then spend some time looking at photos and drawings of adobe dwellings and public buildings in books about New Mexico and the land South of the Border. In dry areas, students may want to experiment with making some adobe sun-dried bricks from mud and straw. A quicker project, and one that soon creates the atmosphere of the Spanish Southwest in the classroom, is the cardboard adobe structure.

While looking at pictures of adobe buildings, students should make sketches and drawings, showing where doors, windows, and other features ought to be placed. They should particularly note the log roof/ceiling beams (called **vigas**) that stick through the top exterior of the adobe walls. Ask them to locate chimneys, hearths, and outdoor baking ovens. Notice the kinds of vegetation that grow near the adobe houses. What do wells look like? These questions will help them transfer their sketches to the sides of their cardboard boxes and to decide what extra features they will make from small food boxes.

Before transferring the designs to the cardboard boxes, ask students to make one good drawing of a typical adobe building. Some students may want to make a dwelling, while others will draw a trading post, council house, or mission church complete with bell tower. When the drawing is complete, perhaps showing architectural elevations from all four sides, guide them in carefully drawing doors and windows on the sides of the boxes (figure 46). Sometimes it is easier for the adult to provide pre-cut templates for doors and windows which students merely trace around.

Mature students can use sharp craft knives to cut out the apertures, but teachers may want to do this for younger artists. To create windows with open-and-close shutters, draw a square or rectangle. Divide this pattern in half vertically and cut through that central line. Cut through the top and bottom lines. To make the shutters fold **out**, score vertically between the ends of the top and bottom cuts **inside the box**. To make the shutters fold **in**, score between the ends of the top and bottom cuts outside.

Some southwestern adobe houses have unusual wooden grid shutters that remain permanently in place, admitting cool breezes but shutting out some of the direct sunlight. To make these, cut out the entire window opening. Then draw enough grids from cardboard to cover the window: in cardboard, five or six should do. Cut them out and glue them to the outside of the window. Later, paint on a window frame to simulate wood. To make an adobe jail for the sheriff and his posse, glue the grids inside the window and later paint them black.

To make doors that open and close, draw the doorway in position, using a ruler to keep it straight. Cut through the top, one side, and bottom. Score along the other side, either on the inside or outside of the box. To make the door open inwardly smoothly, without catching on the bottom of the box, make the bottom cut about two mm above the floor.

Outdoors, find several straight twigs long enough for roof beams. Cut off leaves and small twiglets with a knife but leave the bark intact. Pierce one side of the box with a pencil at regular intervals about an inch from the top. Stick a twig through each hole. When it reaches the other side, mark its place with a pencil, and make a hole there. The twigs should then rest firmly in the box, with an inch or more hanging over each side.

Make a porch, or veranda, for the adobe house under which its occupants can shelter from the blazing sun. Set the box on a larger piece of cardboard which will become the porch floor. Trace around the sides of the adobe house which will not have a porch, and then extend the floor a few inches beyond the porched wall. With a craft knife, cut out the floor. Glue the box to it, securing it with masking tape until it dries. Measure and draw a roof porch the same width as the porch floor. Before cutting it out, draw two tabs which will later be inserted into the wall of the house. Cut it out with a knife and hold it in position against the side of the box. With a pencil, mark slots for the tabs and then cut them out. Insert the porch roof, bend down the tabs inside, tape them in place. Support the roof either with dowel posts cut to size or twigs found outdoors.

Paint the box inside and out with tempera or poster paint. Experiment with mixtures of orange, red, yellow, tan, and white to create the colors of adobe walls found in pictures and photographs. Rather than aiming for a consistent blend, imitate natural adobe by letting individual colors dominate in small patches. After the initial coat of tempera has dried, students may dab small bits of brown, red, yellow, or tan onto the walls with a sponge. Paint the shutters a bright color or brown to represent wood. Paint the door brown, inside and out. Use darker brown or black to paint wood grain and hinges.

The roof of an adobe house may be flat or gabled. Paint a flat roof the same shade as the walls. Paint the gabled roof red to simulate clay tiles. Turn the adobe structure into a church by adding a bell tower made from a cocoa box. Cut out windows on four sides, shape the flaps into a cupola, glue on a cross, and glue the box to the front center of the roof. Add elegance to a tall cardboard adobe house by turning discarded kitchen product boxes into balconies.

Paint the porch floor soft red by first mixing red tempera with a little white and tan to simulate Mexican tiles. When it has dried, paint a faint checkerboard with a small brush, using tan tempera to simulate sand or mortar. Paint the porch roof brown to simulate wood or red to simulate tiles. Paint the porch posts dark brown or leave twigs unpainted.

With kitchen match boxes and discarded cardboard containers, create water barrels, cabinets (called *trasteros*), blanket chests, tables, horse water troughs, and window flower boxes. If the surfaces of these small boxes are slick or highly laminated, students may need to glue paper on or paint will not adhere properly.

Students can make a patio or garden by placing their house on a large sheet of brown or sand-colored oaktag paper. An outdoor

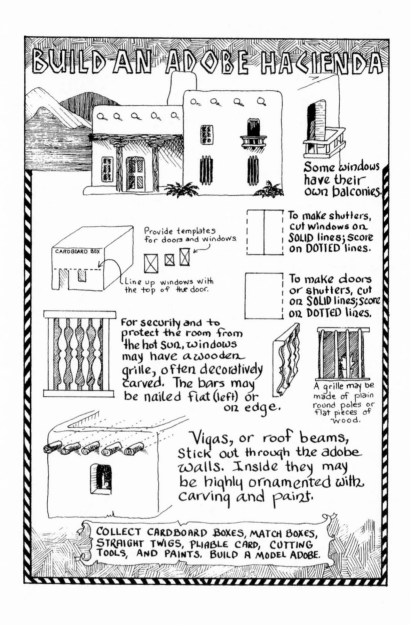

BUILD AN ADOBE HACIENDA

Some windows have their own balconies.

Provide templates for doors and windows.

CARDBOARD BOX

Line up windows with the top of the door.

To make shutters, cut windows on SOLID lines; score on DOTTED lines.

To make doors or shutters, cut on SOLID lines; score on DOTTED lines.

For security and to protect the room from the hot sun, windows may have a wooden grille, often decoratively carved. The bars may be nailed flat (left) or on edge.

A grille may be made of plain round poles or flat pieces of wood.

Vigas, or roof beams, stick out through the adobe walls. Inside they may be highly ornamented with carving and paint.

COLLECT CARDBOARD BOXES, MATCH BOXES, STRAIGHT TWIGS, PLIABLE CARD, CUTTING TOOLS, AND PAINTS. BUILD A MODEL ADOBE.

Figure 46

VIGAS

Collect 6-8 fairly straight twigs. Trim ends straight. Cut off tiny branches.

Insert vigas just beneath top of roof. They must extrude from both sides of the box.

Cut out and glue on sun grille?

Make a Veranda

of twigs or rolled, glued newspaper. Glue the hacienda to a base of cardboard.

Paint terracotta to look like roof tiles

Cut out a piece of card, with two tabs. Cut slits in wall of hacienda and insert tabs. Make porch posts

TAB   TAB

TOP VIEW
LA CASA
PORCH ROOF
BASE

Matchsticks

Una Iglesia

Make towers from small food boxes.

a balcony: glue a match box to the wall.

Bueno!

Paint doors brown

Doors may be very ornate on adobe haciendas. Decorate with cut strips of card.

Mix tempera paint: white ($\frac{1}{3}$), yellow ($\frac{1}{3}$), tan ($\frac{1}{3}$) and sponge onto hacienda. Then sponge again lightly with tan. Last of all, sponge VERY lightly with brown ($\frac{1}{2}$), white ($\frac{1}{4}$), and yellow ($\frac{1}{4}$). ¡Bienvenida! ¡BIENVENIDA A MI CASA!

Figure 46

"beehive fireplace" (*horno*) can be made by coiling clay into an inverted pot shape, smoothing the sides, and adding a chimney made by rolling a small rectangle of clay into a cylinder. The addition of a few small pebbles, a little potted evergreen, and a toy horse will complete the scene.

Los Barcos on Parade: A Craft Project

Many Latin American festivals are Roman Catholic in origin. On feast days, parishioners march in parades with bands, flowers, and singing. Honored members of the church get to carry the statue of the saint on their shoulders. Often they stop at various points along the parade route to let onlookers get a better view of the statue or to rest, for often these statues and their platforms, called *barcos,* may weigh hundreds of pounds.

Create one of **Los Barcos,** literally a boat, to carry in a local festival parade. While the originals are statues of holy men or women or of Jesus or the angels, a *barco* may represent a local hero, animal (such as a school mascot), or figure from folklore.

What You Need:

Old Newspapers and paper towels, some torn into strips
Fabric remnants
Masking Tape
String
Wallpaper paste
Water
Mixing bowls
Cardboard
Scissors
Old leather belt or strips of canvas or twine
Two broom handles or dowels per statue

Keep the scale small by making sure that the statue will fit on a cardboard platform that can be lifted and carried between two broom handles (figure 47). Make the platform from two layers of corrugated cardboard from a large box. Glue and tape them together securely. Pierce sets of holes near each corner of the platform, and thread twine through, tying it into four loose knots. Alternatively, attach pieces of the old leather belt or canvas strips to make support loops. Put broom

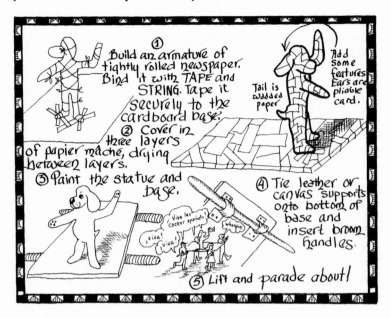

(Figure 47) Los Barcos on Parade

handles through these loops and get four students to practice picking it up and carrying it.

The fun part is making the statue out of papier mâché. Build an infrastructure, or skeleton, from rolled newspaper and bits of wood or wire, formed in the relative pose of the desired statue. This skeleton will look like a child's stick figure. Make the feet especially long, however, in order to secure them to the platform.

Make papier mâché by soaking strips of torn newspaper briefly in wallpaper paste. Other absorbent papers may also be used, such as paper towels. Cotton fabric remnants can be used, especially as the final layer of a clothed figure, for the adhesive impregnated material will retain its shape. An alternative to wallpaper paste is a solution of one part polyvinyl adhesive (PVA) and two to three parts water.

With papier mâché, build up the body of the statue on the platform in layers, allowing to dry thoroughly after the application of from three to five layers. From time to time, wrap long papier mâché strips from the feet of the statue around the platform. If the statue is over two feet high, consider wiring its feet to the platform to keep it from falling off accidentally. Cover the platform with papier mâché, too, top and bottom. When the statue has about four separate, dried layers (up to twenty thicknesses of paper), paint it realistically or fantastically. Refer to the project on ox carts, above, for ideas.

When the statue is not being elevated in procession, give it pride of place in a corner of the library or classroom, much as the originals would be kept in a chapel or side aisle of a Spanish-American church. If students have made a school mascot, organize a mini parade at school before home games. Display it in the main entrance on important days. Make sure a photo of it goes into the newspaper. If the project has centered around a saint or folk hero, make certain that research has produced some identifiable belongings or attributes that will give the statue representational qualities, such as a bird for St. Francis, or an ox for Paul Bunyan, or a bear for Davy Crockett.

When the statue is carried, accompany the parade with drums, cymbals, and maracas (fill empty cans with a few dried beans or pebbles). Play recorded tapes of Peruvian or Paraguayan harp music, of mariachi bands from Texas, or of Cuban, Mexican, or other Hispanic music.

Crack Open a Piñata: A Craft Project

Made to be broken, the piñata is a toy that evokes for many children the party spirit of Latin America. Brought out for children's birthdays, Christmas, and other celebrations, the piñata is hung from a tree branch or rafter, and blindfolded guests take turns trying to break it to release the candies and toys held inside. In Mexico, piñatas are made of pottery, but to prevent danger from flying shards, children can make their own piñatas from papier mâché or plaster-impregnated gauze. Brought to Mexico from Spain by colonists, the piñata has a venerable ancestry. During the Roman Empire, piñatas were simply large clay pots filled with fruit that were ceremoniously broken by vineyard workers to mark the end of the harvest. In Spain, the piñata is not broken; the goodies are released by tapping a false bottom. Piñatas can be made in the shape of animals, a lucky rabbit's foot (a Mexican favorite that looks like a carrot), ships, castles, doll's houses, or stars.

What You Need:

Large party-size plastic soft drink bottles
Vaseline

Torn newspaper or paper towel strips for papier mâché
Wallpaper paste or glue
Water
Mixing Bowl
Craft knife
Edible goodies: wrapped candies, peanuts in shells
Decorative items: fringe, fabric, buttons
Long thread or twine
Sharp knitting needle, or braddle, to pierce hole in piñata
Cleaning rags

The simplest piñata shape can be adapted to take on the character of a historical figure, a car, truck, ship, an animal, a sun, moon, or star. Begin by wrapping papier mâché around a plastic two-liter soft drink bottle that has first been given a **very light** coating of vaseline to keep the papier mâché from sticking when it has dried (figure 48). Apply about three layers of papier mâché and allow them to dry before adding three more and then three more. When all the layers have dried thoroughly, cut the jar in half, either horizontally or vertically, with a craft knife. Remove the plastic jar and wipe off the inside of the papier mâché form to remove any traces of vaseline.

Since the piñata will be filled with small candies, party favors, and "stocking fillers," the maker must decide how to add the goodies, seal up the container, decorate it, and hang it from the ceiling in order to break it open. There are several ways to fill and seal. If the container was cut in half vertically see figure 48 (step No. 5), lay one half of the piñata on a table and fill it full of treats. Place the other half in position on top and seal it with a couple of layers of papier mâché. When it is dry, carefully set it upright on the table to begin decoration.

If the container was cut horizontally, fill the bottom half only. Reattach the top half, securing it with papier mâché—but not so securely that it becomes too difficult to break open. Pierce two holes in the top of the bottle shape with a sharp nail or braddle (awl) and thread a piece of strong twine through. Cover the top of the piñata with papier mâché so that it is sealed completely.

Decorate the piñata with crepe paper, fringed paper, foil gift wrap, ribbons, and paint, depending upon the effect desired. Turn the bottle into a human character by attaching simple papier mâché arms and legs. Turn it into an animal by attaching four feet, wings, mane, or tail, as dictated by species. To suspend a piñata animal such as a

¡Piñata!

① Cover a BIG plastic soft drink bottle lightly with Vaseline.
② Cover with 3 layers of papier mâché.
③ Allow to dry and apply 3 more layers.
④ Allow to dry and apply 3 more layers.

3 x 3 x 3!

⑤ Dry. Cut in two! Remove bottle. ...or...

⑥ Fill with GOODIES and replace top.

⑦ Seal seam with papier mâché.

Pierce neck and thread with LONG twine

⑧ Decorate with more papier mâché; fringe; fabric; paint.

⑨ Hang from a tree limb, basketball hoop, or beam.

⑩ Blindfold players and give them a stick. Spin them around! See if they can break the piñata to get at the goodies!

Figure 48

horse, dog, or pig, thread the twine through the side of the bottle instead of the neck.

In Mexico, the game of breaking the piñata is maddeningly fun, because not only are the players blindfolded, but the piñata is attached to a moveable cord that can be lowered and raised by a master of ceremonies. Adults may want to tie the piñata to a long rope that can be stretched across a hook, pipe, tree branch, or rafter. As players come forward, one at a time to avoid injuring others, to swing their stick at the piñata, the master of ceremonies lowers or raises the rope, moving the candy-filled object out of the way.

Make Papier Mâché Fruits: A Craft Project

What You Need:

Papier mâché mix
Modelling clay
Craft knife
Water-based paints (tempera, latex, acrylic)
Brushes

While making papier mâché piñatas or statues, use some of the mixture to build up a colorful collection of tropical Latin American fruits and vegetables. Students can make bananas, citrus fruits, grapes, sweet potatoes, and chili peppers from modelling clay which in turn are wrapped in several layers of papier mâché. When the papier mâché is thoroughly dry, cut down the middle vertically, remove the clay, and rejoin the paper with more papier mâché. When this has dried, paint the fruits and vegetables with tempera. Display them in baskets. Hang them from Christmas trees. Suspend them in clusters in windows. Fill the decorated cardboard ox carts with papier mâché fruits. Try stringing several papier mâché chili peppers together to make a Southwestern *ristra*.

Sprinkle a Guatemalan Carpet of Flowers: A Craft Project

A particularly Guatemalan art form is the floral carpet, created painstakingly in city streets only to be destroyed by parades on festival days. Sometimes the carpets are made by placing gigantic templates or stencils on the streets. Petals are then dropped through the cut-outs onto the pavement. At other times, floral artists draw designs directly onto the stone pavements and fill them in with petals. Students can make replicas of these Guatemalan floral carpets using color tissue paper and glue.

What You Need:

Newspaper
Felt-tip pen
Photo of oriental carpet
Heavy color construction paper or butcher paper
Scissors
Glue
Color tissue paper, torn into small fragments

To make a pattern, fold a double page newspaper in half (figure 49). With a thick felt-tip pen, draw a large, lacy pattern on one half of the fold. Refer to oriental carpets or to photos of carpets for ideas. Cut out the designs and unfold. Trace the pattern onto a large sheet of butcher paper or construction paper. Fill in the pattern with tissue paper "petals," gluing one corner of a tissue square to the butcher

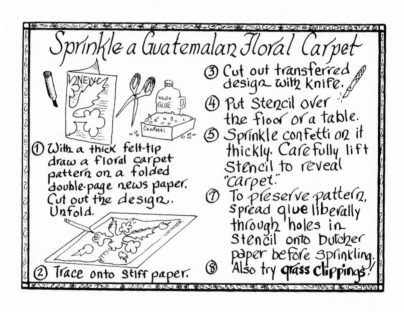

Sprinkle a Guatemalan Floral Carpet

① With a thick felt-tip draw a floral carpet pattern on a folded double-page news paper. Cut out the design. Unfold.

② Trace onto stiff paper.

③ Cut out transferred design with knife.

④ Put stencil over the floor or a table.

⑤ Sprinkle confetti on it thickly. Carefully lift stencil to reveal "carpet."

⑦ To preserve pattern, spread glue liberally through holes in stencil onto butcher paper before sprinkling.

⑧ Also try **grass clippings!**

Figure 49

paper. Glue as many squares as the pattern will hold to create a fluffy carpet.

If you use butcher paper, divide the carpet makers into teams to make one long carpet. Each team can make a different pattern, the size of a sheet of newspaper, for its section. Display the carpet by hanging on a wall.

Open a Hispanic Who's Who

Help students learn about famous or significant Hispanic Americans by creating a Hispanic *Who's Who*. "Sources of Inspiration" at the end of this chapter will reveal famous Latin Americans that ought to be more well-known. Other general biographical reference sources in most libraries will reveal others.

The teacher or librarian can provide an activity sheet with names of several Hispanic artists, musicians and actors, politicians, manufacturers, novelists, and educators. Students can fill in blanks, write short biographies, draw portraits based on photographs, or give short oral reports in class. Written projects can be hung in a "Gallery of Famous Hispanic Americans."

A very attractive *Who's Who* Gallery can be made by painting the names of famous Latin Americans, living and dead, on a wall that has been covered with cheap white wallpaper. Paint the names in large red letters, with a phrase underneath in black, green, or blue that identifies them, such as "Simon Bolivar—liberator," or "Joan Baez—folk singer and political activist."

These are a few celebrities and outstanding Latin Americans to start the list:

Luis Muñoz Marin, Puerto Rico's first elected governor, born February 18, 1898, has lived in New York and Washington, D.C. and has also served as senator from Puerto Rico.

Actor, producer, and singer **Jose Ferrer** was born in San Juan, Puerto Rico, in 1912. A Princeton graduate, he went on to win an Academy Award.

Author of *Down These Mean Streets,* **Piri Thomas** was born in Harlem of Puerto Rican parents.

Among Puerto Rican baseball stars are **Roberto Clemente** of the Pittsburgh Pirates, and **Orlando Cepeda** of the St. Louis Cardinals.

Pablo Casals, one of the world's outstanding musicians, was born in Spain of a Puerto Rican mother but chose to live in Puerto Rico where he played cello and conducted the symphony orchestra in San Juan.

Among Cuban personalities, Revolutionary Premier **Fidel Castro** is perhaps best known. Actor and singer **Desi Arnaz** was from Cuba.

Joseph Montoya (1915–1978) was the first Mexican American elected to the United States Senate.

Mexican-American artist **Octavio Medellín** has worked and taught in the Southwest where he gained inspiration from Indian art.

Author **Luis Valdez** wrote political plays inspired by union conflicts during the 1960's California grape-pickers' strikes.

With strong Mexican roots, actor **Anthony Quinn** has made over 100 films, won two Oscars, and has narrated *The Voice of La Raza,* a documentary about the plight of Mexicans and Puerto Ricans in the United States.

Folk singer **Joan Baez** is the daughter of Mexican-born physicist **Albert Baez.**

Actor **Ricardo Montalban** founded "Nosotros," dedicated to solving injustices and problems of Spanish-surnamed actors, actresses, and technicians in motion pictures.

Guest Speakers and Trips

Schools in areas with high Hispanic populations can find a newspaper or magazine editor, a teacher, a store owner, or an artist to speak about the Latin influence in his or her life and work. Where possible, invite Hispanics from several different Latin American countries to speak so that students can find out firsthand the differences in culture and ways of life. In communities which do not have a large Latin American population, check the telephone directory for Hispanic community centers or clubs or enquire in the state library for information about Hispanic organizations that might provide a speaker.

Most areas have Mexican fast-food restaurants. America is well versed in tacos, burritos, and enchiladas. Make a class trip to a Mexican eatery and savor the spices. Where possible, visit a good Mexican restaurant and order a large mixed plate so that students can sample not only a wide variety of meats, beans, and tortillas, but also the delicate and varied dishes largely unknown outside their regions of origin.

Find out if a state or city museum has any Aztec or Inca relics or artifacts from the days of early Spanish colonization. Take a small group there with sketch pads to draw pottery, statues, and picture-writing.

La Cuchina: Frijoles

Proprietary brands of Mexican-style foods are readily available in the smallest supermarkets across America, so the preparation of refried beans, tacos, and stuffed peppers is easy enough to accomplish. Purists will insist that these are a far cry from authenticity, but instructions are easily printed on the containers, and students will enjoy preparing them.

Mexicans eat vast amounts of red kidney beans. Tex-Mex novels of the old west feature chuck wagons that served vast pots of these beans. Beans are cheap to buy, easy to prepare, and make a healthy, tasty salad that students can concoct in the classroom.

Mexican Bean Salad

This dish takes up to two days to prepare, and the finished product tastes even better after the cooked beans and spices have marinated in the dressing for two or three days more. This recipe will offer tastings to about forty people.

What You Need:

One package dried kidney beans
One package dried garbonzo peas (chick peas)
Jalapeño peppers (canned or fresh, to taste)
Two medium onions (or more)
Two cloves garlic (or more)
Chili powder
Olive oil and vinegar
Mixing bowls and spoons
Cooking pots for beans
Kitchen knives and cutting boards
Lettuce
Avocados
Mild chili peppers
Tomatoes, sliced or quartered
Tortilla chips
Paper plates or cups

Wash the dried beans thoroughly and remove any pebbles or debris. Soak the kidney beans and garbanzos (separately) overnight in water to cover. Next day pour off the water. Cook the beans and peas separately in salted boiling water until they are well done. Kidney beans will cook in about two hours. Garbanzos may require up to four hours. Remove the beans and peas from the heat, cool, and drain.

Chop the peppers, onions, and garlic and add to the beans. Add chili powder to taste and pour on oil and vinegar to taste. Allow the beans to marinate in the dressing for about four hours, or overnight, before serving on a bed of crisp lettuce, chopped avocadoes, tomatoes, and mild chili peppers. A bowl of tortilla chips is an excellent accompaniment.

¡Dígame! Drama and Fun with Spanish!

If there is a strong Hispanic presence in the school or community, speaking Spanish will be easy. The following list of expressions will be too elementary. If, however, Spanish is not widely spoken, encourage use of the language during and before the festival. The following vocabulary provides a foundation for basic communication in greetings and getting about.

Librarians might try using Spanish when checking out materials. A native or fluent Spanish speaker could be invited to spend an hour or two as a user-friendly library assistant. Teachers can use the vocabulary for drama exercises: role-playing students may communicate using only Spanish and gestures; students improvise on imaginative situations using only Spanish. A corner of the library or classroom can be turned into the "Spanish Quarter" where students can take on the roles of merchants, farmers at market, shoppers, teachers, or musicians. The Spanish Quarter can be used throughout the festival to encourage oral use of the language—especially during students' creative learning times.

Good morning!	¡Buenos días!
Good afternoon!	¡Buenas tardes!
Good night!	¡Buenas noches!

Goodbye!	¡Adiós!
Hi!	¡Hola!
How are you doing?	¿Cómo estás?
What's going on?	¿Qúe pasa?
My name is . . .	Mi nombre es . . .
What is your name?	¿Cómo se llamas?
How old are you, pal?	¿Cuántos años tienes, amigo?
I am (ten) years old.	Tengo (diez) años.
Where is . . .	¿Dónde está . . .
Do you like school?	¿Te gusta lá escuela?
Yes! Of course!	Sí! ¡Por supuesto!
No! What a pity!	No! ¡Qué lástima!
I like parties!	¡Me gustan las fiestas!
I do, too!	¡Yo también!
Would you like to join us?	¿Quieres unirte a nosotros?
I don't understand.	No comprendo.
Pardon me, but . . .	¡Oye!, pero . . .
I am looking for . . .	Estoy buscando . . .
the school	lá escuela.
the library	la biblioteca.
a friend (male)	un amigo.
a friend (female)	una amiga.
my book	mi libro.
your magazine	tu revista.
the pencil	el lapiz.
I want . . .	Quiero . . .
to buy a book	comprar un libro
a dozen roses	una docena de rosas
a watch	un reloj
sunglasses	gafas de sol
to visit the school	visitar la escuela
I'd like . . .	Me gustaria . . .
a Mexican flag	una bandera mejicana
two seats	dos asientos
May I introduce . . .	Te presento . . .
my teacher?	a mi profesor/a.
my mom?	a mi madre (a mi mamá).
my friend John?	a mi amigo Juan.
my dad?	a mi padre (a mi papá).
my brother?	a mi hermano.
my sister Lucia?	a mi hermana Lucía.
my granny?	a mi abuela.
my aunt Carla?	a mi tía Carla.

Los Números

1. uno		20. veinte	
2. dos		21. veintiuno	
3. tres		22. veintidós	
4. cuatro		23. veintitrés	
5. cinco			
6. seis		30. treinta	
7. siete		40. cuarenta	
8. ocho		50. cincuenta	
9. nueve		60. sesenta	
10. diez		70. setenta	
11. once		80. ochenta	
12. doce		90. noventa	
13. trece		100. cien, ciento	
14. catorce		200. doscientos/as	
15. quince		500. quinientos/as	
16. dieciséis		1000. mil	
17. Diecisiete		10000. Diez mil	
18. Dieciocho			
19. Diecinueve			

Using the Vocabulary: Some Improvisation Ideas

At the bookshop (or library). Student One is looking for something to read. Student Two tries to help. While speaking the lines, students may assume interesting roles: an old woman, a police officer, a girl walking a dog, a teacher eating a banana, a man asleep on a park bench with his leg tied to a donkey . . .

One   ¡Oye!, pero ¿tienes algunos libros españoles?
Two   ¡Buenos dias, amigo! ¡Sí! ¡Tengo libros españoles!
One   ¿Endónde, por favor?
Two   ¡En la biblioteca!
One   ¿La biblioteca?
Two   ¡Sí! ¡Adiós!
One   ¡Adiós!

Waiting for the school bus. Here students learn some new expressions before the bus arrives. They may pretend that it's raining, that it is very hot or cold, that they are teachers, or that they are sweethearts . . .

One   ¿A qúe hora sale el autobús? (What time does the bus leave?)
Two   A las Cuatro.
One   ¿Que hora es? (What time is it?)
Two   Son las cuatro y cinco. (It is five past four.)
One   Está tarde. (It is late.)
Two   Sí.
One   Quiero ir a mi casa. (I want to go home.)
Two   Yo, también.
One   ¿A mi casa?
Two   No, no a tu casa! ¡A casa! ¿Como se llamas? (No, to my house)
One   ¿Yo? Me llama Carlo (or Carla). ¿Y tú.
Two   Mi nombre es Hector (or Linda).
One   Hector, ahora llega el autobús. (The bus is arriving now.)
Two   Bueno, quiero visitar tu casa, Carlo. (Good! I'd like to visit your house, Carlo.)
One   ¿Esta noche? (Tonight?)
Two   ¡Si! ¿A qúe hora sirven las comidas? (Yes! What time is supper?) ¡Tengo hambre! (I'm hungry!)
One   Pero . . .
Two   Tu eres mi nuevo amigo! (You are my new friend!) ¡Vámonos! (Let's go)

Sources of Inspiration

*Materials About Hispanics, Latin Americans
and Spanish-Speaking Americans*

Fiction

Ardema, Verna. *The Riddle of the Drum: A Tale from Tizapan, Mexico.* Illustrations by Tony Chen. San Diego: Four Winds Press, 1979.
> In this folktale, retold for very young readers, a handsome prince solves a thorny problem to win the hand of the fair princess.

Azuela, Mariano. *The Underdogs: A Novel of the Mexican Revolution.* Translated by E. Munguia, Jr. New York: New American Library, 1967.
> A general in Pancho Villa's army was once a peaceful Mexican peasant, brought into the revolution by force.

Baker, Betty. *Walk the World's Rim.* New York: Harper and Row, 1963.
> Set in colonial Mexico and Texas, this is the tale of Cabeza de Vaca and his black slave's trek through Indian country.

Beatty, Patricia. *Lupita Montana.* New York: Morrow, 1981.
> Two Mexican youths must cross the border to find work in the United States.

Belpre, Pura. *Once in Puerto Rico.* Illustrations by Christine Price. New York: Frederick Warne, 1973.
> The author bases these sixteen retellings of Puerto Rican folktales on her own life there. Another Puerto Rican folktale by this author is *Perez and Martina* (Warne, 1961).

Bethancourt, T. E. *Where the Deer and the Canteloupe Play.* San Diego: Oak Tree, 1981.
> A young Latino from New York City finds out about life for himself in the Wild West.

Bryan, Ashley, ed. *The Dancing Granny.* New York: Atheneum, 1977.
> Spider Ananse, a tall, athletic man, is finally defeated by diminutive Granny Anika in this Carribean tale for beginning readers.

Bulla, Clyde Robert. *The Poppy Seeds.* New York: Harper and Row, 1955.
> A young Indian boy plants poppies throughout his Mexican village in this story for younger readers.

Chardiet, Bernice. *Juan Bobo and the Pig: A Puerto Rican Folk-tale Retold.* Illustrations by Hope Meryman. Walker, 1973.
> A family is tricked by Juan Bobo in this beginning reader story from Puerto Rico.

Clark, Ann Nolan. *Secret of the Incas.* New York: Viking, 1952.
An Inca boy tends a llama herd high in the Peruvian Andes.

Cohen, Miriam. *Born to Dance Samba.* Illustrations by Gioia Fiammenghi. New York: Harper and Row, 1984.
Samba enthusiast Mario gets ready for the annual Rio carnival in a novel that will appeal to middle school students.

Dewey, Ariane. *The Thunder God's Son: A Peruvian Folktale.* Greenwillow, 1981.
Very young pre-readers will savor this tale of Acuri, son of the Thunder God, who visits Peru.

Finger, Charles. *Tales from the Silver Lands.* Illustrations by Paul Honore. New York: Doubleday, 1924.
This Newbery Medal winner is a collection of folktales from South America.

Green, Graham. *The Power and the Glory.* New York: Viking, 1977.
This novel of political terror sets the Mexican government against the Roman Catholic church, especially its priests, whose underground activity reveals much about their private lives.

Jagendorf, M. A. *The King of the Mountains.* New York: Vanguard, 1960.
Lower school readers will enjoy these favorite Latin American folktales.

Kurtycz, Marcos, and Ana Garcia Kobeh. *Tigers and Opossums: Animal Legends.* Little, Brown and Company, 1984.
For lower school readers, this is a pleasant collection of animal folklore from Mexico.

Lawrence, D. H. *The Plumed Serpent.* London: Heinemann, 1974.
Kate Leslie, an Irish widow, rejects the Americanized Mexico presented to tourists and is drawn to a revolutionary movement built around Quetzalcoatl, the pre-Christian snakegod of old Mexico. Lawrence's famous description of a bullfight opens this dramatic novel.

Lowry, Malcolm. *Under the Volcano.* London: Penguin, 1968.
On the Mexican fiesta of Los Muertos, ragged children beg for coins in the shadow of Popocatepetl while a British ex-consul's life crumbles around him.

Madison, Winfred. *Maria Luisa.* New York: Harper and Row, 1971.
When Maria Luisa moves to her aunt's house in San Francisco she finds that neighbors do not like Chicanos.

Mangurian, David. *Children of the Incas.* New York: Four Winds, 1979.
Middle schoolers will enjoy this tale of a poor boy growing up in a Peruvian village.

Martel, Cruz. *Yagua Days.* Illustrations by Jerry Pinkney. New York: Dial Press, 1976.

Adam, a young Hispanic boy, visits Puerto Rico, his parents' homeland, in this picture book for beginning readers.

Morh. Nicholasa. *Felita.* New York: Dial Press, 1979.
A Puerto Rican family meets prejudice when they leave their friendly neighborhood and move into an area where no one speaks Spanish.

O'Dell, Scott. *The Feathered Serpent.* Boston: Houghton Mifflin, 1981.
Julian Escobar assumes the role of the Mayan god Kukulcan and confronts his pagan subjects and priests.

————. *The King's Fifth.* Boston: Houghton Mifflin, 1966.
Estaban, a young map maker, finds that desire for gold gets in the way of this search for knowledge.

————. *The Treasure of Topo-el-Bampo.* Illustrated by Lynd Ward. Boston: Houghton Mifflin, 1977.
Two burros sold to the slave-driving silver mine owner return to save their village and make it rich.

Paulsen, Gary. *The Crossing.* New York: Orchard, 1987.
Mexican orphan and beggar Manual dreams of crossing the Rio Grande into the United States. His friendship with United States Army Sgt. Robert Locke brings both of them hope.

Place, Marian T., and Charles G. Preston. *Juan's Eighteen-Wheeler Summer.* New York: Dodd-Mead, 1982.
In order to save money for a dreamed-for bicycle, a Mexican-American boy works with a truck driver one summer.

Rulfo, Juan. *El Llana en Llamas.* Mexico City: Fondo de Cultura Economica, 1970.
This is a collection of short stories in Spanish.

Steinbeck, John. *The Pearl.* London: Heinemann, 1983.
The good-and-evil story of the great lost pearl is also the tale of Kino the Mexican fisherman, Juana his wife, and Coyolito, their baby, whose fortunes rest on this gift from the sea.

Wojciechowska, Maia. *Shadow of a Bull.* New York: Atheneum, 1964.
This Newbery Medal winner is the story of Manolo, surviving son of a great Spanish bullfighter who has to face his own bull in the ring.

Spanish American Life-styles

American Southwest: An Insight Guide. Englewood Cliffs, New Jersey: Prentice-Hall, 1984.
This colorfully illustrated travel companion delves into many facets of life in the Southwest—geography, history, art, food, and Native Americans, including several good chapters on Hispanic culture.

Ashabranner, Brent. *The New Americans*. New York: Dodd, Mead and Company, 1983.
Chapter Three is about new Americans from Latin America: Cuba, Haiti, Mexico. It documents their legal and illegal entry, the kinds of work they perform, and where they settle.

Coles, Robert. *Eskimos, Chicanos, Indians: Volume IV, Children of Crisis*. Boston: Little, Brown, 1977.
This volume of the Pulitzer Prize winning book deals with three groups of disadvantaged, sometimes oppressed, children in America.

Gruber, Ruth. *Felissa Rincon de Gautier: the Mayor of San Juan*. New York: Crowell, 1972.
This woman, who believed in "the politics of love," was mayor for five terms and was well-loved both in San Juan and New York.

Jacobsen, Peter O., and Sejer Kristensen. *A Family in Mexico*. New York: Franklin Watts, 1984.
Third and fourth graders can use this book to find out how a typical Mexican family earns its living, tends it house, and seeks leisure activities.

Langley, Lester. *Mexamerica: Two Countries, One Future*. New York: Crown, 1988.
While increasing numbers of Mexicans settle in the United States and maintain their culture, Langley shows that the two societies are becoming interdependent.

Lewis, Oscar. *La Vida: A Puerto Rican Family in the Culture of Poverty—San Juan and New York*. New York: Random House, 1966.
Sixteen members of a Puerto Rican family tell their own stories in no uncertain words.

Mayerson, Charlotte. *Two Blocks Apart: Juan Gonzales and Peter Quinn*. New York: Avon Camelot, 1967.
How lives, though lived within close proximity, differ.

Miller, Tom. *On the Border: Portraits of America's Southwestern Frontier*. New York: Harper and Row, 1981.
The unique society along the Rio Grande and west into California links the Anglo and Spanish cultures through food, music, folklore, and traditions.

Palante: Young Lords Party. New York: McGraw-Hill, 1971.
Palante (the Spanish equivalent of "right on!") is the story of the revolutionary and political organization founded in New York City's Puerto Rican community in 1969 that demanded social justice for all.

Ribanoff, M. F. *Mexico and the United States Today*. New York: Franklin Watts, 1985.
Examine the ways in which the two countries differ in economies, politics, international outlook, and immigration.

Ribes Tover, Frederico. *The Puerto Rican Woman: Her Life and Evolution Through History.* New York: Plus Ultra, 1972.
This is a history of Hispanic, black, Taina Indian, and Creole women in Puerto Rico and the United States.

Santiestevan Associates, *The Hispanic Almanac.* New York: Hispanic Policy Development Project, 1984.
This helpful book reveals Hispanic population patterns in the United States, along with other statistical information.

Sterling, Philip. *The Quiet Rebels: Four Puerto Rican Leaders: Jose Celso Barbosa, Luis Rivera, Jose de Diego, and Luis Munoz Marin.* New York: Doubleday, 1968.

Valencia, Humberto. *The U.S. Hispanic Market.* New York: FIND/SVP, 1984.
Market researches reveal much about United States Hispanic buying trends, such as that many Hispanics are slow to purchase telephones because telephone use in their native countries was bureaucratically controlled and therefore difficult.

Weyr, Thomas. *Hispanic U.S.A.: Breaking the Melting Pot.* New York: Harper and Row, 1988.
By the year 2000, demographers predict that Hispanics will constitute the largest minority group in the United States and that over half the nation will be fluent in Spanish. This book shows what makes Hispanics different from Germans, Italians, and other nationalities which have been absorbed into American life.

Yankelovich, Skelly, and White. *Spanish USA.* New York: SIN Television Network, 1984.
This is a study of Hispanic people in the United States that reveals much about language patterns, reaction to commercial advertising in English and Spanish, and day-to-day life-styles.

Latin American Countries

Bailey, Bernadine. *Famous Latin American Liberators.* New York: Dodd, Mead, 1966.
Simon Bolivar (Venezuela), Toussaint L'Ouverture (Haiti), Jose de Martin (Uruguay) and Antonio Jose de Sucre (Venezuela) are among six other heroes featured in this collection of biographies.

Beck, Barbara. *The Aztecs.* New York: Franklin Watts, 1983.
This history of the Aztecs of Mexico and Central America is written for middle school researchers.

———. *The Incas.* New York: Franklin Watts, 1983.
This is an illustrated history of the Inca people.

Bleeker, Sonia. *Inca: Indians on the Andes.* New York: Morrow, 1960.
     For young readers, this is a good introduction to the Inca tribe and culture.

Carter, William. *South America.* New York: Franklin Watts, 1983.
     For readers up to seventh grade, this book offers folklore, history, and religious
     information from all over the continent.

Cheney, Alexander. *The Amazon.* New York: Franklin Watts, 1984.
     General readers in upper elementary school will find many facts and photo-
     graphs of this mighty river here, along with its history and prospects.

Costa Rica in Pictures. Minneapolis: Lerner Publications, 1987.
     Photographs, maps, and brief text introduce the geography, history, govern-
     ment, people, and economy of this Central American republic.

Cuba in Pictures. Minneapolis: Lerner Publications, 1987.
     Colorful, interesting photographs of Cuban people and of the Cuban landscape
     make this short book a worthwhile source for young readers who want to learn
     about this Marxist country in the Carribean.

Dobler, Lavinia. *The Land and People of Uruguay.* New York: Harper and Row, 1972.
     Upper elementary students can learn about life in Uruguay from the text and
     photography of this informative book.

Dominican Republic in Pictures. Minneapolis: Lerner Publications, 1987.
     This country of seven million people shares the island of Hispaniola with its
     neighbor to the west, Haiti. It is a land of mixed African, Spanish, and Indian
     culture, whose life and history is given a general overview in this book for middle
     school readers.

Garcia, Connie. *The Travel Guide to Puerto Rico.* Santurce, Puerto Rico: Puerto Rico
     Almanacs, 1981.
     Beginning with an overview of Puerto Rico, this book tells how to get there,
     where to stay, and what to look for and enjoy in sports, shopping and
     entertainment.

Haskins, James. *The New Americans: Cuban Boat People.* Hillside, NJ: Enslow, 1982.
     Read how various tides of Cuban immigrant refugees crossed the narrow divide
     of water to Florida in 1965, 1971, and 1980.

Huber, Alex. *We Live in Argentina.* New York: Franklin Watts, 1984.
     Citizens from many parts of the country describe their lives there.

Jacobsen, Karen. *Mexico.* Chicago: Childrens Press, 1983.
     For first to third graders, Jacobsen's book uses simple language and good
     illustrations to introduce Mexico to English speakers.

Jamaica in Pictures. Minneapolis, MN: Lerner Publications, 1987.
     Young readers can find out about Rastafarians, Arawak Indians, limbo dancing,
     and Jonkunnu bands in this colorful information book.

Karen, Ruth. *The Land and People of Central America.* New York: Harper and Row, 1972.
    Life may have changed considerably for people throughout Central America since this book was published, yet the background information is still worthwhile.

Kurtis, Arlene Harris. *Puerto Ricans: From Island to Mainland.* New York: Messner, 1969.
    From about fifty BC to the late 1960's here is the history of Puerto Rico, including the problems and contributions of Puerto Ricans who move to mainland America.

Larralde, Elsa. *The Land and People of Mexico.* New York: Harper and Row, 1968.
    Schools and libraries may want to buy a more up-to-date geography book, yet Larralde's account offers good information about festivals, climate, and traditions.

Lindon, Edmund. *Cuba.* New York: Franklin Watts, 1980.
    This is an account of the island communist state since Fidel Castro's takeover in the late 1950's.

Lockwood, Lee. *Castro's Cuba, Cuba's Fidel—An American Journalist's Inside Look at Today's Cuba in Text and Pictures.* New York: Macmillan, 1967.
    This full length portrait of post-revolutionary Cuba and its leaders tries to answer the question: what is he really like?

Lye, Keith. *Take a Trip to Mexico.* New York: Franklin Watts, 1982.
    Pictures introduce various topics about Mexico in a version that complements Elsa Larralde's 1960's work.

Markun, Patricia. *Central America and Panama.* New York: Franklin Watts, 1983.
    General information is coupled with good photographs for each country in Central America.

————. *The Panama Canal.* New York: Franklin Watts, 1979.
    An important book for these days of political uncertainty in Panama; Markun tells about the 1978 Treaty in addition to the construction and value of the canal to world trade.

Mexico. Hong Kong: Apa Productions, 1983.
    This illustrated Insight Guide offers tourists and students interesting information on culture, history, places to visit, and products to buy and enjoy.

Miller, Robert Ryal. *Mexico: A History.* Tulsa: University of Oklahoma Press, 1985.
    From pre-Columbian cultures to modern times, this book reveals Mexican history, architecture, art, music, educational achievements, and economy.

Palazuelos, Susanna, Marilyn Tausend, and Ignacio Urquiza. *Mexico the Beautiful Cookbook.* London: Merehurst, 1991.

Beautifully photographed and written from a historical perspective, this is more than a cookbook: but what a cookbook it is, revealing scores of dishes unknown outside their regions. This is an eye-opener for those who think Mexican food is limited to beans and tortillas.

Perl, Lila. *Guatamala: Central America's Living Past.* New York: Morrow, 1982.
Read about the history, economy, and people of Guatamala.

————. *Mexico, Crucible of the Americas.* New York: Morrow, 1978.
This information book for readers up to eighth grade discusses historical and contemporary life in Mexico.

Puerto Rico in Pictures. Minneapolis: Lerner Publications, 1987.
Pictures of old Puerto Rican landmarks, scenic points, and historic buildings make this a useful book in the study of Latin America.

Shuttlesworth, Dorothy. *The Wildlife of South America.* New York: Hastings, 1974.
The voice of a conservator crying in the wilderness? Read this book for a deeper appreciation for ecological care all over the mountains, plains, and jungles of South America.

Singer, Julia. *We All Come From Puerto Rico, Too.* New York: Atheneum, 1977.
The author's illustrations and text tell what it is like to grow up in Puerto Rico.

Smith, Eileen Latell. *Mexico: Giant of the South.* New York: Dillon, 1983.
Concluding with a useful chapter on Mexican immigration to the United States, this book for upper elementary school readers is packed with information about the United States close neighbor.

Somonte, Carlos. *We Live in Mexico.* New York: Bookwright Press, 1985.
This colorful information book for young readers gives a broad picture of what life in Mexico is like.

Stein, Conrad. *Mexico.* Chicago: Childrens Press, 1984.
Middle school students can learn a great deal about Mexico through this encyclopedia-style book.

Telemaque, Eleanor W. *Haiti Through Its Holidays.* New York: Blyden Press, 1980.
A perfect handbook to consult when planning festival activities, this book explains how Haitian customs and traditions evolved over the centuries and how they are celebrated today.

Warren, Leslie. *The Land and People of Bolivia.* New York: Harper and Row, 1974.
Photographs and text show what Bolivian life was like up to the late 1960's.

Periodicals

Americas
17th at Constitution Avenue NW
Washington, D.C. 20006
    This monthly magazine in Spanish gives good coverage of general interest
Latino topics such as folk art, cooking, tribal life, and geology with excellent
photography and well-written text.

Artes de Mexico
Amores 262
Mexico 12 Distrito Federal, Mexico
    A colorful quarterly, each cheery issue is devoted to a particular Mexican theme
which might be art of the cowboys, colonial architects, mural builders, or
jewellers. Articles are translated into English, and sometimes French, to accompany the Spanish.

Caribbean Review
Barry L. Levine
Florida International University
Miami, Florida 33199
    In English, this is a quarterly that covers social sciences through the arts, crafts,
politics, and foods of the area, pointing out the differences between Chicanos and
Caribbeanos.

Chispa
Inovacion y Communicaciones
Mexico D.F.
Mexico, or EBSCO
POB 4069
Burlingame, California 94010
    A children's monthly, *Chispa* has experiments for kids to do at home, art
projects, Spanish word puzzles and games, and articles in Spanish about the
environment and animals.

Geomundo
De Armas Publications
605 3rd Avenue
Suite 1620
New York City 10016
    Like the *National Geographic* in style, *Geomundo* offers excellent illustrations and
photography with articles in Spanish on social and natural phenomena, particularly in Latin America.

Hispanic
Hispanic Publishing Corp.
111 Massachusetts Avenue NW
Suite 200
Washington, DC 20001

   This upscale monthly features articles in both Spanish and English based upon
the editor's belief that clinging to their native language will only hold Latinos
back socially and economically.

Latino
LULAC Communications
125 S. Kalamath Street
Denver, Colorado 80223

   This monthly bilingual magazine from the League of United Latin American
Citizens carries a wide range of articles about all things Hispanic.

Vista

   Founded by Arturo Villar, this English-language Sunday insert especially for
Hispanics is carried by twenty-four newspapers nationwide.

Chapter Seven

Triumph of the Individual: A Festival of African-American History

The fabric of America is woven from many threads. The 400 year history of European settlement in the New World is a picture painted with a turbulent brush of domination in expansion. Black people arrived in Virginia almost as soon as English settlers did. On August 20, 1619, the colony of Jamestown bought, among other items, twenty Africans from the hold of a Dutch ship. These were not the first Negroes to arrive on the continent. Some historians say that the first Black to reach the New World sailed with Columbus himself. It is certain that subsequent Spanish and Portuguese explorations included black men—not necessarily slaves, but "assimilated" free men who spoke, behaved, and acted as did other Iberians of the time. Most Blacks, however, came in forced servitude. They nevertheless played their part in opening the New World.

Jean Baptiste Point du Sable, a black Frenchman, opened a trading post in 1779 on the site that was eventually to become the metropolis of Chicago. Even earlier a Black named Estevanico came as interpreter with Cabeza de Vaca. A gifted

Focus on
BLACK
HISTORY
marian anderson
· w. e. b. dubois··
alice walker····
······rosa parks
diana ross· grace
bumbry· booker
t. washington
ella fitzgerald
paul robeson·
jessye norman
·james weldon
johnson··le roi
jones··ethel
waters· martin
luther king, jr·
harriet tubman
james baldwin
fats waller···
arthur ashe
julius lester
··· tina turner
duke ellington
zora hurston
willie mays··
·mahalia?·····
jackson····
·chubby checker
A190

237

African-American Bookmark

linguist and interpreter, Estevanico discovered Zuni pueblos in what is today New Mexico, and there lost his life in a skirmish. Blacks, both slaves and free, worked to open the new world to European colonization. Most did this work against their will.

The tragic story of the slave era is well-known. It began in the 1440's when the Portuguese captured black men and women in west Africa to provide cheap labor and, ostensibly, to convert them to Christianity. By 1850, this market in human lives had brought fifteen million slaves to Europe and America, though historians believe that over fifty million captives began the sordid journey in the squalid holds of wooden ships—over half of them died through malnutrition, suffocation, disease, or suicide en route. The system of slavery entrenched a belief among most Whites that Blacks were inferior, suitable only for manual labor.

Throughout the bitter years of slavery, however, individual Blacks distinguished themselves in spite of stifling prejudice and lack of opportunity. Very few Negroes received recognition for their achievements, yet records exist to show that some talented thinkers, writers, and artists did gain favorable attention. Jupiter Hammon, a New York poet, was the first widely read black writer. His fame is eclipsed, however, by Phillis Wheatley (1753–1784) whose *Poems on Various Subjects, Religious and Moral* was praised by prominent people in America and England. Other early black achievers were Lucy Terry, Massachusetts poet (1746), John Derham, America's first black physician, and Paul Coffee, wealthy merchant in Boston who helped to free slaves and repatriate them to Africa. Crispus Attucks was among fighting colonial patriots killed in the Boston Massacre of 1770; he was one of some 5000 blacks who served in the Continental armies during the Revolutionary War. Peter Salem and Salem Poor, two Massachusetts black men, were named heroes at the Battle of Bunker Hill.

Slavery became an entrenched Southern institution, even though the majority of Whites owned no slaves. As the cotton kingdom grew, so did slavery. Blacks outnumbered Whites in many parts of Dixie, from west Tennessee to Arkansas, Louisiana, and Mississippi. The "War Between the States" may have freed the slaves, but racial prejudice continued to bar their exercise of citizenship under liberty. One hundred years passed before the United States government enacted laws to prevent segregation and to encourage Whites to grant their black neighbors an equal chance at what the Constitution calls "the pursuit of happiness." World War II increased Blacks' awareness of the sweetness of freedom. Having served valiantly to liberate the downtrodden of the Old World, black soldiers returned home to face intolerance and racial hatred.

Great steps have been taken since the 1960's in race relations in America, though much has yet to be done to remove old prejudices and barriers. Black men and women continue to excel in all fields of endeavor, from music and theatre to medicine, sports, politics, religion, literature, and education.

A festival of Black history calls attention to past achievements in the face of obstacles, to black celebrities in many walks of life, and to the power of the human spirit. The festival may be centered several ways, focussed on Black Writers, Black Musicians, Heroic Black Women, or Black Sports Figures. A festival to honor black women focuses on the feminine spirit to overcome not only racial antagonism but sexual prejudice as well and can include opera stars, pole vaulters, pop musicians, award-winning authors, and freedom fighters. Black musicians include great jazz originators, Motown superstars, world-class opera singers, and instrumentalists from great orchestras and Mississippi farmlands. And sports? A survey of recent Olympic teams, baseball leagues, track fields, or other athletics will reveal prominent black men and women throughout. A Black Writers Week could focus on poets such as Phillis Wheatley and Langston Hughes, novelists such as Zora Neale Hurston and Alice Walker, and political essayists from Shirley Chisholm to South African Anglican Archbishop Desmond Tutu. Such a festival introduces a sometimes still-ignorant white majority to the significant contributions of Blacks, past and present, to international life in all its forms. It also offers another avenue of historic awareness and pride to Blacks.

Jazz: A Festival Display

Having chosen the theme—Black Women, Black Sports Stars, Great Jazz Artists, Black Writers—decide on an appropriate symbol that can become not only the focus for a display but also a logo for festival printouts. The central artwork can be a black silhouette cut from paper and mounted on light paper. For black women, use a silhouette profile of a woman's face. Ask art students to draw the profile, using a feilow black student as a model, or enlarge a profile from a book jacket, art book, or magazine.

Find a picture of a black athlete—a baseball player, a runner, a decathlon champion, a basketball star, or a swimmer. Using an overhead projector or drawing freehand, trace the outline of the athlete several times larger than the original photo. Cut it out from black paper and mount it on the bulletin board.

For a Jazz Festival (figure 50), locate a photograph of a black musician—a saxophone player, a pianist, or a singer. For a Writers Festival, enlarge a photo from a dust jacket or ask art students to

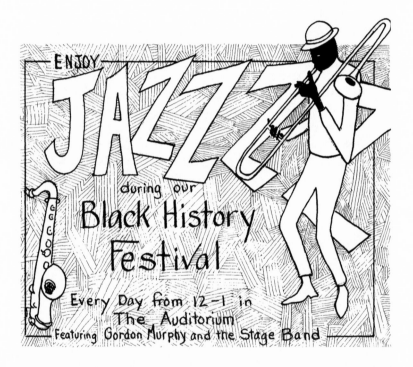

(Figure 50) To focus on a particular theme, create a display that features strong symbols, such as the trombonist and the elongation of the title word. Seek inspiration from photos in magazines and books. Use a photocopier or opaque projector to enlarge them for the bulletin board, or draw them freehand. Materials used in this display include construction paper (background, saxophone, and trombonist), butcher paper (lettering for title), and felt-tip pens (for small lettering.)

draw a silhouette of a child reading a book. If the theme is black politicians, mount photos of the Reverend Jesse Jackson, Archbishop Desmond Tutu, Shirley Chisholm, Dr. Martin Luther King, or other local dignitaries, from mayors and councilpersons to senators or governors. If the theme is black educators, display copies of Booker T. Washington's *Up From Slavery,* along with enlargements of his portrait which is available in most editions of the book.

Beneath the bulletin board display, arrange a selection of appropriate materials—books (of which there are a large number not only in print but readily available to every school and library), recordings, periodicals, pamphlets, artwork, photographs, and newspapers. Even if the theme is limited to one phase of Black life, include materials from a broad spectrum so that potential readers have the opportunity of discovery.

Black History Month: Not the Only Time to Celebrate

Every February, Americans celebrate Black History Month, acknowledging the contributions of black men and women in the arts, sciences, sports, and other fields. Argument has been made that Black History Month should not exist, since it separates Black achievement from the mainstream of American life. Some people of all races would abolish Black History Month in favor of fully integrating the African-American heritage into the larger story. Black Americans have transcended race, transforming American culture and history. Since many periodicals, libraries, and museums will publish articles and mount special exhibitions in keeping with Black History Month, schools may also wish to hold a festival then.

Reference books can reveal important anniversaries and birth or death dates of famous black writers, athletes, or politicians. Hold a festival on Alice Walker's birthday or on the anniversary of Martin Luther King's death (an official holiday in most states on January 18). Remember the founding of Tuskegee Institute or Fisk University, the first date of publication of one of Zora Neale Hurston's novels, or the inauguration of a city's first black mayor with a festival. While any date can be appropriate, linking the festival to an historic event adds special zest.

Festival Activities

Music Appreciation (figure 51): Savor the Variety!

The only truly American music comes from Black history. Combining their native African rhythms and cadences with newly learned Christian hymns, slaves created **spirituals,** often with hidden references to escape and liberty. Made famous in Europe after the Civil War by the Fisk University Jubilee Singers, spirituals are still powerful vehicles of emotion, poetry, and melody, though the tunes in songbooks and in concerts may tend to be white refinements of the originals. Equally, if not more, famous is Jazz, the hot music of the soul—improvisational, rhythmic, communal, and dance-like, divided sometimes into Dixieland and the more intellectual music of Count Basie, Ella Fitzgerald, and Duke Ellington. Pop singers Chubby Checker, Diana Ross, Fats Domino, Aretha Franklin, and Tina Turner followed the greats of the early twentieth century—Ethel Waters, Billie Holiday, Josephine Baker, and Bessie Smith.

(Figure 51) Rooted in Africa, Black music has become a truly American art form. Senegalese musicians Dembo Konte and Kausu Koyateh fuse western and African musical traditions in their performances on harps made from gourds and wire.

Apart from rock and roll or the Motown vocalists, there are the mellow singers like Pearl Bailey and Eartha Kitt, the gospel singers such as Mahalia Jackson and Clara Ward, and the opera singers Marian Anderson, Leontyne Price, and Jessye Norman. Black instrumentalists and vocalists have long been in the mainstream of American musical life. Special displays of their recordings should be available to festival-goers, with lecture "concerts" scheduled for classes or larger audiences.

Festival facilitators should work with music teachers to organize study of various Black music forms prior to and during the festival. Lower school and older students can learn a spiritual. Proficient instrumentalists can learn some Jazz. Solo singers can emulate the recorded work of Ella Fitzgerald, Paul Robeson, or Della Reese. If the area boasts a black gospel community choir or quartet, find out if they could give a concert during the festival, or if a school group could attend a rehearsal with a view to learning style or to performing with the choir.

A Gallery of Black Firsts: Research and Art Project

Through the pioneering efforts of Harriet Tubman, Mary McLeod Bethune (figure 52), Frederick Douglas and Thurgood Marshall, Americans learned to speak a more inclusive language. Billie Holiday, Mahalia Jackson, and Marian Anderson let their music pave the way to better racial understanding, often at a great personal, emotional, and physical price. To honor these and other black men and women, involve students in making a "Gallery of Black Firsts." Using appropriate reference books, back issues of magazines such as *Ebony,* information from book jackets, notes in recordings, and indices such as *The Readers' Guide to Periodical Literature,* compile a list of black firsts, such as:

The **first black man in Congress** was Senator Hiram R. Revels (1822–1901) from Mississippi. He took his seat in Washington on February 25, 1870.

The **first black man in the House of Representatives** was South Carolinian Joseph H. Rainey (1832–1887), who took his seat on December 12, 1870.

The **first United States black newspaper** founded by and edited by and for fellow Blacks was *Freedom's Journal,* in New York City. Its editors were Samuel Cornish and John B. Russwurm.

(Figure 52) Born in 1875 to parents who had been slaves, Mary McLeod Bethune overcame all obstacles to become a prominent educator, champion of race relations, and advisor to U.S. Presidents Hoover and Truman. She was the first black woman in America to establish a school that was to become a four-year accredited college.

Painting by Betsy Graves Reyneau, 1888–1964. Reprinted by permission of National Portrait Gallery, Smithsonian Institution, Washington, D.C. 20560.

The first black man since Reconstruction to be elected to the United States Senate was Massachusetts politician Edward Brooke in 1967.

The first black woman in Congress was Shirley Chisholm, who was elected representative from Brooklyn on November 5, 1968.

The first black cabinet member was Robert C. Weaver, who was President Lyndon Johnson's Secretary of Housing and Urban Development. He took office on January 18, 1966.

The first black mayor of a major American city in the twentieth century was Gary, Indiana's, Carl B. Stokes, who was inaugurated on November 13, 1967.

The first black woman cabinet member was Patricia R. Harris (1924–1985) who became President Jimmy Carter's Secretary of Housing and Urban Development on December 21, 1976.

The first black federal judge was William H. Hastie (1904–1976), who took office in the U.S. Virgin Islands on March 26, 1937.

The first black general in the army was B. O. Davis (1877–1970), who was appointed on October 16, 1940.

The first black woman general in the U.S. Army was Hazel W. Johnson, who was promoted to this office on September 1, 1979.

The first black woman judge was Jane M. Bolin in New York City, appointed to office on July 11, 1939.

The first black Miss America was Vanessa Brown, who won the title on September 17, 1984.

The first black baseball player in the major leagues was Jackie Robinson (1947).

The first Black to win the Nobel Prize was Ralph Bunche (1950).

Gwendolyn Brooks was the first Black to win the Pulizter Prize for poetry (1950).

Marian Anderson was the first black to debut in the Metropolitan Opera House, New York City (1955).

James Meredith was the first black to enroll in the University of Mississippi (1962).

The first black woman to become a pilot in the U.S. Armed Forces was 2nd Lt. Theresa Claiborne, of Emporia, Virginia, who graduated from aviation school in November, 1979.

Ask students to find biographical information, photographs or drawings, political and educational connections, prime achievements, and other relevant information for display. For educational (non-money-making) purposes, it is usually permissible to photocopy printed material. With photocopied illustrations, photos, and appropriate charts or maps, students, teachers, and festival organizers can arrange an attractive wall or table-mounted display of "Black Firsts."

A *Roots* Panorama: Genealogy and More

Perhaps better than any other single event, the publication of Alex Haley's book *Roots* and the subsequent television mini-series stimulated interest in Black genealogy and African-American history, not only among Blacks but also throughout the population of America. With a social studies teacher, a festival facilitator can plan a unit of study in one class that will incorporate materials about ancient African culture, the slave era, and the lives of Blacks in early America. While the students involved will read appropriate materials, and perhaps write papers for their teachers to mark, a culminating event of the unit could be a visual display of drawings and other artwork to illustrate aspects of black history, collected during research and writing.

Books about African art, black music, and literature will reveal information about sculpture—its use in religion and politics; music—folk songs, instruments, dance; and writing. Students may wish to focus on certain tribes and customs or geographical regions, finding as much as possible about language, traditional or historic costume, body decoration, religion, or folklore. They may want to trace their own roots as far as they can into the past, using local archives, government libraries and records, family histories, and church records.

A visual display can include information on how to trace one's genealogy, copies of personal family trees (even short ones), and photos of local places to seek these facts. Larger cities will probably have a museum that contains black African artifacts; usually, postcards that can be put on display during the festival will also be available. Some cities will have shops that sell black African art and clothing. A shop owner may be willing to lend pieces for display. For educational purposes, students may use photocopiers to make posters of historic photographs in magazines and books. Photocopied photographs and artwork can be enhanced with pen and ink, crayons, and other art-room supplies to turn them into more visually appealing items.

To accompany the visual collection of photos and other gleanings of research, students may be scheduled to talk about their papers, either as individual speakers or as part of a panel on Black genealogy and history. Other speakers may be called in from the community (figure 53)—professors, art collectors, travellers, historians—to talk to groups about their special interests. Elderly black residents may be able to talk about changes they have seen through their lives or about their own childhood reminiscences. Students can be encouraged to talk to older black residents of the neighborhood and to record their conversations as mini-documentaries to be shared through journalism or informal discussions during the festival.

How Does Our Library Rate? A Survey

Find out how many books in your school or local library are multi-ethnic or multi-racial in outlook. Start with materials for the very young. Ask a sociology class to look at illustrations, text, forms of speech, and references to historical characters or events in a cross section of books for young children. This is also a good opportunity

(Figure 53) During the African-American Festival, invite speakers who can trace their roots back to Africa. Here, Shakiru-Deen Aremu Ekemode demonstrates the function of the talking drum from his ancestral Yoruba village near Lagos, Nigeria.

for middle or high school students to learn, and put into practice, good bibliographic style. Students can also learn proper note-taking skills in this project. The results of their findings can be presented in charts, formal papers, or oral presentations that give practice in speech-making and demonstrations.

Researchers may hold these points in mind:

1. Do the illustrations show white children only? Is this appropriate for the text? How could people from other ethnic or racial backgrounds be introduced into the illustrations? Why would this be appropriate? How do you react to these illustrations personally?

2. Does the book show racial prejudice in illustrations or text? Are non-whites presented in an unfavorable light?

3. Does the book show people of many races and ethnic backgrounds in illustrations or text?

4. Do the illustrations show black children only? How do you react to these illustrations personally?

5. Which books best represent the multiracial, multiethnic makeup of America? Give author, title, city of publication, publisher, and date of publication, followed by a short annotation.

Some students might survey the holdings of the middle or high school library, or of the public library, to look at the books and materials available on black people and history. Interviews with librarians might help locate these materials more easily.

Points for discussion:

1. What percentage of the total library collection is devoted to black history? How does this figure relate to the ethnic or racial makeup of the total community or school population?

2. List twenty biographies of black people in the library.

3. List twenty recordings of black music in the library.

4. How many books or other publications on black art are in the library?

5. Name ten black women novelists represented in the library. Ten black male novelists. Ten non-American black novelists.

Ads on TV Watch: Is Racial Stereotyping Dead?

A related project leads students to look at newspaper and magazine advertising or to ads on television. Ask participating students to keep a journal in which they record the name of the product being advertised, the audience to which the ad is aimed, and other details, such as (1) race, sex, and approximate age of models in the ad; (2) specific location of the ad—magazine or periodical date and page number; television station, program, date and time of day; (3) approximate cost of product; (4) what the product does.

Over a period of time, from one week to a month, ask students to make charts or graphs showing:

1. Number of white models/actors in ads.
2. Number of black models/actors in ads.
3. Number of other racial or ethnic groups in ads.
4. Number of ads for various products, such as:
   a. Household goods
   b. Cars
   c. Alcohol
   d. Tobacco
   e. Dog food
   f. Toys
5. Number of black models/actors in ads for specific products.

In group discussions, ask students to decide why products are advertised the way they are. Through advertisements, who are the ideal American people? What do advertisements do to make people want to buy the products? Imagine a particular advertisement done with actors of a different racial background. Would the ad be as effective?

Another project surveys the number of black characters on television programs in proportion to those of other races. Keeping record of names of programs, networks and channels, times of transmission and product sponsorship, students should be able to:

1. List roles of Blacks in particular programs.
2. Identify position in society of these roles.
3. Show black people as leaders of the community.
4. Identify any racial stereotyping or prejudice.

Besides listing Black sit-coms or music programs with all-Black bands or groups, students should be able, at the end of the project, to discuss the role of Blacks in television, how Blacks are presented in tv dramas, and how many Blacks are news or sports broadcasters. Has stereotypical portrayal of African Americans ceased today?

Edible Soul: Festival Foods

It might be rightly said that, while there is Mexican, Indian, Chinese, or Vietnamese food in America, there is really no such thing as a distinctive Black food. While there is Soul Food, Southern-born in the slave quarters of antebellum plantations and come-of-age in trendy restaurants in major cities, it differs little from the victuals eaten on White tables across the Southern states. Cheap, simple, and reflecting well its humble origins, Soul Food was (and is) the nourishment of most rural Southerners, black and white. Only the rich plantation owners dined more elegantly and on more refined fare.

From Africa the slaves brought with them skills in cooking that soon changed the tastes of Euro-American planters and their families. In parts of the South, French, Spanish, and African styles combined to form what is known today as Creole cooking. Everywhere Blacks settled, either by force or as free people, their own cooking traditions melded with that of the White culture around them.

On the plantation, turnips and ham went up to the big house; turnip greens and offal remained behind in the slave quarters. Like many African dishes, the food of slaves was based on peas and beans, and in some areas, rice. It tended to be fatty, overcooked, and often not very well-seasoned. Poor Whites, too, ate collard greens, cornbread and cornmush, yams, okra, fried chicken, and perhaps one of the greatest dishes of all, chittlins, or more properly, "chitterlings," the small intestines of pork, marinated, covered in hot sauce, boiled or fried, and served with turnip greens, black-eyed peas, and cornbread. Blacks, like other poor people, learned to make do with what was available, and in the warm climate and fertile soil of the South, where long growing seasons produced an abundance of vegetables and livestock, greens, peas, okra, sweet potatoes, catfish, and corn turned into a distinctive cuisine.

If confined to individual classrooms, teachers and students can come up with their own meals, either prepared as a class event or cooked at home and shared as a picnic during the festival. Some teachers, students, or parents may like to demonstrate food preparation as a scheduled festival event, perhaps with student aides to prepare vegetables, dice cooked meats, or serve the finished products.

A black restaurant owner or cook may be engaged to talk about Soul Food or representative dishes from Africa or the Caribbean.

Festival organizers may decide not to serve food at all since African Americans do not adhere to any one cuisine. If food is to be served during the festival at any time, it should not be implied that it is standard food in the Black household, but that it is a typical American, Kenyan, or Caribbean dish, prepared and cooked by people of many races. Soul Food is tasty, nevertheless, if often high in cholesterol, and traditional Southern Black cooking creates a festive table. Cooking was one of the few rewarding avenues of creativity open to slaves. In the kitchen, whether cooking for their owners or for themselves, black women (there were few male chefs) became artists in the preparation of food. For their own consumption, this artistry was vital, for out of little much was created.

Hushpuppies
(Makes 10–20)

No one knows why they are called hushpuppies, though some folk historians maintain that they were originally made to feed the dogs during a fish fry to keep them from begging for handouts. Popular throughout the South as an accompaniment to fried fish, these little savory breads are easy to prepare and use ingredients readily available in most places. They should be fried in deep oil, so if hushpuppies are prepared as a festival event with a demonstration, an adult should be in charge of the actual cooking.

1 cup cornmeal
3/4 cup flour
4 tsps baking powder
1 tsp sugar (optional)
1 tsp salt
1/2 tsp black pepper, freshly ground
3 cloves garlic, crushed
1/2 finely chopped bell pepper
2/3 cup milk (or buttermilk)
1 egg, beaten
1 finely chopped medium size onion
Vegetable oil for cooking

Mix the first six ingredients together in a bowl. Stir in the milk, garlic, bell pepper and onion until well blended.

Heat the oil in a deep fryer or kettle to 375° F. Drop the hushpuppy mixture into the hot oil by spoonfuls and fry until they are golden brown, from 3 to 4 minutes. Drain on paper towels and serve hot.

(Originally, hushpuppies would have been fried in animal fat.)

Black-eyed Peas
(Up to 20 Small Servings or Tastings)

Like many pulse recipes, this dish may be formed loosely around the following recipe, with added quantities of some ingredients, deletions of others, and additions of still others. Black-eyed peas may be enhanced with whatever happens to be in the kitchen. Paprika, hot pepper sauce, bell peppers, corn kernels, pre-cooked turkey or chicken, shrimp or fish, diced potatoes, tomatoes, or other vegetables, meats, herbs or spices may be added, thus creating different emphases. The following basic recipe is a good framework for peas and may be used as it stands. Black-eyed peas may be served in small dishes during the festival and eaten with hushpuppies.

2 (or more) cups dried black-eyed peas
2 (or more) smoked ham hocks or
8 (or more) smoked link sausages
2 (or more) quarts of water
3 chopped or sliced medium onions
4 (or more) chopped celery sticks
3 to 5 crushed garlic cloves
1/2 to 1 teaspoon red pepper
1/2 to 1 teaspoon salt

Soak the peas overnight in plenty of lightly salted water. As part of the festival proceedings, teachers should help students in various classes prepare their own peas just before school is out for the day. Before cooking, the peas should be drained and rinsed in cold water in a sieve. Combine the meat, onion, and other vegetables in the water in a large pot. Cover and bring to the boil. Simmer over reduced heat for about half an hour. Add the pre-soaked peas and cook over low heat, covered, for up to two hours or until the peas are tender. Student volunteers can apply taste tests periodically to ensure that the dish is just right.

Hocks and Greens
(Makes up to 30 small tastings)

3/4 to 1 pound of salt pork, smoked ham, or pork chops
6 cups water
1/3 teaspoon crushed red pepper or several dashes Tabasco
2 lbs mustard greens
3 lbs turnip greens or collard greens

Add meat to water and bring to a boil. Lower the heat and simmer, covered, for an hour. Skim the surface of the water for fatty residues. Add seasonings and greens and cook up to an hour. Serve with black-eyed peas, hushpuppies, sliced tomatoes, and onions.

Animals of Africa: A Research and Art Project

What You Need:

Cardboard boxes of various sizes
Craft knives and scissors
Pencils
Artroom water-based printmaker's ink, or household latex paint
Printing brayers or rollers
Butcher paper or construction paper
Pictures of African animals for reference
Old newspapers for worksurface
Old rags (socks, towels, clothing with buttons removed)
Wear old work clothes, or cover clothing with smocks or aprons
Drying line suspended across the room
Clothes pins

Create a frieze of African animals around a classroom, down a hallway, or in the library with cardboard printing blocks which provide silhouettes that are reusable, storeable, and sturdy (figure 54). Africa is rich in animal life, but with human populations growing, native habitats are shrinking. National governments have set up programs to combat poaching on game reserves to protect elephants, rhinos, and other animals in danger. In addition, some animals are threatened by drought. Let this animal art project be the focus of research on African wildlife. Students can find out where animals flourish and where they are threatened. Locate the nearest office of the World Wildlife Fund for detailed information about how your school could help publicize the plights of endangered species.

1. Each student chooses the animal he or she wishes to adopt for study. The teacher can facilitate this by putting the names of African animals on slips of paper which students pull out of a hat. Students can be encouraged to study any animal they wish. The latter approach may be better since students' personal input may be greater. Artistically, too, the results may be richer if there are herds of elephant (drawn by different students) and zebra. Look in reference sources for photographs and drawings of these animals.

2. Choose a large piece of flat corrugated cardboard. In pencil draw the animal, making it as large as the cardboard will allow. Draw in features such as eyes, nostrils, wrinkles in the skin, stripes and spots, toes and other identifiable characteristics.

Figure 54

3. The cardboard animal will be a printing block; therefore, to give the final print characteristic details, students will have to cut away the features they have drawn. If they have drawn in simple lines, these will have to be widened slightly to make any effect on the print. The teacher will need to supervise young children closely during this process.

4. Cut out the animal silhouette. Remove any small scraps of cardboard still adhering to the cuts. Hold the silhouette up to a light source, or prop it against a window. Are there enough characteristic features cut out? Does the elephant have enough wrinkles? Has the leopard enough spots? Could you give the lion two more whiskers?

5. To print:

a. Where space allows, set up two types of work areas. One should be for inking, the other for printing. Cover both areas with clean newspaper. Each student should have one inking area, but they can all share the printing space.

b. Place the silhouette on a work surface covered with plenty of old newspapers. Squeeze water-based printing ink directly onto large cutouts or into small paint trays. With the roller or art-room brush spread the ink all over the cardboard until it is evenly coated. (You can use household latex paints or tempera, but generally they are too runny and too messy.)

c. Pick up the silhouette carefully by holding the sides tightly between outstretched fingers. Carry it to the printing area and place it flat on the surface. Lower a piece of construction paper onto the silhouette. Start by placing one edge of the construction paper on the work surface beside the silhouette, lowering gradually and evenly until it lies flat.

With an old sock or rag, or with a clean roller, rub the animal silhouette (gently at first) through the paper. When the entire cutout has been rubbed, test to see if a good print has been made. Place one hand on the edge of the paper and lift the other side gently off the cardboard printing block. If the ink has not covered well, lower the paper into position and rub some more.

d. Lift the finished print off the cardboard and hang it on a line to dry. Depending upon the thickness and condition of the ink, drying will take up to a day. Prints drying on the line make a cheerful display themselves, so you might consider this method of hanging the work around school.

6. Experiment with variations:

a. Mix different colors to get different effects. Use inks to make realistic animals or create fantastic colors. Use single colors to make silhouettes. Paint on details after the printing ink has dried.

b. Make three or four prints from one inking. Successive prints will be fainter, more delicate.

c. Create herds of animals by overprinting, both while the print is wet and after it has dried.

d. Print on one long roll of butcher paper. This takes some judicious juggling, with students holding the printed section until it is long enough to clip to the clotheslines, but this is an exciting way to make a frieze without seams.

e. Cut out the dried prints and mount them on color paper or on a background that shows the habitat.

f. Mount the finished print as a frieze. Show the animals going to the watering hole. Draw on trees and shrubs, the sun or moon. Show human beings—poachers hidden in scrubland, villagers hunting, even tourists on a mini-bus. Put school pictures of the students involved in the project inside the windows of a schoolbus labelled "On Safari."

g. When the cardboard block has dried, make prints from the reverse side. Mount the dried cardboard block on color paper as part of the exhibition. Peel off one side of the cardboard to reveal the corrugations, and make prints from that.

h. Let students use each other's printing blocks to create designs of their own with different animals. Create fantasy animals with the body of one print and the head of another by placing cover sheets between the block and the paper when printing.

i. Reduce the finished, dried prints on a photocopy machine and turn them into greeting cards (see figure 82, page 350, in the chapter "Dance With Dragons"). Give the students one card from every print, with envelopes, or sell the cards for an animal conservation project.

j. Print on different papers. Try newspaper, absorbent kitchen towels, rice paper, gift wrap. Make prints on squares cut from old cotton sheets or towels or handkerchiefs.

How Much Do You Know? A Festival Contest

A "test" like the following helps motivate students to use reference materials in the library, to read books about African Americans, and to search through appropriate periodicals. Some festival organizers will want to offer prizes for the first answer sheets turned in with the most correct answers. Place copies of the quiz in an accessible box or wall-mounted display pouch with rules for completion. These may include writing neatly, documenting answers that ask for clarification, where to turn in completed entries, and how to identify the paper—name, homeroom, or teacher/advisor. Classroom teachers can also use the "test" for assessing student awareness of the Blacks' contributions to American life.

HOW MUCH DO YOU KNOW?

To see how much you know about Black history, answer the following questions with the correct answers.

I. MATCH the column on the right with the names on the left by writing the correct letter of the alphabet in the blank.

Famous Black Women

1. Leontyne Price ⎯⎯⎯⎯
2. Marian Anderson ⎯⎯⎯⎯
3. Billie Holiday ⎯⎯⎯⎯
4. Diana Ross ⎯⎯⎯⎯
5. Ethel Waters ⎯⎯⎯⎯
6. Josephine Baker ⎯⎯⎯⎯
7. Harriet Tubman ⎯⎯⎯⎯
8. Phillis Wheatley ⎯⎯⎯⎯
9. Alice Walker ⎯⎯⎯⎯
10. Clara Ward ⎯⎯⎯⎯

a. *Lady Sings the Blues* is her autobiography.
b. Famous as a gospel singer.
c. A major twentieth century black author.
d. She was the lead singer with the "Supremes."
e. A famous operatic soprano.
f. This singer-dancer moved to France to escape racial harassment.
g. Although she sang jazz early in her career, this woman was a singer on Billy Graham crusades.
h. This famous operatic contralto was once kept from singing at Constitution Hall in segregation days.
i. She was a conductor on the underground railroad.
j. Wrote the first book of poems published by an African-American woman.

II. Write TRUE or FALSE in the blank following these statements. If you think the statement is false, and you correct the facts so that it becomes true, you get an extra five points each.

1. Mary McLeod Bethune is the first black woman to establish a four-year college. _____

2. Hattie McDaniel played Scarlett O'Hara in the film "Gone with the Wind." _____

3. The Shirelles' famous Motown hit, "Dancing in the Streets" was banned from airplay. _____

4. Shirley Chisholm helped start the Civil Rights Movement by riding in the white section of a Montgomery, Alabama, bus. _____

5. Maya Angelou, author of *I Know Why the Caged Bird Sings,* was brought up in Chicago. _____

6. Bessie Coleman was the first African-American woman to receive her air pilot's license. _____

7. Grace Bumbry is famous for her rhythm and blues interpretations of 1920's hits. _____

8. Sojourner Truth was the first black woman ever to lecture for the abolition of slavery. _____

9. Zora Neale Hurston was a writer during the Harlem Renaissance. _____

10. *Uncle Tom's Cabin* was written by a black woman. _____

African-American Men and Women

III. FILL IN THE BLANKS or CIRCLE THE CORRECT CHOICE in these sentences.

1. _____ is a famous African-American country musician and singer.

2. (Paul Robeson, Jackie Robinson, Clifton Davis) was the first African-American big league baseball player.

3. (Martin Luther King, Dr. George Washington Carver, Booker T. Washington) brought prosperity to Southern industry through his research on the peanut.

4. _____ was a poet during the first half of the twentieth century in the Harlem Renaissance.

5. What does NAACP stand for? _____

6. (Shirley Chisholm, James Meredith, Ralph Abernathy) was the first black man to enroll in the University of Mississippi.

7. (Wilt Chamberlain, Arthur Ashe, Willie Mays) was an outstanding baseball player.

8. Black Panther (Eldridge Cleaver, Stokely Carmichael, Angela Davis) wrote *Soul on Ice.*

9. Dr. Martin Luther King was assassinated in (Chicago, Nashville, Memphis).

10. (Julian Bond, Jesse Jackson, Dick Gregory) was not nominated for the office of United States Vice President.

To help students (or teachers) answer these questions, either as part of a festival competition or just for fun, some libraries will want to display "Sources of Inspiration"—reference books, novels, *Readers' Guides,* and magazines prominently, or perhaps adjacent to the quiz sheets. Alternatively, bibliographies of helpful materials can be appended to the question sheets, giving location and library numbers.

Answers

I. Matching 1. e, 2. h, 3. a, 4. d, 5. g, 6. f, 7. i, 8. j, 9. c, 10. b.

II. True and False 1. True, 2. False: She played the role of Mammy; Vivien Leigh was Scarlett, 3. False: it was a popular hit of Martha and the Vandelles, 4. False: Rosa Parks is the woman who integrated the bus system; Shirley Chisholm is a New York politician, 5. False: she was brought up in Arkansas, 6. True, 7. False: she is an opera diva, 8. True, 9. True, 10. False: Harriet Beecher Stowe was a white abolitionist.

III. Multiple Choice and Fill-in-the-Blanks 1. Charlie Pride, 2. Jackie Robinson, 3. George Washington Carver, 4. Countee Cullen, Langstone Hughes, Claude McKay, and James W. Johnson may be among the answers, 5. National Association for the Advancement of Colored People, 6. James Meredith, 7. Willie Mays, 8. Elridge Cleaver, 9. Memphis, 10. Dick Gregory is the odd man out.

Wordsearch: A Names Puzzle Just for Fun

(This puzzle may be used as a "test" for students to see how many famous black men and women they can recognize. For extra points, players may write down a one- or two-word character definition beside the names of men and women in the list, identifying them by profession or contribution to society.)

The names of twenty-three famous African-American men and women are hidden in the puzzle on page 263, with the answers circled on page 264. Find the names by reading forward, down, or backwards. When you find a name, draw a circle around it, and cross it off the list.

1. Crispus Attucks	13 Leontyne Price
2. Shirley Chisholm	14. Charlie Pride
3. Bill Cosby (appears twice)	15. Della Reese
4. Bo Diddley	16. Diana Ross
5. Duke Ellington	17. Bessie Smith
6. Virginia Hamilton	18. Harriet Tubman
7. Jesse Jackson	19. Nat Turner
8. Mahalia Jackson	20. Tina Turner
9. Michael Jackson	21. Cicely Tyson
10. Martin Luther King	22. Alice Walker
11. Hattie McDaniel	23. Ethel Waters
12. Rosa Parks	

```
F D G N B I L L C O S B Y L P E R W Z Q P A S R T
X C I S P W E A H A T T I E M C D A N I E L S J P
C B J X V M A H A L I A J A C K S O N T Y B X W D
R O K D E L L A R E E S E R E A Z I L O S W P X I
I D I D D L E Y L O A Z D Y T H A R R I E T S S A
S W Y P Z M A R T I N L U T H E R K I N G T P L N
P W I E D I R P E T O M K D E R P X S V B U X W A
U B I L L C O S B Y R T E F L W A T E R S B R T R
S Y T R W S X I B N R T E L L I N G T O N M Z V O
A L I C E W A L K E R R W Q P X R O S A P A R K S
T R Z B N M I W S R J E S S E J A C K S O N W C S
T R W T I S P V I R G I N I A H A M I L T O N V B
U B E S S I E S M I T H A T I N A T U R N E R M E
C C V B N A S P O C D G T T U R N E R T R Y P C B
K S I D M I C H A E L J A C K S O N F G T C P S L
S H I R L E Y C H I S O L M C I C E L Y T Y S O N
```

```
F D G N B I L L C O S B Y L P E R W Z Q P A S R T
X C I S P W E A H A T T I E M C D A N I E L S J P
C B J X V M A H A L I A J A C K S O N T Y B X W D
R O K D E L L A R E E S E R E A Z I L O S W P X I
I D I D D L E Y L O A Z D Y T H A R R I E T S S A
S W Y P Z M A R T I N L U T H E R K I N G T P L N
P W I E D I R P E T O M K D E R P X S V B U X W A
U B I L L C O S B Y R T E F L W A T E R S B R T R
S Y T R W S X I B N R T E L L I N G T O N M Z V O
A L I C E W A L K E R R W Q P X R O S A P A R K S
T R Z B N M I W S R J E S S E J A C K S O N W C S
T R W T I S P V I R G I N I A H A M I L T O N V B
U B E S S I E S M I T H A T I N A T U R N E R M E
C C V B N A S P O C D G T T U R N E R T R Y P C B
K S I D M I C H A E L J A C K S O N F G T C P S L
S H I R L E Y C H I S O L M C I C E L Y T Y S O N
```

Sources of Inspiration

Books By and About African Americans

Fiction

Bess, Clayton, *Story for a Black Night.* New York: Parnassus, 1982.
A village in Liberia faces decimation by a smallpox epidemic.

Billington, Elizabeth. *The Move.* New York: Frederick Warne, 1984.
For middle school readers, this is a story of prejudice in action for an African-American family who move from New York City to the suburbs.

Bontemps, Arna. *Sad Faced Boy.* Boston: Houghton Mifflin, 1937.
Slumber, a sad-faced harmonica player from Alabama, forms a band with his brothers which takes Harlem by storm.

Brooks, Bruce. *The Moves Make the Man.* New York: Holt, Rinehart, and Winston, 1984.
Basketball star Jerome Foxworthy is the first Black in his southern white high school. His white pal Bix, a fellow athlete, helps the school face the problems of integration.

Bunting, Eve. *Face at the Edge of the World.* Boston: Clarion, 1985.
Jed tries to find the reasons for the suicide of his best friend, a gifted black writer.

Collier, James. *Who is Carrie?* New York: Delacorte, 1984.
Carrie, a young slave in the 18th century, learns about the new American government being formed around her while listening to the conversations of men such as Washington and Jefferson.

Crutcher, Chris. *The Crazy Horse Electric Game.* New York: Greenwillow, 1987.
A black benefactor helps a permanently-injured athlete back to physical and mental health.

Emecheta, Buchi. *Adams' Story, a Novel.* London: Allison and Busby, 1983.
In two parts, this novel talks about the second class citizenship which many Blacks have to endure.

————. *The Moonlight Bride.* London: Braziller, 1983.
Readers of middle school age and up will enjoy this story of two African girls' encounter with a python in the jungle.

Green, Bette. *Philip Hall Likes Me, I Reckon Maybe.* New York: Dial, 1974.
Blacks in Arkansas face racial prejudice which black and white youngsters do not necessarily understand.

Hamilton, Virginia. *A Little Love.* Jacksonville, Florida: Philomel Books, 1984.
  Black motherless teenager Sheena wanders through the South to find the father she never knew.

————. *Arilla Sundown.* Greenwillow, 1976.
  A young girl of mixed Black and Native American blood has trouble growing up.

————. *The Magical Adventures of Pretty Pearl.* New York: Holt, Rinehart, and Winston, 1983.
  Curious about human beings, a goddess descends to earth where she observes a Georgia black colony.

————. *The Planet of Junior Brown.* New York: Macmillan, 1971.
  Eighth-grade dropout Junior Brown retreats into his own hiding space, or planet, but keeps a grip on reality through the help of his chum Buddy.

————. *Zeely.* New York: Macmillan, 1967.
  Zeely helps a young black daydreamer turn toward reality.

Hentoff, Nat. *Jazz Country.* New York: Harper and Row, 1965.
  A talented white boy longs to enter the world of black Jazz musicians so that he can become a great trumpter.

Howard, Ellen. *When Daylight Comes.* New York: Atheneum, 1985.
  A white captive in a Virgin Islands slave rebellion comes to understand why her captors have risen against oppression.

Hurston, Zora Neale. *Jonah's Gourd Vine.* London: Virago Press, 1987.
  Sometimes funny, often full of pathos, this is the beautifully written story of John Pearson, who works his way up to the pastorate of Zion Hope Church in the all-Black town of Sanford, Florida. Hurston, novelist, anthropologist, journalist and critic, was one of the most important writers of the Harlem Renaissance, and deserves to be rediscovered today.

————. *Their Eyes Were Watching God.* London: Virago Press, 1986.
  This reissue of the 1937 original is the poetic, rhythmic tale of Janie's quest for fulfillment and self-discovery. The world holds much mystery for the protagonist who discovers that husbands are just things she "grabbed to drape dreams over."

Jones, Toeckey. *Go Well, Stay Well.* New York: Harper and Row, 1980.
  In spite of the official restrictions of apartheid, a black girl and a white girl become friends in South Africa.

Klein, Norma. *Bizou.* New York: Viking, 1983.
  Bizou, whose father is a French white man, learns about her African roots from her African-American mother.

Lester, Julius. *This Strange New Feeling.* New York: Dial, 1982.
Three couples fight for freedom from slavery in this novel of pre-Civil War America.

MacKinnon, Bernie. *The Meantime.* New York: Houghton Mifflin, 1983.
Young black student Luke Parrish becomes a victim of racial tension, antagonism and strife in his high school.

Mathis, Sharon. *Teacup Full of Roses.* New York: Viking, 1972.
Can three black boys rise above their ghetto environment and the devastation of drugs to find life's deeper meanings? Yes!

Miles, Betty. *All It Takes Is Practice.* New York: Alfred A. Knopf, 1976.
Stuart and the entire fifth grade are upset when an interracial family moves into the neighborhood.

Monroe, Mary. *The Upper Room.* London: Allen and Busby, 1989.
This first novel mixes witty patois with a plot of amazing mayhem in which Mama Ruby dispatches unwanted visitors with a knife concealed beside a crucifix beneath her dress in the swamps and citrus fields of the Deep South.

Myers, W. D. *Fallen Angels.* New York: Scholastic Books, 1988.
It is 1967, and Richie Perry, 17, leaves his Harlem high school for the Army and a tragic year in Vietnam.

Tate, Eleanora. *The Secret of Gumbo Grove.* New York: Watts, 1987.
Young Raisin Stackhouse discovers her family's South Carolina background in this story of Black heritage and pride.

Thurman, Wallace. *The Blacker the Berry.* New York: Collier, 1970.
Facing discrimination and rejection by her own friends and family because of her ebony skin, Emma Lou runs to Los Angeles, then to Harlem, to discover that truth and beauty can be found in many ways. This is a classic in African-American literature, first published in 1929.

Walker, Alice. *The Color Purple.* New York: Harcourt Brace Jovanovich, 1982.
Set in the harsh world of the Deep South between the wars, this is the powerful story of Celie's rise from child abuse and an ill-fated, loveless marriage to a life of self-sufficient dignity.

————. *In Love and Trouble.* New York: Harcourt Brace Jovanovich, 1973.
Thirteen short stories explore the desires and fears of African-American women.

West, Dorothy. *The Living Is Easy.* London: Virago Press, 1987.
Using her own "charming insincerity" and her husband's wealth and generosity, Cleo Judson stops at nothing to win a place for herself, her daughter, and her sisters' children in Boston Black society. First published in 1948, this is a portrait

of a woman for whom social respectability never has too high a price. She becomes both victim and oppressor.

Wilkinson, Brenda. *Ludell.* New York: Harper and Row, 1975.
  Middle schoolers will learn about the painful days of segregation in this novel set in a southern fifth grade. Sequels are *Ludell and Willie* (Harper, 1977) and *Ludell's New York Time* (Harper, 1980).

————. *Not Separate, Not Equal.* New York: Holt, Rinehart, and Winston, 1987.
  This story of the 1960's Civil Rights Movement focusses on the cruel harrassment endured by Malene Freeman when she and five other black students integrate a white Georgia high school.

Williams-Garcia, Rita. *Blue Tights.* Lodestar, 1987.
  Joyce, 15, learns to be comfortable with herself in this story of a young black dancer's growth into self-respect and maturity.

Biography

Albertson, Chris. *Bessie.* London: Barrie and Jenkins, 1976.
  The "Empress of the Blues," Bessie Smith, was a proud black singer whose biography is based on research in black periodicals, interviews with family, and friends.

Angelou, Maya. *I Know Why the Caged Bird Sings.* New York: Random House, 1969.
  Angelou's story of her Arkansas childhood reveals in moving language the joys and sorrows of growing up Black in the South. The continuing biography includes *The Heart of a Woman* (1981).

Brooks, Sara. *You May Plow Here: The Narrative of Sara B.* New York: Norton, 1986.
  Sara Brooks describes her life in Alabama from childhood to domestic service and talks about discrimination.

Buchi, Emecheta. *Our Own Freedom.* London: Sheba Feminist Publications, 1981.
  Photos by Maggie Murray and text by Emecheta Buchi depict the lives of some African black women.

Cade, Toni, comp. *The Black Woman, an Anthology.* New York: New American Library, 1970.
  This book tells of the parallel growth of black pride and feminism in the 1960's. Included are stories, poems, and essays by twenty black women, including Shirley Williams, Alice Walker, and Audre Lord.

Calderon, Erma. *Erma.* New York: Random House, 1981.
  Erma tells about her bittersweet life as an 11-year-old bride, apartment manager, fruit picker, and servant. She writes with poetic imagery of her life in the South and her trip to New York.

Davis, Angela. *Angela Davis, an Autobiography.* New York: Bantom, 1974.
Once the FBI's most wanted criminal, Davis—communist, feminist, intellectual symbol of the revolutionary sixties—tells about her motivating hopes and her struggle for Black liberation.

Davis, Daniel S. *Mr. Black Labor: The Story of Philip Randolph, Father of the Civil Rights Movement.* New York: Dutton, 1972.
This is the story of Randolph's lifelong struggle for equality for his race.

Gilliam, Dorothy B. *Paul Robeson, All-American.* Washington, D.C.: New Republic Book Company, 1976.
The skillful author shows why American racism led singer and actor Robeson into deep involvement in social protest long before the Civil Rights Movement.

Gregory, Susan. *Hey, White Girl!* New York: W. W. Norton, 1970.
This record of a white girl's senior year in a Chicago West Side black high school speaks of love, suffering, and intimate knowledge of life in the ghetto and how that life shaped the destinies of its inhabitants.

Holiday, Billie, with William Duffy. *Lady Sings the Blues.* London: Barrie and Jenkins, 1973.
This autobiography reveals that Holiday's increasing fame and wealth from music could not make her forget a painful childhood nor overlook constant racial prejudice.

Horton, James Oliver. *Black Bostonians: Family Life and Community Struggle in the Antebellum North.* New York: Holmes and Meier, 1979.
Horton tells about lives, family structures, culture, and religion of urban Blacks in Boston before the civil war.

Franklin, John Hope, and August Meier. *Black Leaders of the Twentieth Century.* Chicago: University of Illinois Press, 1982.
The authors write about fifteen African-American men and women, including Mary McLeod Bethune.

Garrow, David J. *Bearing the Cross: Martin Luther King, Jr., and the Southern Christian Leadership Conference.* New York: Morrow, 1986.
Garrow tells the story of Dr. King's policy of peaceful, non-violent opposition to oppressive U.S. segregation laws, and the important role played by the Southern Christian Leadership Conference in bringing about change.

Griffin, John Howard. *Black Like Me.* London: Panther, 1984.
This is the now famous story of a White who darkened his skin to walk the back streets and farms of the Deep South where he discovered the world of narrow-minded whites.

Gwaltney, John Langston. *Drylongso: A Self-Portrait of Black America.* New York: Random House, 1980.

Blacks from across the American social spectrum tell how they feel about religion, oppression, welfare, slavery, and race relations in this remarkable book by a distinguished Black, and blind, anthropologist.

Harris, Trudier, ed. *Dictionary of Literary Biography, Volumes 33, 38, 41, 50, and 51.* Detroit: Gale Research, 1984–1987.

This lengthy collection offers biographical and bibliographical information specifically about black writers of fiction, drama, and poetry in five volumes.

Harrison, Nancy. *Winnie Mandela, Mother of a Nation,* London: Grafton Books, 1985.

The wife of once-imprisoned African National Congress leader Nelson Mandela struggles for Black freedom in South Africa.

Johnson, Robert E. *Bill Cosby: In Words and Pictures.* Chicago: Johnson, 1987.

This is a lavishly illustrated biography of the successful television actor. It follows Cosby from his birth in a Philadelphia housing project to the pinnacle of the entertainment industry.

Kuzwayo, Ellen. *Call Me Woman.* London: The Women's Press, 1985.

Can a black grandmother look on quietly while the young people of Soweto face the tanks and bullets of apartheid? This is a true story of courage and dignity that covers seventy years of one woman's personal and political history.

Lee, Helen Jackson. *Nigger in the Window.* New York: Doubleday, 1978.

A college-educated black woman tells of her struggles to find a job in the '30's and '40's, long before the Civil Rights Movement could have improved her lot.

Lefontant, Newel. *A Salute to Black Historic Women.* Chicago: Empak Publishing Company, 1984.

Twenty-four great black women's one page biographies, accompanied by a pen and ink portrait, concludes with activities for youngsters—crossword puzzles, word searches, and multiple choice quizzes. Women included in this small book span the length of American history, from the late 18th century to the present.

Mebane, Mary E. *Mary.* New York: Viking, 1981.

Mary grew up in 1930's North Carolina, which was for her a world without options. She strove against the odds to escape the drudgery of domestic service to graduate summa cum laude from a black university. The equally extraordinary chronicle of her later life is written in *Mary Wayfarer* (Viking, 1983).

Metcalf, George R. *Black Profiles.* McGraw Hill, 1970.

Here are biographies of thirteen black champions of integration and emancipation.

Metzger, Linda, Hal May, Deborah Straub, and others. *Black Writers.* Detroit: Gale Research, 1989.

Over 400 black writers are included in this well-written reference source which offers bibliographies and biographical information.

Ortiz, Victoria. *Sojourner Truth, a Self-Made Woman.* Lippincott, 1974.
This is the true story of a remarkable black woman's struggles in the 1800's against slavery.

Page, James, and Jae Min Roh. *Selected Black American, African, and Caribbean Authors: A Bio-Bibliography.* Littleton, Colorado: Libraries Unlimited, 1985.
This is a handy, compact, one volume book about writers of African descent.

Shockley, Ann Allen, and Sue P. Chandler. *Living Black American Authors.* New York: R. R. Bowker, 1973.
Brief biographical information about black writers in the United States gives statistics, educational achievements, family and professional information, memberships in organizations, awards received, a list of publications, and corresponding address at time of publication. There is also a list of black publishers.

Sterling, Philip, and Raymond Logan. *Four Took Freedom.* Garden City, New York: Doubleday, 1967.
The life stories of Harriet Tubman, Frederick Douglas, naval hero Robert Smalls, and United States Senator Blanche Bruce illustrate the courage it took to forge ahead in the 19th century.

Washington, Booker T. *Up From Slavery.* New York: Airmont Publishing Company, 1967.
Booker Talaiferro Washington, born a slave, made the American Dream come true through devotion to ideals. This is the autobiography of the founder of Tuskegee Institute, his own struggle for education, his travels in Europe, and his many honors.

Webb, Constance, *Richard Wright.* New York: G. P. Putnam's Sons, 1968.
Based on the author's personal friendship with Wright, and access to his diaries, letters, and unpublished novels, this is the life story of the prophetic author of *Uncle Tom's Children, Black Boy,* and *Native Son.*

Life and History

Adams, William. *Afro-American Literature: Drama.* Boston: Houghton-Mifflin, 1970.
Including "Raisin in the Sun" by Lorraine Hausberry, the first play by a black woman to receive the New York Drama Critics Circle Award, this collection also offers "A Land Beyond the River" by Loften Mitchell and "Purlie Victorious" by Ossie Davis.

Chafe, William H. *Civilities and Civil Rights: Greensboro, North Carolina, and the Black Struggle for Freedom.* New York: Oxford University Press, 1980.

Chafe shows the contrast in methods of traditional Southern civility and black activism in achieving equality of races.

Chapman, Abraham. *Black Voices, an Anthology of Afro-American Literature.* New York: Mentor, 1968.
This anthology contains fiction, poetry, autobiography, and criticism by authors such as Richard Wright, Gwendolyn Brooks, Margaret Walker, Ann Petry, and nearly twenty others.

Cottle, Thomas. *Black Children, White Dreams.* Boston: Houghton Mifflin, 1974.
Cottle records the daily lives of black children in a northern city who talk intensely of their experiences in what they perceive as a White world.

Davidson, Basil. *Black Mother, Africa: The Years of Trial.* London: Longman, 1970.
Black Mother is about the course and consequences of the long African-European connection of trade, empire, slavery, and forced immigration.

Haber, Louis. *Black Pioneers of Science and Invention.* New York: Harcourt, Brace, and World, 1970.
This biography reveals the lives of fourteen African-American scientists and industrialists against the background of their work and environment.

Haley, Alex. *Roots.* London: Hutchinson, 1977.
This famous study of continuities, grounded in twelve years of research, neither romanticizes nor glosses over the story of Black history in America.

Haskins, James. *Black Theater in America.* Crowell, 1982.
Broadway stars, playwrights, singers and dancers tell the story of Black theatre from the 1700's to the late 20th Century.

Hirshey, Gerri. *Nowhere to Run—The Story of Soul Music.* New York: Time Books, 1984.
From Motown to Memphis, Hirshey interviewed dozens of black singers and instrumentalists who shaped American music in the 1960's. That story is revealed here.

Huggins, Nathan, ed. *W. E. B. Du Bois: Writings.* New York: Library of America, 1987.
This collection includes three full-length books, *The Suppression of the African Slave Trade, The Souls of Black Folk,* and *Dusk of Dawn.*

Johnson, James Weldon. *Black Manhattan.* New York: Atheneum, 1969.
Johnson views the Harlem Renaissance of the 1920's as a close observer, impressed by the music and vitality of poetry, literature, and theatre, but concerned about its "primitive" quality.

Jones, Leroi. *Blues People: Negro Music in White America.* New York: Morrow, 1971.
Jones, a musician himself, places jazz and blues within the context of American social history.

Kaplan, Sidney. *The Black Presence in the Era of the America Revolution, 1770–1800.* Washington, D.C.: Smithsonian Institution Press, 1973.
Pictures and documents record the role of African Americans in the revolution.

Leuzinger, Elsy. *The Art of Black Africa.* New York: Rizolli International Publications, 1979.
Majestic photographs by Isabelle Wettstein and Brigitte Kauf reveal over 200 art objects from sub-Saharan Africa. Statues and sculptures of chieftains' ancestors and of gods and goddesses were an expression of African religion. This artwork survives today, not only in museums, but in the contemporary practice of sculpting in the traditional ways.

Long, Richard, and Eugenia W. Collier. *Afro-American Writing: An Anthology of Prose and Poetry.* Pennsylvania Park, Pennsylvania: University of Pennsylvania Press, 1985.
This comprehensive and up-to-date collection is divided into five parts: To the Civil War, Civil War to World War I, World War I to World War II, '40's to '70's, and '70's and After.

Low, Augustus, and Virgil Clift, eds. *Encyclopedia of Black America.* New York: Da Capo Press, 1987.
This wide-ranging reference book offers a broad history of African-American life in the United States.

Meltzer, Milton. *The Black Americans: A History in Their Own Words.* New York: Thomas Crowell, 1984.
Meltzer collected documents that portray more than 350 years of Black life in America, from anonymous sharecroppers after the Civil War to famous writers of the late twentieth century.

Raines, Howell. *My Soul Is Rested: Movement Days in the Deep South Remembered.* New York: Putnam, 1977.
Interviews with black and white men and women who took part in the Civil Rights Movement in the 1960's shows their determination to win equal opportunities for all despite prejudice and danger.

Rollins, Charlemae. *Christmas Gift.* Chicago: Follett Publishing Company, 1963.
This anthology of Christmas poems, songs, and stories, written by and about Blacks, also includes holiday recipes from plantation cabins. The line drawings by Tom O'Sullivan are dignified and full of vitality.

Seaberg, Stanley. *The Negro in American History.* New York: Scholastic Book Services, 1968.
This is an examination of the origins and history of the unresolved problems of racial tension in the United States, from Columbian America to Reconstruction.

Skidmore, Thomas E. *Black Into White: Race and Nationality in Brazilian Thought.* New York: Oxford University Press, 1974.

Skidmore shows how Brazilians dealt with race relations over the centuries in a manner different to that of the United States and provides a new vantage from which to view race relations in the New World.

Stanford, Barbara Dodds, and Karina Amin. *Black Literature for High School Students.* Urbana, Illinois: NCTE, 1978.

This comprehensive survey of black writers and their literature begins before the Civil War, and includes the Harlem Renaissance, contemporary and new black writers, analyzes young adult Black fiction, and discusses goals and objectives in studying Black literature.

Sterling, Dorothy, ed. *We Are Your Sisters: Black Women in the Nineteenth Century.* New York: Norton, 1984.

This annotated volume portrays the lives of African-American women in their own words before and during the Civil War.

Thorpe, Earl. *Black Historians, a Critique: A Revision of Negro Historians in the United States.* New York: Morrow, 1971.

This critical analysis observes the contributions, achievements, and writings of 19th- and 20th-Century African-American historians.

Webb, Sheyann, and Rachel Nelson. *Selma, Lord, Selma: Girlhood Memories of the Civil Rights Days.* Montgomery: University of Alabama Press, 1980.

Firsthand accounts of two African-American women who were young girls during the turbulent demonstrations in Selma, Alabama, in 1965 make for gripping reading.

Williams, Juan. *Eyes on the Prize: America's Civil Rights Years, 1954–65.* New York: Viking, 1986.

Here are the stories of largely unknown activitists who motivated the civil rights movement.

Black Women

Bogle, Donald. *Brown Sugar—Eighty Years of America's Black Female Superstars.* New York: Harmony Books, 1980.

Legendary African-American actresses and singers reveal their private lives and public selves in this profusely illustrated history.

Bryan, Beverley, et al. *The Heart of the Race: Black Women's Lives in Britain.* London: Virago Press, 1985.

Using history, analysis, and interviews, this book describes black women's celebration of their culture and their struggle to create a new social order in Britain.

Lerna, Gerda. *Black Women in White America.* New York: Vintage Books, 1972.

In this documentary history, African-American women tell about oppression and survival.

Sterling, Dorothy, ed. *We Are Your Sisters.* New York: Norton, 1984.
Documents, letters and photos reveal the lives of 19th-century black women and their relations to family, job, and women's rights.

Tate, Claudia, ed. *Black Women Writers at Work.* New York: Continuum, 1983.
Tate interviews Maya Angelou, Toni Morrison, Alice Walker, and other black authors.

African-American Food and Cooking

Darden, Norma Jean, and Carole Darden. *Spoonbread and Strawberry Wine: Recipes and Reminiscences of a Family.* Garden City, New Jersey: Anchor Press, 1978.
Compiled by two sisters, this collection of foods for all occasions offers triple-decker butterscotch pie, outstanding cakes, and traditional picnic and table fare.

Eldon, Kathy, and Eamon Mullan. *Tastes of Kenya.* Nairobi: Kenway, 1984.
This book looks at the many cooking styles of Kenya, from use of exotic tropical foods to barbecues to curries. Measurement by grams and/or ounces, but not by American cups and spoons, helps would-be cooks become familiar with weighed food preparation. Recipes include hot mango delight, yogurt soup, and coconut prawns.

Ferguson, Sheila. *Soul Food: Classic Cuisine From the Deep South.* London: Weidenfeld and Nicolson, 1989.
Ms. Ferguson, lead singer with The Three Degrees, offers a beguiling collection of anecdotes and recipes from her extended family. Written in a jive-talkin', finger-lickin', cotton-pickin' style, it is fortified with photographs and histories among the recipes for cornbreads, biscuits, fried chicken, greens and fatback, and other cholesterol-rich goodies.

Gaskins, Ruth. *A Good Heart and a Light Hand.* New York: Turnpike Press, 1968.
Learn how to make possum casserole and potato wine by referring to this reader-friendly compilation.

Gibrill, Martin. *African Foods and Drink.* Hove, England: Wayland Press, 1989.
For middle school students, this exploration of the cuisine of Africa offers geological and anthropological insight into the cultures of several tribes and countries. The text is lively and accompanied with maps and high quality color photos. The recipes can be prepared at home or school with items from the local supermarket. Try Maharagwe (spiced red beans), Bidia (cornmeal mush), or peanut stew (an interesting soup), washed down with ginger beer and lemon grass drink.

Hultman, Tami, ed. *The Africa News Cookbook: Cooking For Western Kitchens.* London: Penguin, 1985.
Recipes from all over Africa are clearly explained and translated into metric

measurements. Representative items include Spinach Stew (Central African Republic), Mango Snow (Tanzania), Baked Curried Fish (Kenya), Coconut Pudding (Angola), and Pounded Corn (Zambia), making this an excellent source for authentic food preparations for a festival.

Kaiser, Inez. *Soul Food Cookery.* Pitman, 1968.
Nearly three hundred recipes include soul sandwiches and soul TV snacks.

Wolfe, Linda. *The Cooking of the Caribbean Islands.* New York: Time-Life, 1974.
Fritters, vegetables, meats, and exotic treats from the tropics show how many native African dishes were transported to the islands by slaves.

Periodicals

Black American Literary Forum. c/o Joe Weixlmann, Indiana State University School of Education, Statesman Towers, Room 1005, Terre Haute, Indiana 47809.
Since 1967 this quarterly journal has published scholarly research in many fields of black literature.

Ebony. Johnson Publishing Company, 820 S. Michigan, Chicago, Illinois 60605.
This venerable monthly photo-news magazine features excellent Black history articles, interviews with celebrities, news of sports, entertainment, religion, health, and food in the Black tradition.

Essence. 1500 Broadway, New York City 10036.
Since 1970 this magazine especially for African-American women has offered film and book reviews, recipes, and articles relating to health and home.

Interracial Books for Children Bulletin. 1841 Broadway, New York City 10023.
Published eight times a year since 1967, this magazine writes about racial stereotypes, good and bad character portraits, biases, and curriculum suitability in newly published children's books.

Jet. Johnson Publishing Company, 820 S. Michigan, Chicago, Illinois 60605.
Special features on black history, television listings, and interviews with African-American celebrities make this one of the most popular magazines.

Chapter Eight

The Way of the Prophet: A Festival of Islam

During the last two decades of the twentieth century, the religion of Islam began a renaissance. Part of this resurgence in faith and pride originated in Iran, where Muslims wished to eradicate what they saw as decadent western influences on their ancient culture and way of life. There, politics and religion became as one, and an Islamic republic was established with ideologies that were often at odds with those of the United States and other western countries. Islam is not limited, however, to Iran or the Middle East. Much of southern Asia, Africa, and the Far East is Islamic, and there are large Muslim communities in England, France, and the United States. Minarets now mingle with church spires in many western cities as Islamic people follow their religion with pride and faith. Nor is Islam to be judged by the standards of Iran, which follows the Shi'ite denomination. Nearly ninety percent of Muslims are Sunnites and do not emphasize the Shi'ite reverence for martyrdom, sacrifice, and mystical, hidden meanings in the Qur'an.

A Festival of Islam

The Way of the Prophet

277   Islamic Bookmark

(Figure 55) Separated by a park, these two ancient mosques in Istanbul contain some of the most impressive Islamic art in the Middle East. The interior of Hagia Sofia (left), originally the Orthodox Church of Holy Wisdom, still possesses some of the richest Byzantine mosaics in the world. They were whitewashed when the building became a mosque hundreds of years ago and were covered with calligraphic inscriptions from the Qur'an and with geometric and floral patterns. The mosiacs have been restored to public view. The gigantic Blue Mosque (right), flanked by four graceful minarets, is covered outside with ornate stone tracery, while inside the thousands of blue and white tiles have led some art historians to call this one of the seven wonders of the Islamic world.

In order to understand this major world religion, schools and libraries should offer periods during which Islam can be studied, read about, and celebrated as a cultural force. Islam, which is an Arabic word meaning "submission," is founded on the holy book the Qur'an (or Koran) whose name is Arabic for "recitation." A Muslim, or follower of Islam, is one who submits to the will of God as revealed to the prophet Muhammad and recorded in the holy scripture, the Qur'an. Unlike Christianity, Islam has few rituals, with only Friday prayers in the mosque to compare with a Christian or Jewish worship service. There are few festivals, reflecting, perhaps, the early conservatism of Muhammad and his followers who were most concerned in stamping out pagan practices. While the early Christian church incorporated pagan celebrations into its calendar, the Muslims sought to eradicate them. While some Muslim nations celebrate certain events in the lives of the Prophet and his followers, others do not. Most Islamic festivals are celebrated chiefly with prayers, both at home and in the mosque, and do not have as many secular manifestations (gifts, decorations, greeting cards, and commercialization) as those which occur in western Judaism and Christianity. Muslims across the world are united in their allegiance to the "Five Pillars of Faith."

These Five Pillars are:

1. The duty to recite the creed: "There is no God but Allah, and Muhammad is His Prophet!"
2. The duty to pray to the One God five times each day, preceded by ritual ablution.
3. The duty to give of one's wealth for the use of the needy or for pious purposes, such as building a mosque or an Islamic school. This is called **Zakat**, which is a "purification" of wealth through sharing.
4. The duty to keep the fast of the month of Ramadan from sunrise to sunset.
5. The duty to make the pilgrimage **(Hajj)** to the city of Mecca, which, according to Islamic faith, is where Adam lived after his expulsion from the Garden of Eden.

Additionally, Muslims are forbidden pork, alcohol, gambling, and usury (or loaning money for profit); they are enjoined to honesty, fortitude, and generosity. They are noted for their respect for animal life, their strong family ties, and their sense of obedience to their elders.

Christians may be surprised to find that the Qur'an and its followers honor Jesus Christ and his mother Mary. Jews and Christians share with Islam the belief in one God, the early stories of the Garden of Eden, the Flood, Abraham and Isaac, and other Old Testament characters. A "Festival of Islam" can highlight the things which these religions share, as well as featuring things which make Islam unique. Since Muslims are not only immigrating to other parts of the world but are also attracting converts among native inhabitants, it is time that people of other beliefs learn about Islam. The suggestions for celebration which follow focus on a few pan-Islamic festivals, some forms of Arabic art, and a study of the world map. Since Islam, like Christianity, encompasses many cultures, there is no

such thing as "Islamic cuisine"; festival recipes are included, however, which reflect the Arabic origins of this religion.

Festival Display: A Global Map Project

What You Need:

Rolls of white art paper
Felt-tip pens
Map of the world from reference book
Pictures of a mosque

To show the global importance of Islam, draw a large outline
world map on the bulletin board, including every country. In the
Atlantic and Pacific oceans, place silhouettes of a typical mosque:
square base topped with dome partnered with a slender tower, or
minaret.

Turn this display into a learning center by asking individuals or
groups to label the countries and their capitals. Provide color pencils
or felt-tips so that students can shade in the countries which have
large Muslim populations.

Prepare small world maps (figure 56) identical to the display map
for each student, asking them to:

a. identify each country (or select countries) and their capital
cities.

b. label mountain ranges, rivers, seas, plains or other geographical
features.

c. color with felt-tips the countries with large proportions of
Islamic people.

Surround the display with paper tiles inspired by those of the
Islamic Middle East, instructions for which follow below.

Activities Based on Muslim Art

Some of the world's great art is Islamic. Visitors to Cairo, Istanbul,
and other Muslim capitals marvel at the beauty of ceramic tiles,
carpets, silk scarves, wood carvings, and great palaces and mosques
such as the Topkapi Palace and the Suleyman Mosque in Istanbul,
the Dome of the Rock in Jerusalem, and the Masjid-i-Jami in
Isfahan.

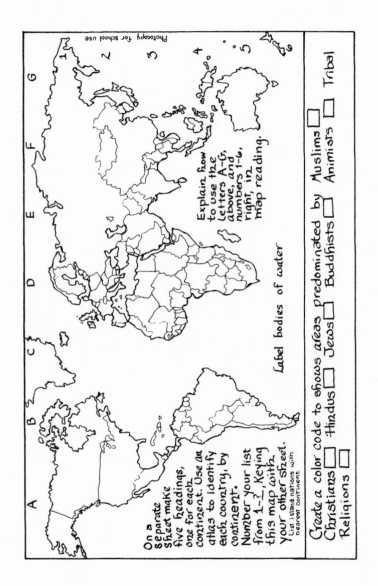

On a separate sheet make five headings, one for each continent. Use an atlas to identify each country, by continent. Number your list from 1-?, keying this map with your other sheet.

List island nations with nearest continent.

Label bodies of water

Explain how to use the letters A-G, above, and numbers 1-6, right, in map reading.

Create a color code to show areas predominated by
Christians ☐ Hindus ☐ Jews ☐ Buddhists ☐ Muslims ☐
Religions ☐ Animists ☐ Tribal ☐

Figure 56

Westerners, brought up on the heady outpourings of ancient Greece and Rome and Renaissance Europe and used to the work of contemporary photographers, ceramicists, and painters, may be unfamiliar with Islamic forms. Since artistic portrayal of God and the human form was forbidden by Muhammad, Islamic art has focussed on geometric design, bold use of color, and representations of foliage and animals. Mosques may be ornately decorated, but none of them will represent Allah nor the Prophet nor any other human being. Even in Islamic palaces, there are very few western-style portraits. The glory of Islamic art lies in its use of pattern, texture, and color. To experience some of the qualities of Islamic art and architecture, students can design a carpet, make a tile, and learn about the design and function of a mosque.

Create a Collage of Symbols: A Symbolism Project

Islam, as students will find out when they work on the map project, spans much of north Africa, the Middle East, and southern Asia as far as the kingdom of Brunei in the Pacific. There are also Muslims in most other countries. Islamic art, which developed in the Arab states and was originally based on classical themes, represents the cultures of many nations. While there are specific themes which are Islamic, there are other themes which are peculiar to specific nations. From reference sources, students can see how the middle eastern use of tiles and carpets is common throughout the Islamic world, while elements from the antique culture of Greece may occur only in Asia Minor.

What You Need:

Materials required will vary, depending upon the method chosen to complete the project.

Drawing Paper
Butcher Paper
Pencils and erasers
Black Felt-tips
India ink and pens
Paints (watercolor, tempera, acrylic, latex)
Glue
Reference sources for photographs and drawings

Create either a mural or a collage of drawings, based upon references in books about the Islamic world or visits to a local Islamic center. Use certain Islamic symbols, such as the crescent moon, and include everyday tools and utensils, such as the *cezva* (see figure 65, page 300), or animals, such as the sheep and the camel. Think architecturally, too, and incorporate the dome of a mosque or a classical column from one of the ancient ruins in Turkey, such as Ephesus (figure 57). Try incorporating Arab calligraphy, pictured in tiles and plaques on the walls of mosques. Use opaque projectors or photocopy machines to enlarge source materials.

Variations

1. Each artist plans a separate collage or mural on a sheet of paper, after which they discuss their designs. Students point out symbolism, architectural features, and design, then pick two elements from each collage and combine those in one giant mural, working in a medium of their choice, from paper cutouts to acrylics.

2. Each artist completes his or her design as a photocopiable bookmark, using black ink.

3. One artist, either student or teacher, draws the outline of a large mural on butcher paper on the classroom, library, or corridor wall, and students fill in the tempera colors with sponges and brushes. This may seem less than satisfactory in educational terms, but it is **not** paint-by-number. This method was used, in fact, prior to and beyond the European Renaissance in art and craft workshops of the masters. This is also a good way to involve many people in making short work of an eye-catching festival display.

4. All artists follow instructions (see pages 349–350, figure 82) to make greeting cards, using black ink or black felt–tips.

Figure 57

Make a Mosaic Canister: An Art Project

What You Need:

Empty tin cans
Construction paper
Glue
Scissors

The blue-domed Mosque of Masjid-i-Jami in Isfahan, Iran, is famed for its mosaics of glass, tiles, and precious stones. Throughout the Middle East, Islamic artists have enhanced their houses, palaces, public buildings, and mosques with mosaics, using traditional designs of the Tree of Life, animals, and foliage. Students can have fun with this art form by creating a pencil holder from a tin can.

First, cover the empty tin can with plain construction paper and glue it in place. Lightly sketch a simple motif on the paper with a pencil.

To make the mosaics, cut up lots of color paper from the scrap box. With white glue, build up the design with fragments of paper (figure 58).

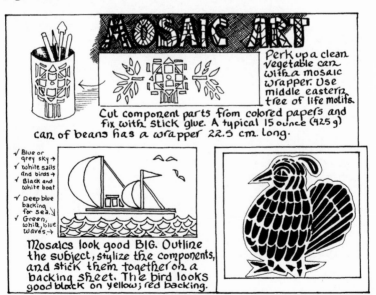

Figure 58

Several traditional Islamic designs can be used to decorate table place mats, as designs for woven carpets, or for collages of scrap paper and cloth. These include:

The Tree of Life: Used by many cultures, from the Celtic to 19th-century Shakers in America, the tree of life symbolizes eternity, and is usually represented by a large tree trunk and branches lightly covered with stylized leaves and fruit.

A Camel: This desert animal, which is still very much used throughout north Africa and the Middle East as a beast of burden, represents wealth.

A Dog: A dog preceded Muhammad into Mecca and today represents protection from sickness.

A Heron: This bird represents a long life.

A Rooster: This familiar barnyard bird signifies victory in battle.

A Carnation: This flower stands for happiness.

The color blue: The symbol of heaven and eternity.

The color white: Mourning, or grief.

The Harem: Build a Wall of Decorative Tiles

What You Need:

Squares of plain paper (all the same size, preferably 6 inches square)
Photos of Turkish tiles from reference books
Pencils and black felt-tip pens
Photocopy machine
Scissors
Color construction paper
Glue

Among other predominately Islamic countries, Turkey is famous for both its medieval and contemporary ceramic tiles. This no-fail art project can be used to create a faux tile surround for the world map display or to create a harem wall in a classroom or library (figures 59–62). The ancient cities of Turkey were built in the style which we know as classical. After the reign of Constantine and the conversion of Asia Minor to Christianity, the Byzantine style developed. Despite some iconoclastic opposition, churches were decorated with mosaics, frescoes, and statues of religious figures. The Muslims, on the other hand, took their scriptures literally and forbade representation of human or supernatural beings in their artwork. Hence, there devel-

Masters of Creative Art

(Figure 59) Many of the walls of the Inner Harem of Istanbul's Topkapi Palace (top) are totally covered with blue and white Turkish tiles with interlocking geometric designs and phrases from the Qur'an written in calligraphy. This particular wall is part of a courtyard, or **avlu**, which is a pedestrian avenue connecting various chambers. The only people who walked here were women in the Sultan's household, their female or eunuch servants, and the Sultan himself. The magnificent Blue Mosque (below), so called because it too is completely covered inside with blue and white tiles and tile mosaics, is perhaps the richest example of this artform in the Middle East. This photograph of the central dome was taken from the floor through a hanging worked iron candelabra.

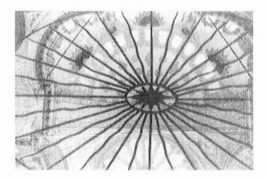

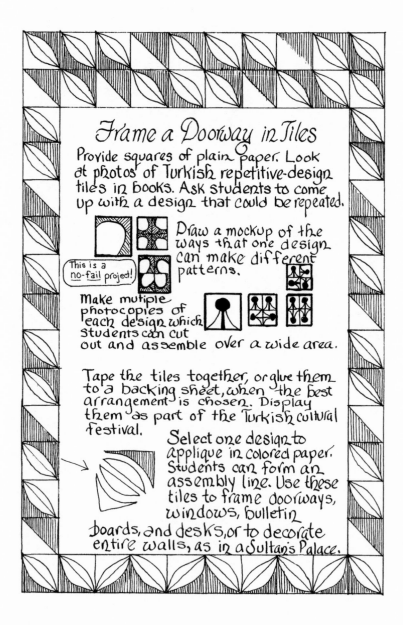

Frame a Doorway in Tiles

Provide squares of plain paper. Look at photos of Turkish repetitive-design tiles in books. Ask students to come up with a design that could be repeated.

Draw a mockup of the ways that one design can make different patterns.

This is a no-fail project!

Make multiple photocopies of each design which students can cut out and assemble over a wide area.

Tape the tiles together, or glue them to a backing sheet, when the best arrangement is chosen. Display them as part of the Turkish cultural festival.

Select one design to applique in colored paper. Students can form an assembly line. Use these tiles to frame doorways, windows, bulletin boards, and desks, or to decorate entire walls, as in a Sultan's Palace.

Figure 60

Students who enjoy a challenge can make floral-inspired designs based upon Turkish tiles, such as these from Topkapi Palace in Istanbul. To complete the design, trace this pattern onto a sheet of paper. Fold the paper and trace the design on the other side. Color with felt tip pens. Or, trace the design once, fold the paper, and cut out. Unfold, and glue to a contrasting sheet of paper.

Making symmetric, intricate patterns is relatively easy. Draw a geometric or floral design on paper. Fold the paper, and cut out the design.

Draw a line in the center of the paper. Make a pattern, beginning at the line. Fold, trace; or fold and cut out.

fold↓

fold↗

Figure 61

(Figure 62) These tiles, from the Topkapi Palace, show how Turkish and Islamic art combines floral motifs with geometric shapes. These tiles are basically blue and white, with pastel shades of red, gold, green, and brown used sparingly to highlight petals, leaves, and borders. Using these designs to inspire a festival display joins traditional Turkish artwork with contemporary student interpretation.

oped in Turkey a rich artistic tradition based upon geometric and floral patterns.

Build a wall of paper tiles, colored with traditional Turkish blues and greens, to set a festival ambience. Begin by drawing a shapely line from one side of the square of paper to the other. Shade in one side of the design. Photocopy the design several times, and arrange them together to see the different combinations that can be made. Use one of the tiles as a template, cutting along the shapely line. Use one side of the design as a pattern around which to trace on color paper. Cut out the color paper and glue the design onto white squares.

To create a cohesive design, select only one of the student designs to use in building the faux tile wall or display frame. A more advanced project for the art room would be to make these tiles in clay, slip glazing, and firing to use in a permanent wall decoration or to use as tabletop coasters.

A Magic Carpet? Design an Eastern Rug

What You Need:

Graph paper
Pencils
Coloring media (felt-tips, crayons, pencils)
White paper for tracing
Light box (if available)
Color construction paper (for mounting)

Beautiful silk and woolen carpets are very important to Muslims. Shoes may not be worn inside a mosque, and it is a real pleasure to walk on soft, highly patterned carpets which completely cover the floors inside. Some mosques may have as many as five hundred valuable carpets laid side by side, not only to beautify the interior, but also to make being there more comfortable. Today, carpets from Turkey, Iran, Egypt, and other Muslim countries may cost several thousands of dollars. They use traditional Islamic designs and are woven not only in factories, but in private homes and by nomads in tents where it may take up to one year to complete just one carpet.

Rather than weaving a rug (which might take years), students can design a carpet on graph paper with felt-tips, crayons, or pencils. A combination of symmetrical and floral patterns will produce a realistic effect. Most carpets have a border around all four sides. This border will usually be of one color, with a vine or geometric patterns (see figures 61 and 63, pages 289 and 293).

The interior of the carpet should be balanced, well-organized, and repetitive. Some carpets tell a story, while others depict desert animals, flowers, vines, or geometric patterns. Look in reference books for pictures of Middle Eastern carpets or ask if a parent could bring in a small Persian carpet for study.

After designing the carpet on graph paper with pencil, trace onto white paper with fine-point felt-tip pens, using a light table where possible. Mount the finished designs on color construction paper and display on a wall in the festival space.

Calligraphy: An Art Project in Illumination

What You Need:

Poems
Pencils
Rulers and erasers
Felt-tip pens
Felt-tip calligraphy pens
White Paper
Reference sources: books of Islamic design

Poetry is very important to Middle Easterners. The Qur'an itself is poetic in form, and Islamic schools teach not only the holy scripture but also the poetry of Firdowsi and Omar Khayyam.

For this project, students may either write a short poem on any topic of their choice or choose a favorite short verse. Using special calligraphy pens and India ink (or calligraphic felt-tips), students should write their poem carefully and with good penmanship. Most art stores can suggest basic instruction pamphlets in the use of calligraphic pens. If calligraphy seems beyond the scope of the project, just ask students to write carefully. Following the ancient eastern tradition of painting miniatures to illustrate manuscripts, students can frame their poem with an "illumination" (figure 63). The frame should be symmetrical and contain a flowing pattern of stylized foliage, animals, geometric designs, or a combination of all

Figure 63

three. No human figures should be included since Islam does not approve of this.

Learn About the Mosque: A Research Project

What You Need:

Reference books with descriptions of mosques
Handout sheets (figure 64)
Rolls of art paper
Pencils, rulers, and felt-tip pens

A mosque is not just a "church." It can be a place of meeting, of buying and selling, and of relaxation from the heat of the Middle Eastern day. They are based upon the design of Muhammad's house in the seventh century, with a courtyard for assemblies of a non-religious character, a fountain for drinking and washing, and a house for praying.

Besides studying photographs of mosques in reference books, students can be given a diagram of a typical mosque (figure 64) with

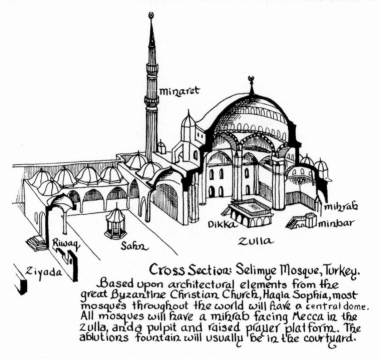

Cross Section: Selimye Mosque, Turkey.
Based upon architectural elements from the
great Byzantine Christian Church, Haqia Sophia, most
mosques throughout the world will have a central dome.
All mosques will have a mihrab facing Mecca in the
zulla, and a pulpit and raised prayer platform. The
ablutions fountain will usually be in the courtyard.

Figure 64

a list of architectural features so that they may become familiar with buildings important in this culture. Where possible, a trip should be arranged to a nearby mosque where guides will be happy to explain the function and design of the building.

Most mosques traditionally include these architectural features:

Sahn: an open courtyard, usually surrounded with colonnades and arches for relief from the sun's heat. In the center of the sahn is a fountain, often built in marble, of ornate design.

Riwaqs: the shady arcades built on three sides of the courtyard where people read, talk with friends, or do anything else, provided it does not disturb their neighbors.

Ziyada: an outer courtyard, built to separate the sahn from the hustle and bustle of the surrounding town.

Zulla: the prayer hall, which includes only these essential items:

Mihrab: a niche, rather like a blocked doorway, which indicates the direction of Mecca, toward which Muslims turn to pray, first introduced in the 8th century. These niches may be plain or decorated with mosaics, marble, and intricate stucco and surmounted with ornate lamps.

Minbar: a high, raised pulpit from which the Friday sermons are delivered by the **imam** (an elder, spiritual leader in the mosque), said to be based on the three-stepped chair used by Muhammad when he spoke to large crowds. A minbar may be highly decorated with wood carving, precious stones, marble, gold, or alabaster.

Dikka: a platform supported on columns above the floor of very large mosques. Since Muslim corporate prayer follows ritualistic body movements, some members of the congregation climb to the top of the dikka to see what the imam is doing. They follow the actions of the imam, and the congregation follows theirs.

Minaret: The tower, usually round, which stands beside a mosque and is used by the **muezzin** (a male official who proclaims the hour of prayer through traditional Muslim chant or song) to call the faithful to prayer. Muslims followed the pattern of the Jews (who used a ram's horn) and the Christians (who used a clapper or bell) to signal prayer times. A typical minaret consists of a hollow round tower surmounted by a small dome, with a small porch near the top from which the muezzin may call.

Line a wall with art paper. After discussing the architecture and inner arrangement of a typical mosque, assign a team of students to draw an enlargement of the mosque in figure 64, or another mosque of their choice from a reference source, on the wall as part of the festival display.

Activities Based on Muslim Holidays

The First of Muharram: On New Year Shake the Tree of Paradise

What You Need:

Small cardboard box or plastic bowl
Small paper leaf shapes, enough for everyone in the class or group

For Muslims, the new year begins on the first day of the month of Muharram. Tradition states that on this day the Book of Life is balanced, and that on the basis of the preceding year's record, a person's future is inscribed. Additionally, an angel shakes the Tree of Paradise, which has as many leaves as there are people on earth. Many leaves will fall, every one bearing the name of a man or woman who will die during the coming year. The Muslim year begins, therefore, with prayers for mercy and for the dead and with readings from the Qur'an about the certainty of the life hereafter.

Although this legend persists throughout Islam, the First of Muharram is celebrated in contrasting ways in different countries. In some cultures, Muslims wear mourning clothes and erect black tents which they decorate inside and out with lamps, flowers, draperies, and swords. Before evening prayers in the mosque, they walk in the streets to greet their friends, wishing them a good new year and hoping that their leaves will not be shaken from the Tree of Paradise.

To illustrate how this heavenly lottery works, place paper leaf-shapes bearing the names of every child in the class into a box or bowl. Ask one student to be the angel who shakes the container, perhaps a set number of times so that not all the leaves will fall out. Do this near the end of a class session, so that those whose names do not fall out get to leave first; those whose leaves do fall out get to remain behind and pick up litter, tidy the tables, put away books, or sharpen pencils. The next class meeting can discuss the fairness (and randomness) of this method of casting lots.

(Students can cut out the leaf shapes themselves, and write their names, or the teacher can do this before they arrive.)

After Ramadan Comes Edi-al-Fitr: Fast for Charity and Bake a Cookie

During the Muslim month of Ramadan, the faithful may eat nothing from sunrise to sunset. In common with many other religions, a period of fasting is kept to renew spiritual values. The Qur'an was delivered to the Prophet Muhammad during Ramadan, the ninth lunar month of the Muslim year, making this the most solemn period of Islam. During the fast it is customary to pray in the mosque and to read the Qur'an, yet businesses, schools, and shops continue to function as normal.

From sundown to sunrise, one may eat. Some Muslim cultures have turned the nights of Ramadan into revelries, with parties and celebrations, while other countries practice moderation. At the end of Ramadan comes three days of festival, however, called Eid-al-Fitr (Festival of Fast-Breaking), introducing the month of Shawal.

Ritual prayers (*Salat*) in the mosque and alms-giving form a major part of the celebrations. A more secular manifestation of this *Eid* is the wearing of new clothing, the giving of candies and money to children, and the eating of special sweets (which vary from culture to culture) at home. Families open their houses to entertain friends and relatives.

To experience fasting on a small scale, organize a "Fast for Charity." Form a committee of students and teachers to find a worthy charity, which could range from Save the Children to famine and disaster appeals to the American Cancer Society. Encourage middle and high school students to forfeit the price of one lunch and to go without eating on the fast day. Provide a collection box in the library for fast donations or appoint a collector in each homeroom.

To make the fast more meaningful, organize a speaker from the designated charity during the lunch period, show a relevant film, or organize an hour of sustained quiet reading. As an alternative to a real fast, offer a "famine meal" of boiled rice and kidney beans to participants. Turn the fast into a celebration by creating and wearing costumes from Africa, the Middle East, or Asia, based upon illustrations in books.

To relate the Muslim fast of Ramadan to a Christian season, hold the fast during Lent. Consult a local mosque (in the telephone directory) to find out when Ramadan occurs, and have the fast then. Discussion groups prior to and during the fast can focus on the benefits (or lack thereof), reasons for, and insights gained through fasting.

Conclude the fast with a traditional Moroccan cookie:

Ghoriba Mughrabi
(Moroccan Pastry Balls)
Recipe makes about 30 cookies

What You Need:

8 ounces unsalted butter, melted and white sediment discarded
4 ounces confectioners sugar, sifted
12 ounces plain flour (or fine semolina)
Mixing bowls
Cookie baking trays

Preheat the oven to 350° F, 180 C.

Pour the melted butter into a large bowl and add the confectioners sugar and flour. Knead until the mixture easily forms a ball. Cover and let the dough rest for up to three hours.

Knead vigorously until the dough is soft and pliable. Take walnut sized lumps and pass them from one hand to another until they are very soft. Place them one by one on a baking tray, gradually using up all the mixture. (These procedures are easily done by cleanly washed student hands.)

Bake in the oven for 10–15 minutes or until the cookies are golden. Remove and cool thoroughly. Dust generously with confectioners sugar and store in an airtight container.

(The teacher may prepare the cookie dough at home the night before, refrigerate overnight, and bring to school next day for student participation. Alternatively, begin the mixing process with students early in the morning, and bake the cookies early in the afternoon.)

Lailat al-Qadr: The Night of Power

Lailat al-Qadr (the Night of Power) celebrates the first revelation of the Qur'an to Muhammad. Although the date is not known, the event is commemorated during the last ten days of the month of Ramadan with special prayers. Some Muslims remain awake all night, reading the Qur'an

During the season of Ramadan, display the Qur'an, along with scriptures from other religions. Using indices or concordances which most scriptures have, mark references to fasting, or write excerpts on poster board to hang above the book display. If the festival occurs outside Ramadan, make a small poster describing Lailat al-Qadr to display beside a copy of the Qur'an.

Bake an Egyptian Pastry

Another sweet pastry popular throughout the Islamic Middle East and north Africa is **Tulumba Tatlisi**. Some cooks make these choux pastries from rice flour, while some even include wine. They all involve a sugar syrup bath. The following recipe, from Cairo, makes a perfect conclusion to a fast:

Tulumba Tatlisi

What You Need:

For the sugar syrup bath:

1 1/2 cups sugar
1 cup white grape juice
1/4 cup water
Saucepan

Boil the sugar, grape juice, and water for about fifteen minutes or until it forms a slightly thick syrup. Remove from heat and set aside.

For the pastry:

1/2 cup unsalted butter, melted
Dash salt
1 1/4 cup water
2 rounded cups flour
1 tsp sugar
4 eggs
Vegetable or olive oil
Large mixing bowl
Damp dish towel
Pastry bag with large star nozzle
Electric frying pan

Younger students can do procedures 1–3 without constant supervision, but an adult should be in charge of procedures number 4 and 5.

1. In a bowl, add salt to melted butter. Stir in the water and gradually sift in the flour and sugar, stirring constantly. When the dough is soft and thoroughly blended, let it rest for up to an hour in a cool place, covered with a damp dish towel.

2. Next, beat the eggs into the dough. Knead the mixture in the bowl until it is evenly blended and glisteningly soft.

3. Spoon the dough into the pastry bag (fitted with a large star nozzle).

4. Heat about an inch of oil in the frying pan, making certain to use special care around younger students. Pipe in two-inch lengths of pastry. When they begin to swell, increase the heat. Turn the pastries to cook evenly on both sides. If cooking more than one batch, allow the oil to cool slightly before adding succeeding pastries and only increase heat after the swelling has begun. If you have no piping bag, drop walnut–size lumps of batter into the oil instead. The taste will not be impaired.

5. Toss the tulumba lightly in the sugar syrup where they remain "to bathe" for five or ten minutes. Remove them to a serving plate. Tulumba tatlisi may be served with sliced bananas but they are especially enjoyed by adults when accompanied by middle eastern coffee (figure 65).

Eastern Mediterranean and North African cultures enjoy thick, strong coffee, drunk from demitasse cups with sugar. Try making this delicious beverage. If ground Turkish coffee is not available in your area, place ordinary dark roast coffee beans in a grinder and pulverize them until they resemble powder. For a single cup of coffee, place two teaspoons of the ground beans in a *cezva*, an Eastern

(Figure 65) During the festival, make time to enjoy Tulumba Tatlisi, pictured here with a cup of strong, sweet coffee.

coffee pan shown in figure 65, along with sugar to taste (optional). If no *cezva* is available, use the smallest sauce pan you have.

Put a demitasse of cold water onto the coffee and place the coffee pan over low heat. Bring it just to the boil, stirring until the sugar is dissolved. Allow the coffee to froth and then remove it from the heat. When the froth subsides, return pan to the heat and bring just to boil once more. Allow the froth to subside and repeat, bringing the brew to boil three times in all. Pour the coffee into the demitasse and drink.

Grounds in the bottom of the cup are part of the pleasure. Some people like to sip them, while others leave just a little liquid in the bottom to ensure that they don't drink them. If you are lucky enough to be near a Turkish or Lebanese fortune-teller, he or she will ask you to rotate the coffee grounds three times, then turn them upside down onto a saucer. When they are quite cold, your fortune may be told by interpreting the designs the grounds make as they fall down the inside of the cup.

Serve Lassi, a Yogurt-based Drink

Students will enjoy making this Islamic Asian drink to accompany cookies or pastries. It is reminiscent of the taste of buttermilk, and it is easy to make at school.

Ayran, or Lassi

What You Need:

2 cups of plain yogurt
2 cups cold water
Pinch of salt
Mint leaves
Ice cubes
Whisk or electric blender
Cups

Mix equal portions of plain yogurt and water with just a pinch of salt. Beat it with a whisk or place it in a blender to make it really foamy. Rub mint leaves against the side of the cups and add ice cubes. Pour in the Ayran, as it is known in Asia Minor, or Lassi, as it is called in India, and sip.

(Figure 65a) The famous *souks*, or markets, of middle eastern and African Islamic cities are warrens of pedestrian thoroughfares between shops selling daily necessities and tourist trifles. Some souks are covered by tents and awnings, while others are sheltered beneath overhanging roofs of houses on narrow stone streets. This is the famous Egyptian souk in Istanbul, covered by a series of domes supported by arches ornamented with tiles and geometric painting.

Go Shopping in the Souk: Turn a Corner of the School into an Eastern Market

To create the atmosphere of a souk during the festival, line up rows of tables in the library or classroom. Students can sell homemade cookies, secondhand books, handmade crafts, or attic treasures. Teachers and parents could sell Tulumba Tatlisi and Ayran, while art students could offer handmade tiles.

Offer prizes for the most authentically decorated stall. Students can make awnings and table frontals from cloth or paper and canopies from bedspreads. They can decorate with paper Islamic tiles.

Add some excitement by hanging a clothesline between two uprights. With clothespins, attach small favors: stuffed toys, a package of cookies, pocket calculators, watches—which have been donated by businesses or from household clear-outs. Bazaar shoppers can try to "ring" their favorite favors by throwing rubber seals from home canning jars. If a seal remains on a clothespin, the student wins what the pin holds.

The Feast of Ashura

The Qur'an devotes much space to a number of people familiar to Jews and Christians, including Abraham, Moses, and Noah. On *Ashura*, the tenth day of the first Muslim month, Noah's safe landing of the ark is celebrated with prayers and a rich pudding based upon the fruits which Noah's wife used. To celebrate Noah's triumph, display an ark with animals (figure 66) and read the story of the flood, both from the Bible and from the Qur'an. According to the story, the ark came to rest on Mount Ararat in present day Turkey, a country with a predominately Muslim population.

Noah's Ark Sails Again: A Craft Project

What You Need:

Empty, discarded cardboard boxes
Glue
Masking tape
Craft staple gun

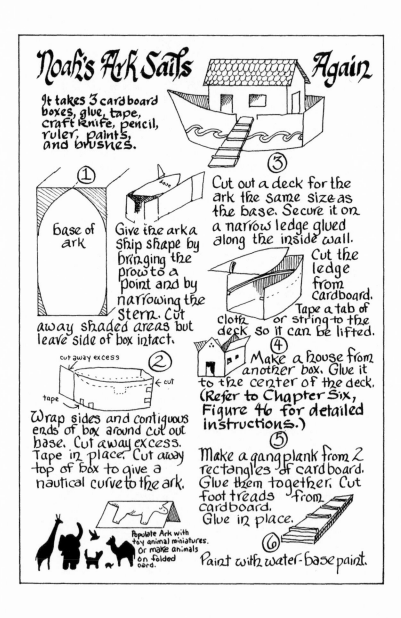

Noah's Ark Sails Again

It takes 3 cardboard boxes, glue, tape, craft knife, pencil, ruler, paints, and brushes.

① base of ark — Give the ark a ship shape by bringing the prow to a point and by narrowing the stern. Cut away shaded areas but leave side of box intact.

② cut away excess — tape — cut — Wrap sides and contiguous ends of box around cut out base. Cut away excess. Tape in place. Cut away top of box to give a nautical curve to the ark.

Populate Ark with toy animal miniatures. Or make animals on folded card.

③ Cut out a deck for the ark the same size as the base. Secure it on a narrow ledge glued along the inside wall. Cut the ledge from cardboard. Tape a tab of cloth or string to the deck so it can be lifted.

④ Make a house from another box. Glue it to the center of the deck. (Refer to Chapter Six, Figure 46 for detailed instructions.)

⑤ Make a gangplank from 2 rectangles of cardboard. Glue them together. Cut foot treads from cardboard. Glue in place.

⑥ Paint with water-base paint.

Figure 66

Pencils
Rulers
Water-based paints (tempera, household latex)
Acrylic or oil-based varnish (optional)
Brushes
Stiff card or construction paper for animals
Coloring media (paints, felt-tips) for animals
Scissors
Old newspapers to cover worksurface

Make an ark for the festival with cardboard, glue, and paint. Depending on the size of the boxes, you can make an enormous ark to leave at school for use in other activities throughout the year or several small arks for the students to take home at the end of the festival.

1. To make the hull of the ark, use the largest of the boxes available. Cut away the top of the box. Make the box ship-shaped by cutting slits as shown in the illustration. Gently bend the cardboard into a curve for the prow. Join the ends together with masking tape. For the stern of the ark, cut away just enough of the base to create a slight inward curve when you bring the rear sides of the boat toward each other. Secure the sides to the base and to the back of the boat with masking tape. Cut away extra cardboard.

2. Give a nautical curve to the deck "railing" as shown in the illustration, letting the point of the prow be the highest part. Cut away a gate for the gangplank along one side.

3. Cut a deck for the ark. Trace around the base of the ark onto a piece of cardboard. Cut out this shape slightly larger than the tracing to ensure a snug fit when you place it on top of the ark. To secure the deck inside the hull, glue and staple a cardboard ledge just below the level of the gangplank gate. Tape or staple a durable tab of cloth, leather, or string to one end of the deck so it can be lifted off later.

4. Using a smaller cardboard box, make a boat house to glue onto the center of the deck. Refer to the instructions on pages 207–212 (building an adobe house), for ideas.

5. Make a gangplank by cutting two rectangles of corrugated cardboard, long enough to make a gentle slope from the deck to the floor or tabletop on which the ark will rest. Glue these two rectangles together back to back to keep the gangplank from

bending in the middle. Cut narrow strips of cardboard as wide as the gangplank and glue them at intervals to make realistic foot treads.

6. Paint the ark as imagination dictates. For further protection, coat the dry painted surface with one or two layers of acrylic varnish (or oil-based varnish). Make simple animals for the ark by folding paper in half. Draw a side view of the animal with its backbone touching the fold, feet touching the cut side of the paper. Cut out the animal and place it on the ark.

Improvised Drama: The Flood

Invite small groups of students to act out parts of the flood story. Besides Noah and his family, there are parts for the neighbors who scoffed at Noah's ark-building scheme, and for as many animals as there are students. The teacher or another student can be the narrator, setting the scene for the story. When it comes to dialogue, let the actors and actresses make that up at the right time.

Noah's Wife Made a Pudding: So Can We

Finally, serve dishes of *Ashura,* the pudding which Noah's wife served her family on Mount Ararat when the ark came to rest.

"Ashura" or Noah's Ark Pudding
(Makes about ten average servings)

1 1/3 cup crushed wheat
1/3 cup white beans
1/3 cup garbanzo beans (chick peas)
1/3 cup rice
1 1/3 cup sugar
1/3 cup raisins
1/3 cup chopped dried apricots
1/3 cup chopped dried figs
1/3 cup blanched almonds
1/3 cup chopped walnuts
1 pomegranate
2 Tbsp rosewater
2 Tbsp potato flour
Water for soaking and cooking

Soak wheat, white beans, and garbanzos separately the day before cooking begins. After soaking, simmer the wheat for five to six hours. Check the water frequently to make sure that it always covers the wheat.

Bring the white beans and garbanzos to a boil. Then cook gently for one and a half hours. Pour the cooked wheat and beans into a sieve over a large bowl. Remove the sieve and pour the liquid into a saucepan. Top with water to make about 4 1/2 to 5 cups. Add the sugar, bring to a boil, and cook until the sugar has dissolved.

Stir in the potato flour gradually to avoid lumping. Add the contents of the sieve. Stir in the chopped fruits and nuts. Pour in the rosewater and simmer for twenty minutes.

Put in dessert bowls and refrigerate. Remove from refrigerator a few minutes before serving. Garnish with pomegranate kernels and chopped nuts.

(Alternatively, simply serve bowls of dried fruits and chopped nuts.)

The Prophet's Birthday

Muhammad's birthday is celebrated on the twelfth day of the Muslim month of Rabee Al-Awwal, which is more accurately the day of his death since no one knows when the Prophet was born. Some Islamic cultures celebrate with fairs, fireworks, and general feasting, while others spend the time chiefly in prayer and thanksgiving for the Prophet's life. It is generally customary to tell the story of his birth in Mecca and of the miracles which took place that night. Just as many legends have grown up around the story of Jesus's birth, so there are many traditional tales associated with the birth of Muhammad. One story tells that when he was born the mountains danced and sang, "There is no God but Allah," the trees responding, "and Muhammad is his prophet." Then every living thing—birds, fish, and every creature—called out together, "How bright is the star over Mecca! Now the world has a light to lead it." Seven thousand angels brought a golden basin of heavenly dew to Muhammad's mother, Amina. She bathed the infant in the dew, and he was thereafter clean. Soon afterwards, people from all over the East came to see the baby, and when his face was uncovered they had to shield their eyes from the dazzling light. Amina, too, has several legends attached to her life, including whispers from Allah that her son was to become a great lord of the people. One story tells that Muhammad's mother shone with a great light that enabled her to see places hundreds of miles away.

Another legend tells that reviving rain fell on the land surrounding Mecca as soon as Muhammad was born, relieving pestilence and drought. Another story tells that while travelling with his uncle in Iraq, a Christian monk, Bahira, told the boy that trees would bow down before him and that he would become a great prophet.

As a drama activity, act out some of the legends of the birth of Muhammad. Compare the stories of Muhammad's birth with those of Moses, Jesus, Zoroaster, and Sidhatta Gautama (the Buddha). Serve these cookies from Algeria as part of the birthday celebrations.

Helilat El-Louze: Bake Muhammad's Birthday Cookies
(Crescent Cookies, Muhammad's Birthday Cookies)
Recipe makes about 30

What You Need:

1/2 cup softened butter
1/2 cup sugar
Zest of one lemon
1/2 cup ground almond
1 large egg (or two small eggs)
1 1/2 cups plain flour
1 egg yolk

Garnish

1/4 cup vanilla sugar or plain sugar

Preheat oven to 350° F, 180 C.

Place softened butter and sugar in a bowl and beat until smooth and creamy. Add lemon zest, almonds, and egg(s), blending thoroughly. Sift in the flour gradually, kneading with hands to form a smooth ball of dough. Remove walnut-sized lumps and roll in the hands to form "sausages" about three inches long. Curve them into crescent shapes.

Place on a greased cookie sheet and brush with egg yolk. Bake for 15 minutes or until lightly golden. Remove from oven and sprinkle with sugar. Bake a further 10 minutes or until golden brown. Cool on wire racks.

Eid al-Adha: The Feast of Sacrifice

About seventy-five days after Eid al-Fitr following Ramadan, Muslims commemorate Abraham's sacrifice of a sheep in place of his son Ishmael, a Qur'anic story illustrating a man's total submission to God. In some countries, Muslims sacrifice an animal, giving one third of the meat to neighbors, one third to the poor, and keeping one third to eat at home. In all Muslim communities, this Eid is a time of feasting, parties, and gift–giving to children. Because Abraham almost sacrificed his son when God required this as a test of faith, Eid al-Adha is also a time of remembering the dead through visits to cemeteries. Graves are marked with flowers and palm leaves, and families spend several hours there, reciting passages from the Qur'an in honor of the dead.

Ishmael, son of Abraham's maid Hagar, is considered to be the father of the Arab people, just as Isaac, son of Abraham's wife Sarah, is regarded as the father of the Jews. Several legends relate to Ishmael's piety. When his mother could find no water, Ishmael kicked the sand, and a spring gushed forth. Very near to this spot is the *Ka'aba*, a stone structure about fifty feet high, which contains the sacred Black Stone, the Ruby of Heaven which Adam brought from Eden, marking the center of the earth. Today this is a center of Muslim pilgrimage, or *Hajj*, for the city of Mecca grew up here, the site of Muhammad's birth and death and the holiest site in all Islam.

Sketch a Sheep

As a creative art project related to the stories of Abraham and Ishmael (or Abraham and Isaac in the Judaeo-Christian tradition), visit a sheep farm and draw pictures of young lambs, ewes, and rams. In parts of India, youngsters paint their pet sheep with vegetable dyes as part of the celebrations. Encourage students to create colored designs for their sheep sketches, using geometric patterns or inscriptions copied from Arabic calligraphy.

A Glossary of Islamic Terms

Since many of these words will increasingly occur in daily newspapers and magazine articles about Islam, encourage library users to become conversant with them. Reproduce the vocabulary list and make it available during the festival of Islam. Familiarity with even a few words and phrases helps international and intercultural understanding.

Ahl al Kitab: people of Scripture, that is, Jews, Christians, and Muslims.
Allah: the Arabic name for God.
"Allahu Akbar": Arabic for "God is greatest," a phrase which begins most Muslim prayers.
"Assalamu alaikum wa rahmatallah": "Peace be on you and God's mercy!," a traditional Muslim greeting spoken both on arrival and leave-taking.
Eid: festival (pronounced halfway between "eed" and "id").
Hajj: the obligatory pilgrimage to Mecca.
Hijab: the covering dress of Islamic women.
Iftar: breaking the fast at sunset during Ramadan.
Injeel: the divinely revealed scripture given to Jesus.
Imam: leader.
Isa: the Arabic word for Jesus, who is revered as a prophet.

(Figure 67) In accordance with strict Islamic law, this woman wears *hijab*, a plain coat-like dress and a scarf. Traditions vary from country to country. In some places, women cover themselves totally when they venture into public places, leaving only tiny eye-slits from which to see. In other countries, Western dress is prevalent and accepted.

Jihad: striving, either within oneself or in society, for righteousness.
Mosque: an Islamic place of meeting, rest, and prayer, based in design upon the house of Muhammad in Medina, Saudi Arabia.
Qur'an: divinely revealed scripture given to Muhammad. It means, literally, "that which is revealed."
Salat: the divinely instituted five daily prayers.
Taurat: the divinely revealed scripture given to Moses.
Wudu: ablutions in water preceding salat.

The Muslim Calendar

Based on the lunar cycle, the Muslim year is shorter by ten or eleven days than the solar year. Lunar months are not fixed to the seasons. Because of this, fasting and festivals will sometimes take place in winter and sometimes in summer. And a Muslim's birthday will occur on a different day every year according to the western calendar.

The Prophet Muhammad had a revelation in which he was told that Muslims must adopt the lunar calendar, so that each month has twenty-nine and a half days, and each year consists of 354 days. Once every thirty-three years the Islamic lunar calendar aligns itself with the solar calendar.

The Muslim era began with the *Hijrah*, or Emigration of the Prophet Muhammad from Mecca to Medina (Qur'an, 8:30; 9:40) because of persecution. The twelve Islamic months are:

Muharram
Safar
Rabee' Al-Awwal
Rabee' Al-Thani
Jumada Al-Oola
Jumada Al-Thaniyah
Rajab
Sha'ban
Ramadan
Shawwal
Thul-Qa'dah
Thul-Hijjah

Every week has one special day to observe. This is Friday, commemorated as the Islamic day of congregational prayer in the mosque, since Adam was born on this day. Friday roughly compares to the Jewish Sabbath and the Christian Lord's Day.

The Lunar Calendar: A Research and Art Project
What You Need:

Photocopies of Figure 68 (see page 314) (12 per student)
Pencils and felt-tip pens
Almanacs and commercially available calendars for the coming year
Yarn, string, ribbon, or loose-leaf binders
Color construction paper or poster paper
Plain drawing paper

Using an almanac in the library which shows moon phases, ask students to determine how many full moons there are every year. Does any month ever have two full moons? Find out why the moon changes appearance. Why did ancient civilizations watch the changing moon very closely? How did they tell the time by looking at the moon?

Make a calendar for the coming year. The festival organizer or teacher in charge will need to reproduce the month chart (figure 68) and then provide twelve copies for each student. Before photocopying, cover the instructions at the top and bottom with a piece of plain paper. Referring to a commercially available calendar for the upcoming year, students can carefully fill in the days and dates. Weeks can begin with Sundays, the first day of the western week; Mondays, the first days of the business week; or Friday, the Muslim day of prayer. Students may want to work in pencil first, then fill in with felt-tips later when any mistakes have been corrected. Think of items to include in the calendar, such as dates of the new and full moons, important holidays and birthdays, and school events.

Mount the calendar pages on rectangles of color construction or poster paper. Students can illustrate each month with appropriate drawings, mosaics, or photographs of friends or people in their families who have birthdays then. Use a paper-punch to make holes in the top of the calendar mounts and tie them all together with yarn, ribbon, or string or hold the pages together with commercially available loose binder rings. If time permits, students can make two calendars, one to keep and one to give away.

A Calendar Project

While discussing lunar calendars, kept by Jews and Muslims, provide photocopies of this calendar month for students to use in making their own diaries and schedules.

SUNDAY	MONDAY	TUESDAY	WEDNESDAY	THURSDAY	FRIDAY	SATURDAY

CALENDAR ART

Students can turn their best artwork into a calendar. Help them mount their work on a rectangular sheet of colored paper. Give them twelve calendar sheets to fill in. These may be suspended from the bottom of the mount with loose-leaf binder rings, or each one glued atop the other along the top edge and glued to the mount.

Figure 68

Sources of Inspiration

Books About Islam

Aggaral, Manju. *I Am a Muslim.* New York: Franklin Watts, 1984.
A young British Muslim boy of Pakistani origin describes his faith and life in this photographic documentary.

Al Faruqi, Ismail Ragi. *Islam.* Niles, Illinois: Argus Communications, 1979.
This small book with color illustrations provides a good overview of the religion and its followers.

Ali, Asghan. *The Origin and Development of Islam.* Selangor, Malaysia: Iraq, 1980.
The author's readable history of his religion includes valuable social and cultural information.

Edmonds, I. G. *Islam.* New York: Franklin Watts, 1977.
An informative book for schools, it explains the basic beliefs and practices of Islam and recounts the spread of the faith and its empire.

El Droubie, Riadh. *Islam.* London: Ward Lock Educational, 1978.
El Droubie tells the story of the Muslim's heritage, with emphasis on modern Islamic life.

Goldziher, Ignaz. *Introduction to Islamic Theology and Law.* Princeton, New Jersey: Princeton University Press, 1981.
Scholarly lectures of Muhammad and the Qur'an, Islamic holy laws, asceticism, sects, and modern life reveal in detail the nature and practices of this world religion.

Haneef, Suzanne. *What Everyone Should Know About Islam and Muslims.* Lahore, Pakistan: Kazi Publications, 1979.
Written by an American Muslim who was a devout Christian during girlhood, the book presents a brief yet comprehensive survey of the basic teachings of Islam for the Western reader.

Hitti, Philip K. *Islam and the West: A Historic Cultural Survey.* Huntington, New York: R. E. Krieger, 1979.
Hitti dips into many facets of life, from political conquests of old to ascetic literature that rivals that of medieval Christianity.

Iqbal, Muhammad. *The Way of the Muslim.* Amersham, England: Hulton Educational, 1973.
For middle schoolers, this is a handy and practical introduction to Islam.

The Islamic Tradition. Niles, Illinois: Argus Communications, 1978.
This book is accompanied by a sound cassette and two color filmstrips about Islam, the Hajj, and cultural tradition.

Jansen, G. H. *Militant Islam*. New York: Harper and Row, 1979.
Penetrating insight into the dangerously sensitive Middle East by a former correspondent for *The Economist*, this book reveals from the inside why contemporary Islam is influenced by the minority Shi'ite wing.

Khuri, Fuad I. *Imams and Emirs: State, Religion and Sects in Islam*. London: Saqi, 1990.
Khuri tells the story of a religion divided by politics, country, and denominational loyalty.

The Koran. Translated into English from the original Arabic by George Sale. London: Frederick Warne, n.d.
The sacred book of over 720,000,000 people deserves to be read in the West, especially in these days when space and time are being constantly redefined by technology.

Lampros, Susan. *Byzantium and Moslems*. St. Louis, Missouri: Millikin Publishers, 1970.
This teacher's guide to the history of Christian Byzantium and the Muslim Ottoman Empire provides basic classroom projects, transparencies, and duplicatable activity sheets. The book shows the contributions which Muslims have made to the world culture: chess, medicine, astronomy, cuisine, and mathematics.

Leacroft, Helen. *The Buildings of Early Islam*. Reading, Massachusetts: Addison-Wesley, 1976.
Through line drawings, architects' plans, and color illustrations, this book shows the great beauty of mosques, minarets, castles, and palaces from the eighth century to the 1500's.

Lewis, Bernard. *Istanbul and the Civilization of the Ottoman Empire*. Norman, Oklahoma: University of Oklahoma Press, 1963.
On May 29, 1453, Constantinople fell to the young Sultan Mehemmed the Conqueror. The Orthodox capital became an Islamic center. The Muslims did not sack the city, however, but preserved it and enlarged it as befitting the headquarters of an Empire. This is the story of Istanbul from the 15th to the 17th centuries.

Liebetrau, Preben. *Oriental Rugs in Color*. New York: Macmillan, 1963.
This book shows students many Islamic patterns and decorative styles and is most helpful in planning a creative drawing or weaving project.

Lippman, Thomas. *Understanding Islam: An Introduction to the Moslem World*. New York: New American Library, 1982.
This "primer" on Islam traces it origins in the seventh century to modern day headlines in international news.

Lovejoy, Bahija. *Other Bible Lands*. New York: Abingdon Press, 1961.
Venture into the realms outside Palestine and modern day Israel to glimpse how the people live and how their religions and traditions set them apart.

The March of Islam, AD 600–800. Amsterdam: Time-Life, 1988.
This well-illustrated history of the foundation and spread of Islam also shows what was going on in India, China, Japan, and Europe at the same time.

Mortimer, Edward. *Faith and Power: The Politics of Islam.* New York: Vintage Books, 1982.
Mortimer shows not only the history of Islam, but also its manifestations in modern Turkey, Saudi Arabia, Pakistan, Iran, and Russia.

Naipaul, V. S. *Among the Believers: An Islamic Journey.* New York: Alfred A. Knopf, 1981.
This award-winning journalist novelist describes the lives, faith, and renewal in Islam of people from Iran to Indonesia.

Nasr, Seyyed. *Ideals and Realities of Islam.* New York: Beacon, 1972.
What are the doctrines, beliefs, and practices of traditional Islam? How does Islam relate to Christianity and other world religions? The answers are here.

Pipes, Daniel. *In the Path of God: Islam and Political Power.* New York: Basic Books, 1983.
Pipes examines Islam as a world political force, describes its origins, and assesses its future.

Powell, Anton. *The Rise of Islam.* New York: Warwick Press, 1980.
Powell traces the history of Islamic civilization from Muhammad's revelations in the seventh century to 1700.

Rice, David Talbot. *Islamic Art.* London: Thames and Hudson, 1965.
Islamic art is a supreme triumph of pattern and color. Without the Western media of oil paint, fresco, and figure sculpture and without representing the human form, Islamic art is a rich tableau of ceramics, woodwork, carpets, textiles, relief and miniature painting.

Robinson, Francis. *Atlas of the Islamic World Since 1500.* New York: Facts on File, 1982.
Maps, color charts, and photographs augment this informative study of the development and spread of Islam and Arab power.

Said, Edward. *Covering Islam: How the Media and the Experts Determine How We See the Rest of the World.* New York: Pantheon, 1981.
Said says that American misconceptions about the Middle East are promoted by distorted news coverage.

Serjeant, R. B. *The Islamic City.* Paris: UNESCO, 1980.
This is a series of papers from the colloquium of the Middle East Centre, Cambridge, England, in July, 1976, on how to preserve the priceless heritage of Islam artistic and architectural civilization without turning cities into museums.

Shafaat, Ahmad. *The Gospel According to Islam.* New York: Vantage Press, 1979.
This is an attempt to bridge the gap between Christianity and Islam, using modern critical research, the Christian New Testament, and the Qur'an to form the story of Jesus as it is known by Muslims.

Smith, Wilfred C. *Islam in Modern History.* New York: New American Library, 1957.
A thought-provoking study of Turkey, Pakistan, Muslim India, and the Arab States shows that many people are torn between an ancient faith and a modern world.

Stevens, Cat. *Islam, My Religion.* London: Ta-Wa Publishers, 1981.
This former rock singer describes how conversion to Islam changed his entire mode of thought and living.

Tames, Richard. *The Muslim World.* London: MacDonald, 1985.
Especially for elementary students, this small book of color illustrations, maps, photographs, and text gives a brief and lively introduction to the parts of the world where the Islamic faith predominates.

Watt, Montgomery. *Muhammad: Prophet and Statesman.* London: Oxford University Press, 1975.
Using the social and political background into which the Prophet was born and showing the influence of Judaism and Christianity, Dr. Watt's biography is a good introduction to Islam as well as a very readable biography of its founder.

Weekes, Richard W., ed. *Muslim Peoples: A World Ethnographic Survey.* Westport, Connecticut: Greenwood, 1978.
These profiles of over a hundred distinct groups of Muslims from all parts of the world, including American Black Muslims, shows how folk culture accompanies Qur'anic belief.

Books About Some Muslim Countries

Ellis, Harry. *The Arabs.* New York: World, 1958.
Ellis offers a very readable history of the Prophet Muhammad's unification of the Arab empire and concludes with a brief overview of that world at mid-century.

Glubb, John. *Syria, Lebanon, and Jordan.* London: Thames and Hudson, 1967.
This pre-war introduction to the geography, climate, history, religion, and government of these three Middle Eastern nations paints a picture of cultural antiquity and contemporary grappling with modern problems.

Kiernan, Thomas. *The Arabs: Their History, Aims, and Challenge to the Industrialized World.* Boston: Little, Brown, 1975.
Written by a journalist who lived in the Middle East, this book presents chapters on Islam, social and political developments, language, and the wealth of oil reserves.

Nelson, Harold, ed. *Libya, A Country Study*. Washington, D.C.: American University, 1979.
After a comprehensive history of the country, this book explores postrevolutionary Libya and the role of its leader, Colonel Qudaffi, in internal and global politics.

Nyrop, Richard, ed. *Saudi Arabia, A Country Study*. Washington, D.C.: U.S. Government Printing Office, 1985.
Offering a useful history of the country, the book goes on to describe Saudi Arabia's current economy, climate, government, oil wealth, and religion.

Taheri, Amir. *The Spirit of Allah: Khomeini and the Islamic Revolution*. Bethesda, Maryland: Adler and Adler, 1986.
Taheri examines the man behind the Shi'ite explosion which engulfed Iran and is sweeping the Middle East, returning millions of Muslim fundamentalists to a medieval way of life.

A Select List of Islamic Periodicals

Arts and the Islamic World
5-A Bathurst Street
London W2, England
Published quarterly, this glossy arts periodical reviews contemporary work in stained glass in mosques, ceramics, architecture, paper money design, calligraphy and other areas in which Muslims work.

Azure, The Review of Arab Literature, Arts and Culture
Arab Cultural Trust
13-A Hillgate Street
London W8 7SP, England
This is an excellent source for contemporary Islamic short stories, poetry, drama, and reviews.

Islamic Horizons
P.O.B. 38
Plainfield, Indiana 46168
This attractive monthly is very readable, with variety, humor, advertisements and articles from around the world. Very much like other American publications, yet noticeably different.

Islamic Quarterly
146 Park Road
London NW8, England
This small magazine contains varied articles on economics, theology, roles of women, and Islam in different countries, with book reviews.

The Muslim
Federation of Students' Islamic Societies in the United Kingdom and Eire
38 Mapesbury Road
London NW2 4JD, England
Published three times a year, this magazine debates theological issues, offers interpretations of the Qur'an, and includes a children's section with games and puzzles.

Muslim Education Quarterly
23 Metcalfe Road
Cambridge CB4 2DB, England
Along with appropriate book and media reviews, this magazine profiles Muslim schools and education in different countries, from the United States to the third world.

For Help in Calligraphy

Lings, Martin. *Qur'anic Art of Calligraphy and Illumination.* Brooklyn, NY: Interlink Publishing Group, 1987.
The book examines historic illuminated editions of The Qur'an, and provides help in reproducing classic Arabic calligraphy.

Shepherd, Margaret. *Basics of the New Calligraphy.* Wellingborough, England: Thomas, 1988.
After mastering the basic alphabet with this easy to follow manual, students can learn twenty-six variations, from deco to Gothic.

Thomson, George E. *The Calligraphy Work Book—How to Master Broad Pen Scripts.* New York: Sterling Books, 1985.
With full instructions, from how to pick up a pen to production of illuminated manuscripts, this books is a must for would-be calligraphers.

For further help, write to the manufacturers of Rotring calligraphy pens:
Rotring-Werke
Riepe KG
D-2000 Hamburg, Germany

For Further Assistance

These two organizations in the United States can provide further help and materials. Please write to them.

The American Institute of Islamic Studies
P.O. Box 10191
Denver, Colorado 80210

Founded in 1965 to promote knowledge and understanding of the faith, history, and culture of Islam and the contemporary Muslim world and to create a climate of mutual respect and friendship among people of diverse races, cultures, and religions, this organization has a research center library that offers films, books, lectures, and other materials.

The Islamic Center of New York
1 Riverside Drive
New York, NY 10023 (Phone 212-362-6800)

Since 1966 the Islamic Center of New York has served the religious and cultural needs of the large Muslim community of New York as well as providing information about Islam, its history, civilization, and people. They maintain an extensive library.

Chapter Nine

Dance with Dragons: A Festival of the Orient

To travel in the beautiful lands of Southeast Asia is to touch paradise on earth. Abundant vegetation carpets the lowlands, rising to high peaks blue in the distance. Flowers vie with birds and animals to create striking colors and shapes that are echoed in the architecture of thousand-year-old temples. The sea washes thousands of islands and forms idyllic coastlines from India to the Koreas.

For all their beauty, some of the nations of Southeast Asia are not wealthy by western standards. Some few are still torn by ideological conflict and overt warfare, repression and civil war. To escape the dangers of combat and to find a peaceful life, thousands flee their Eden: Vietnamese boat people, Burmese refugees, Cambodians from the tyranny of the Khmer Rouge. Many other Asians, through the logical progression of their professions, have made America their home. Every immigrant brings centuries' old traditions that speak through religion, art, language, and social customs.

While the United States has made great strides since the Civil Rights dec-

323   Oriental Bookmark

ade of the 1960's, minorities still face prejudice from time to time. In America many immigrants have to overcome language barriers and cultural differences to forge the new lives they seek.

Because America is a nation built by immigrants, the U.S. has more cultural diversity than any other land. The world community is mobile, and millions of people leave the lands of their birth, for whatever reasons, to live elsewhere. Since the mid-1960's, increasing numbers of Southeast Asians have settled in America, bringing with them their art, their drama, literature, foods, and ways of life. As they adapt to mainstream American ways, so should Americans learn from them. Schools can encourage Americans of all backgrounds to discover the heritage of Southeast Asia by celebrating a festival of the Orient, discovering that diversity is richer in potential than uniformity.

To celebrate the ancient culture which East Asian immigrants have brought with them to America, schools can create some of the forms of paradise associated with those countries. We can experiment with batik printing, dance with dragons, write pictographically, build a miniature Thai temple, prepare some authentic foods, learn geography, and help weave this culture into that of our own.

Two Dancers: Variations on a Display

What You Need:

Butcher paper
Color construction paper
Map of Eastern Asia from atlas
Scissors
Pencil and felt-tip pens
Opaque projector (optional) for enlarging map
Magazine articles and/or travel brochures

A display will establish the oriental focus, whether the festival celebrates recent Asian immigrants to a region or a particular country's culture. Make a large outline map of Southeast Asia as a bulletin board attention-getter for a general festival of the Orient. Enliven the simple outline map by cutting out the shape of each country from different color paper and put the whole together like a puzzle. Refer to encyclopedias to find major crops, industrial products, and natural resources. Make symbols of these agricultural and manufacturing goods and staple them to the map, along with drawings to represent capital cities, tourist attractions, homes of famous artists or authors, and rivers and mountains. The map can also be tied into a festival activity, outlined below.

If the festival is limited to one ethnic group or country, use the outline map but show the chosen country alone in color, limiting the rest of the region to black and white (figure 69), or pick an especially identifiable art form, such as the Indian dancer (figure 70) in front of eastern arches. Look at pictures of writing from that country and identify ways of adapting some forms onto the western alphabet to give visual color to the display. Enlarge a photograph from a magazine of a folk dancer or artist or of a piece of artwork. With a

Figure 69

group of students make a dragon (see figure 72) to bring good luck to the festival; when not in use, the dragon can make an eye-catching display. Use a single letter from a manuscript in oriental calligraphy. Ask someone literate in Japanese or another oriental script to choose letters to spell out the name of a country, ethnic group, or slogan.

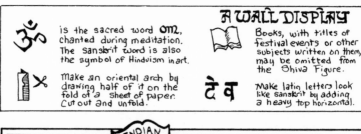

(Figure 70) To focus on oriental culture, enlarge a map of East Asia. To celebrate the culture of a specific country, highlight its geographical area with a special color. Copy a work of art that is unique to the culture and place it over the area map. The map is framed with a stylized temple gateway. India is featured in a display centered on three oriental window frames, with enlargements of sanskrit text found in reference books.

Causes for Celebration

While it is not essential to link this festival to an established national, cultural, or ethnic holiday or period of commemoration, there are good reasons for doing so. Research the national holidays of the countries in Southeast Asia to find especially appropriate periods for celebration. Chinese New Year, the Buddha's birthday, or the end of a war are good centerpieces for a festival. Additionally, other events, such as these which can be found in "Sources of Inspiration" at the end of the chapter, can stimulate interest:

February: Chinese New Year (exact dates vary according to lunar calendar).

April 13–15: International Kite Festival in Pattaya, Thailand, attracting many United States participants.

May 5: Coronation Day in Thailand when the nation honors the king in a public holiday.

May 10: In 1869, Chinese construction crews of the Central Pacific Railroad met Irish crews of the Union Pacific Railroad in completing the first railway to span the North American continent.

May 15: Celebration of the Buddha's birth, death, and enlightenment.

June 4: Commemoration of the 1989 massacre of students seeking democratic reform by the People's Liberation Army in communist China.

June 15: This is the annual celebration of Farmer's Day in Korea.

August 15: In Korea, this is Liberation Day, commemorating the end of World War II and Japanese domination of their country.

September 15–16: International Swanboat Races in Thailand, centering on Bangkok.

October 9: Han'gul Day, celebrating the establishment of the written Korean alphabet in the 15th century.

October 15: Diwali, Hindu festival of lights (Date varies slightly according to lunar calendar).

December 5: Maulidin Nabi (Birthday of the Prophet Muhammad) celebrated in Singapore, Brunei, southern Thailand, and Indonesia.

Trips to Take

In areas which have attracted growing communities of Asian immigrants, schools should organize small trips to shopping centers and restaurants to get a flavor of the culture. In Alexandria, Virginia, "Little Saigon" boasts numerous Vietnamese restaurants, groceries, and hardware stores selling items not generally available in mainstream stores. Both Los Angeles and Honolulu have over 50,000 residents of Japanese descent. New York City also has a large Asian population, over half of which is Chinese. "Chinatown," "Little Seoul," or "New Manila" will more than likely be in a large metropolitan area, and it will be easier for urban students to visit restaurants, communities, temples, and museums that offer insights into the oriental way of life.

In addition to visiting ethnic communities, schools should invite immigrants to talk about their culture to small class groups. Recent refugees from Laos, Vietnam, or Cambodia can share their stories with student journalists. Asian teenagers can talk about how their home culture differs from that of mainstream America.

The entire festival, including visits to ethnic communities and seminars with Asian speakers, will show how much Asian Americans add to United States society. This may also point out that success in chosen fields of trade and business runs the risk of diluting cultural identities. Just as German or English immigrants in the nineteenth century have lost virtually all their national traditions, so will the Asians lose theirs. They will become simply Americans. Even small festivals in schools and libraries will help make other Americans aware of Asian traditions and culture and will help to keep these things alive.

Activities

Get Your Bearings: Research and Art

Provide some outline maps as activity sheets (figure 71) so that students can orient themselves and learn about Southeast Asian agriculture and natural resources. Reference books and encyclopedias can help students fill in extra details, such as rivers, mountain ranges, and cities.

Display the maps as students complete them.

Dance with a Dragon: A Craft Project

In the folk-myths of Japan, Malaysia, and other Southeastern Asian cultures, the dragon is a powerful recurring image. Unlike the

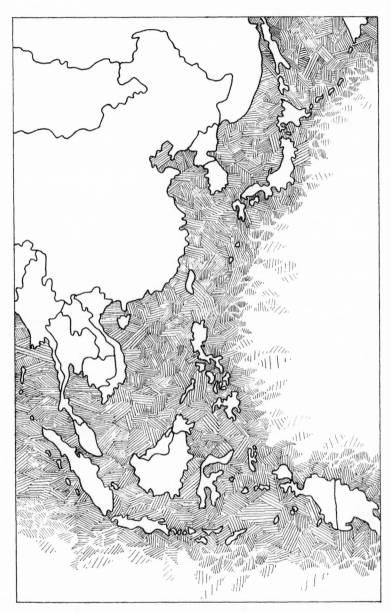

(Figure 71) Get to know eastern Asia and the western Pacific. Provide students with copies of this outline map for an assignment: (a) identify each country, using an atlas; (b) pinpoint major cities; (c) draw in some natural features, such as rivers, lakes, mountains, and forests; (d) color code with felt-tips for language spoken or products exported, religions, or political systems.

European legends which cast the dragon in the role of the bad guy, in the Orient, the dragon is not only friendly but is a portent of good luck and wealth. Most frequently seen during New Year celebrations when young men of the community put on the snake-like dragon costume for parades through streets with firecrackers and sounding cymbals, the curling, twisting dragon evokes tales of long ago.

Students can make a dragon for a festival without expensive materials or tools. The basis of the dragon is a collection of cardboard boxes which will be inverted and decorated with paper, glue, and paint to form the head and torso. The dragon can be as long as the entire student body of a school—each student makes his or her own segment. The length can be limited to one box per class or homeroom, club, or activity group.

What You Need:

Cardboard grocery boxes
Craft papers: newspaper, crêpe paper, construction paper, foil
Fabric remnants (optional)
Glue
Staples and staple gun
Scissors
Craft knife
Felt-tip pens
Glitter, sequins
Old mops and brooms (optional)

To make a dragon segment, turn a cardboard box upside down and decorate with paper and paint. Look at several suggested patterns (figure 72) for a decoration. Decide whether every segment should look alike or whether they can vary according to artists' prerogatives. A single standard pattern for each segment will create a sophisticated dragon. If each group decorates its box as desired, a highly original, colorful dragon can be created when all the individual parts are connected.

Make scales by cutting patterns A or B (figure 72) from fabric or paper: newsprint, construction paper, foil, or gift wrap. Fix them to the box with glue and/or staples, beginning at the bottom and overlapping them like roof tiles. Further enhance the scales by cutting fringes into them, gluing sequins or glitter in patterns or random configurations or by painting oriental designs on them.

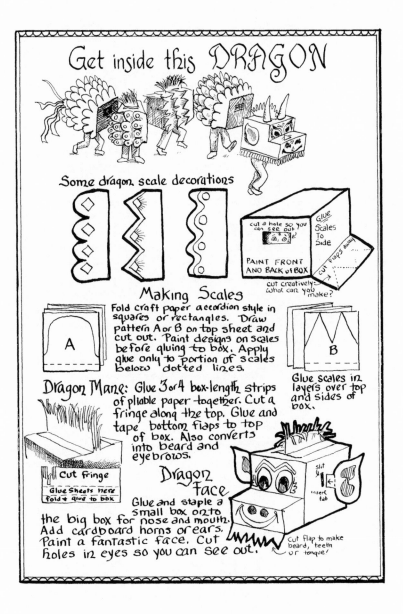

Get inside this DRAGON

Some dragon scale decorations

cut a hole so you can see out
PAINT FRONT AND BACK of BOX

Glue Scales To Side

Cut Flaps away

cut creatively — what can you make?

Making Scales

Fold craft paper accordion style in squares or rectangles. Draw pattern A or B on top sheet and cut out. Paint designs on scales before gluing to box. Apply glue only to portion of scales below dotted lines.

A

B

Glue scales in layers over top and sides of box.

Dragon Mane:
Glue 3 or 4 box-length strips of pliable paper together. Cut a fringe along the top. Glue and tape bottom flaps to top of box. Also converts into beard and eyebrows.

Cut Fringe
Glue Sheets here
fold + glue to box

slit
insert tab

Dragon Face
Glue and staple a small box onto the big box for nose and mouth. Add cardboard horns or ears. Paint a fantastic face. Cut holes in eyes so you can see out.

Cut flap to make beard, teeth or tongue!

Figure 72

Make a mane along the top of the box by attaching old mop heads, brooms, or fringed paper. Make a paper fringe by cutting several lengths of paper, one at a time. Glue them together along the bottom and staple for extra security. Fix them onto the top of the box with strong packing tape.

Before making the head, find pictures of oriental mythical figures in books. Using these for ideas, make up a fierce face with large eyes, huge nostrils, and a sweeping tongue. Paint the features onto the box with tempera or cut them from construction paper and glue them on.

Practice walking in formation as a dragon before having a dress rehearsal with the boxes over students' heads. The dragon procession is really just a case of following the leader, but the participants and observers will enjoy the scene more if the dragon weaves in a wave-like pattern as it walks down the school playing field, through the hallway, into the principal's office, or along the sidewalk.

To help students see where they are going, cut a slit in the front of the box, level with their eyes, either before or after decoration. The boxes may be linked with a segment of twine or ribbon, but for greater choreographic possibilities, they should be left detached. A clever dance instructor can come up with formation marches for the dragon that lets the segments split up, reunite, rotate individually, and wobble formidably.

Good Luck! Make a Tassle

In the Orient, tassles are given to friends on special occasions as a wish for good fortune. The tassles, made of silk threads suspended below a jade or metal ornament, will be hung in doorways, on picture frames, or in windows. Students can make good luck tassles, using yarn, cardboard, and found items.

What You Need:

Yarn or embroidery thread in various colors
"Ornaments" such as buttons, bells, wooden beads, old earrings
Scissors
Craft knives
Stiff card or cardboard, cut into rectangles about 2 × 6 inches (5 × 15 cm)
Poster board
Pencils and felt-tip pens

To Make the Medallion

The tassles will be suspended from a medallion drawn into and cut from poster board. The medallions should represent a favorite animal or inanimate object. They should be no more than two inches (5 cm) square. The teacher may want to provide a set of templates of animal faces and silhouettes, stars, circles, or other geometric shapes around which students may trace. Teachers may also want to give assistance in cutting, especially if craft knives are used. When the medallions are cut out, pierce two holes, one at the top, another at the bottom. With felt-tips, draw on textural features.

To Make the Tassle (Figure 73)

First, place a six-inch piece of yarn along the top of a piece of cardboard. Tape it in place at either end. With scissors, cut through the bottom of each strand of the looped yarn. Wind the yarn around the cardboard from twenty to thirty times, looping around the six-inch strand. Tie the short piece of yarn in a knot and remove the

Figure 73

loop from the cardboard frame. With scissors, cut through the bottom of each strand of the looped yarn. Wind another piece of yarn around the top of the loop and tie it in a secure knot. Add beads or bells to the six-inch piece of yarn and thread it into a medallion. Tie another piece of yarn into the other hole and hang the tassle over a doorway to provide good fortune to everyone who passes beneath it.

Batik a Banner: Patterns to Dye for

Southeast Asia is home to many crafts now famous the world over. Calligraphy is a great art form. Puppetry in Thailand and Japan is a skill handed down from master puppeteers to apprentices. Printmaking, painting, and carving are also practiced throughout the region. Indonesia is famous for its fabric decoration called *batik,* a word which means "wax writing." Skilled batik artists, both in Asia and America, can produce incredibly intricate designs on silk and wool, using wax, dyes, and patience. Students can also make a batik wall hanging as part of a festival of the orient.

What You Need:

Old (preferably white) cotton sheets, or
White handkerchiefs
Canning wax (parafin wax)
Household dyes
Saucepan
Hot plate
Art brushes or *tjaps* (*batik* wooden stamps) (see below)
Water
Trays for dye and water
Cold running water
Electric iron
Old newspapers
Paper towels

What is required? Some old cotton sheets, canning wax (parafin) from the grocery store, and household dyes. A saucepan in which to melt the wax, an electric hot plate, some paintbrushes, and running cold water. An iron and a stack of newspapers. Some cardboard and creativity.

Some teachers may wish to use *tjanting,* the specialized *batik* pens, or *tjaps,* the wooden stamps that can be dipped in wax and pressed onto the cloth. If these are unavailable, wax can be applied with an ordinary artist's paint brush.

Prior to introducing the unit with young people, mix the dye according to manufacturer's instructions. Most *batik* artists will, however, recommend using less water in mixing the dye in order to achieve deeper fabric coloration. Try mixing the dye in boiling water, three times normal strength. Allow the dye to cool and store it in a lidded jar. The dye will keep for about a month, but if it is allowed to sit on a shelf, strain it through cheesecloth prior to use to filter out lumps.

First, talk about *batik* with students. Ask them to look up articles about this art form in encyclopedias and craft books. Show them examples of *batik* scarves and wall hangings. Find Indonesia on the map and talk about vegetable dyes, silk worms, and costume. Next ask students to decide on a theme for their *batik* cotton square. They can use felt-tip pens to make quick sketches of autumn leaves, animals, a smiling face, or a line of trees (figure 74, number 1). Using books and other materials about Southeast Asian countries, they can copy oriental motifs and designs, from alphabet characters to stylized temple ornaments.

Cut the old cotton sheets into one-foot squares. Then make a frame from cardboard (figure 74, numbers 2 & 3) and pin the square on securely. Carefully melt the wax in the saucepan.

Using a small paint brush, transfer the melted wax to the cotton sheet, painting a silhouette picture with wax (figure 74, number 4). Wax cools quickly, so dexterous movements will be necessary. Japanese or Chinese calligraphy brushes, available from good educational supply houses, are excellent. To create sparkle, students can splatter wax onto their cotton square by shaking a wax-laden brush over it. Care must be taken, however, so that clothing and work surfaces are not coated with wax! Although molten wax can present a safety hazard, normal precautions should prevent disaster.

After the wax on the cotton square has dried, remove the fabric from the frame. Pour dye into a flat pan or tray. Place the cotton square into the tray of dye. To get rich coloration, leave the fabric in the dye for several hours (figure 74, number 5). Remind students that wet, dyed fabric will look much darker than it will when dried. When the desired color has been achieved, lift the fabric from the tray and rinse it in cold running water (follow the dye manufacturer's instructions). Hang the squares on a rack or clothesline to dry.

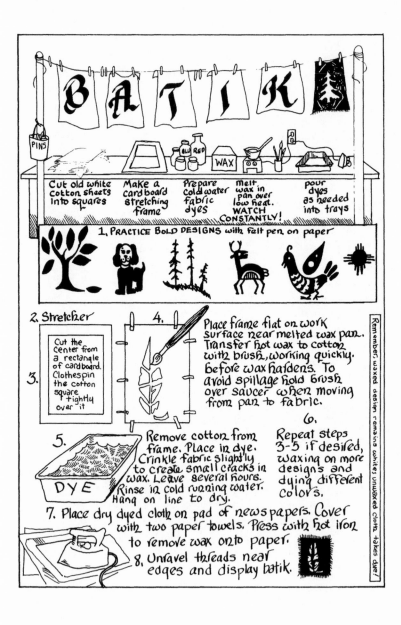

BATIK

Cut old white cotton sheets into squares

Make a cardboard stretching frame

Prepare cold water fabric dyes

Melt wax in pan over low heat. WATCH CONSTANTLY!

pour dyes as needed into trays

1. PRACTICE BOLD DESIGNS with felt pen on paper

2. Stretcher

3. Cut the center from a rectangle of cardboard. Clothespin the cotton square tightly over it

4. Place frame flat on work surface near melted wax pan. Transfer hot wax to cotton with brush, working quickly before wax hardens. To avoid spillage hold brush over saucer when moving from pan to fabric.

5. Remove cotton from frame. Place in dye. Crinkle fabric slightly to create small cracks in wax. Leave several hours. Rinse in cold running water. Hang on line to dry.

DYE

6. Repeat steps 3–5 if desired, waxing on more designs and dying different colors.

7. Place dry dyed cloth on pad of newspapers. Cover with two paper towels. Press with hot iron to remove wax onto paper.

8. Unravel threads near edges and display batik.

Remember, waxed design remains white; unwaxed cloth takes dye!

Figure 74

For a more complicated pattern, stretch the cloth once more on the frame. Paint a complementary design in wax beside the existing pattern. When this is dry, dip the fabric in another dye color, and repeat the process of rinsing and drying (figure 74, number 6). To remove the wax, place the dry fabric on a pad of newspapers and cover with two thicknesses of paper towels. Apply a hot iron, moving the paper towel from time to time to soak up the wax as it melts (figure 74, number 7).

Finish off the small banners by pulling a few threads from each of the four sides to create a ravelled appearance (figure 74, number 8) or sew a hem on the top and suspend the banner on a wooden dowel.

Pictographs: A Creative Writing Project

The venerable alphabets of China, Japan, Korea, and other Southeast Asian countries are far older than the Roman letters used in America. Based on pictographs, or hieroglyphics similar to those developed in ancient Egypt and Phoenicia, many of the modern oriental letters differ little from their originals. Careful examination can reveal their origins, and once the "code" is broken, students can begin to recognize how these picture-letters achieved meaning. They can also invent their own pictographs.

The Chinese symbol for man (figure 75) is like a child's stick figure. Surround it with a box, and the symbol represents a prisoner.

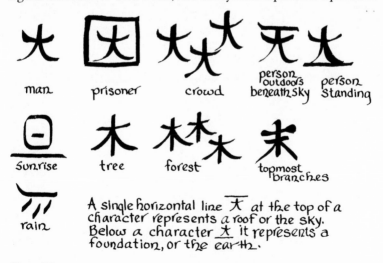

man   prisoner   crowd   person outdoors beneath sky   person standing

sunrise   tree   forest   topmost branches

rain   A single horizontal line 大 at the top of a character represents a roof or the sky. Below a character 大 it represents a foundation, or the earth.

Figure 75

Write three of these figures, and it means "a crowd." Draw one symbol immediately after another, and the implication is the verb "to follow." The symbol for tree is also quite literal. Two tree shapes means "forest."

In Japanese script, which is based on the ancient Chinese, the character for rain is an easily understood pictograph. Drops of water fall from a cloud in the sky to earth. In pictographs like this, the single horizontal line at the top of the character represents a cover or roof, which might be a forest canopy, the sky, or heaven. Placed below the character, the horizontal line represents a foundation, such as the earth. Drawn beneath the symbol for man, this line simply means "to stand."

Provide an activity sheet for students that includes examples of oriental script. Ask them to invent their own pictographs to represent things that are important to them. How many students can make complete sentences with pictographic writing?

Questions such as this (figure 76), in English, can help students begin pictographic writing:

The dog ate supper under the tree.

He went to sleep.

It began to rain.

The dog went indoors to join his family by the fireside.

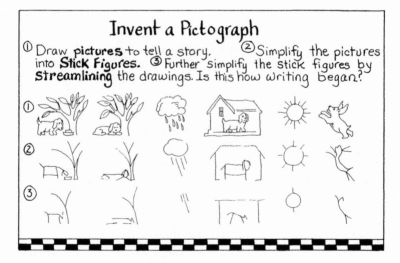

Figure 76

For the Birds: Build a Thai Spirit House

Throughout Buddhist Thailand, visitors comment on the many ornate "birdhouses" at the edge of property boundaries. These pinnacled and colorfully painted little structures are found in hotel gardens, factory forecourts, and on the lawns of private dwellings. They are, in fact, traditional spirit houses, built in the style of ancient temples and dwelling houses with peaked gables topped with stylized swans (the symbol of royalty) and open walls. The houses, positioned on a central post like an American birdhouse, are gaily painted in bright colors. Here, residents of the property offer incense, food, and drink to the spirits of the land whose ownership they may have displaced and to their ancestors. Thai spirit houses are built of either wood or pressed concrete. There are, in fact, large cottage industries devoted to their manufacture.

Points for discussion to tie this project into the festival include comparison of religious practices and beliefs from various parts of the world. In resource books, find floor plans of Buddhist temples. Compare these to synagogues, mosques (see figure 64, page 294), or to churches. Study statues of the Buddha and learn the iconographic meaning behind the several stylized postures used to portray contemplation or teaching. Contrast the Thai use of spirit houses with Christian practices on November 2 in Mexico.

As a permanent reminder of the oriental festival, and to make a colorful bird-feeder for the school grounds, build a little wooden house in Thai style (figures 80–81, pages 343–344) from as few as thirteen pieces of sawn timber or plywood. For an indoor Thai house, the patterns (figures 77–79, pages 340–342) can be transferred onto corrugated cardboard.

What You Need:

Paper (for drawing patterns)
Photocopy machine (to enlarge patterns)
Wood glue (or white glue for cardboard model)
Masking tape
3-ply plywood
3/4 inch pine plank
5-ply plywood
Wooden post and 3" or 4" nails (for mounting wooden model, optional)

Make two of these gable end-walls from 3-ply plywood.

Enlarge these plans on a photocopier, to any size you wish to make. Figures given here refer to the author's own bird feeder.

26.8 cm

Cut out this opening as a front door. Cut to the dotted line only to make a window for rear wall.

The floor should be this wide

20.5 cm

Figure 77

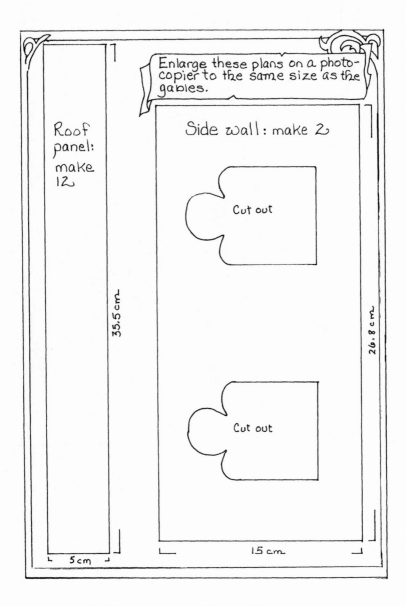

Roof panel: make 12

Enlarge these plans on a photo-copier to the same size as the gables.

Side wall: make 2

Cut out

Cut out

35.5 cm

26.8 cm

5 cm

15 cm

Figure 78

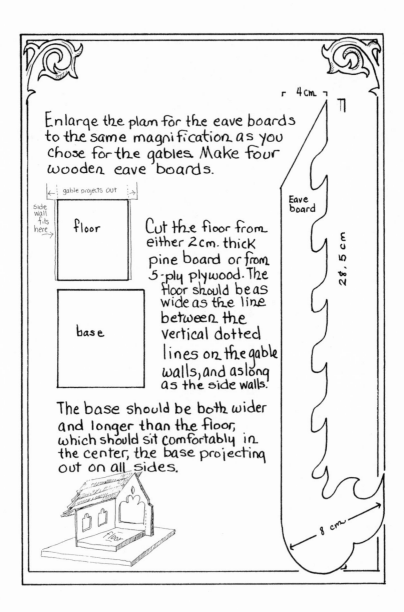

Enlarge the plan for the eave boards to the same magnification as you chose for the gables. Make four wooden eave boards.

4 cm

Eave board

28.5 cm

← gable projects out →

side wall fits here →

floor

base

Cut the floor from either 2 cm. thick pine board or from 5-ply plywood. The floor should be as wide as the line between the vertical dotted lines on the gable walls, and as long as the side walls.

The base should be both wider and longer than the floor, which should sit comfortably in the center, the base projecting out on all sides.

8 cm

Floor

Figure 79

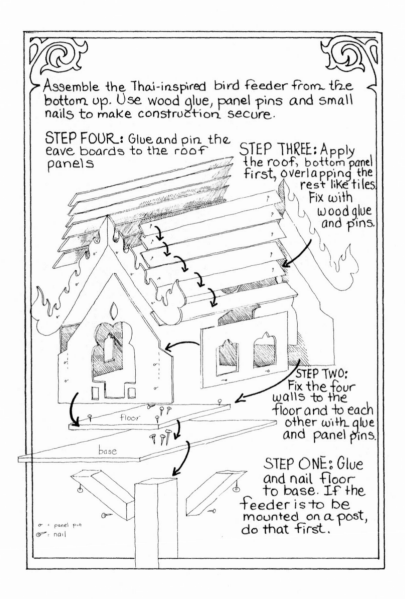

Assemble the Thai-inspired bird feeder from the bottom up. Use wood glue, panel pins and small nails to make construction secure.

STEP FOUR: Glue and pin the eave boards to the roof panels

STEP THREE: Apply the roof, bottom panel first, overlapping the rest like tiles. Fix with wood glue and pins.

STEP TWO: Fix the four walls to the floor and to each other with glue and panel pins.

STEP ONE: Glue and nail floor to base. If the feeder is to be mounted on a post, do that first.

floor

base

σ = panel pin
⌀ = nail

Figure 80

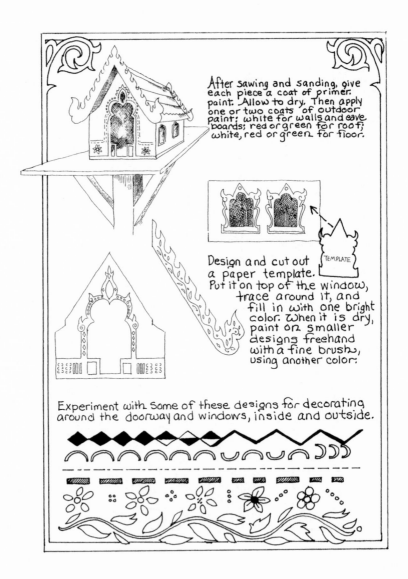

After sawing and sanding, give each piece a coat of primer paint. Allow to dry. Then apply one or two coats of outdoor paint: white for walls and eave boards; red or green for roof; white, red or green for floor.

TEMPLATE

Design and cut out a paper template. Put it on top of the window, trace around it, and fill in with one bright color. When it is dry, paint on smaller designs freehand with a fine brush, using another color.

Experiment with some of these designs for decorating around the doorway and windows, inside and outside.

Figure 81

Nails (fine panel pins, 1″, 2″, and 3″ nails)
Hammer
Electric jigsaw or scroll saw (or manual fret saw)
Electric drill
Sandpaper
Oil-based outdoor paints (including white primer paint)
Artists' and household paintbrushes
Turpentine or turpentine substitute to clean brushes
Scissors
Pencil
Cardboard grocery boxes (for cardboard model)
Waterbased paints (for cardboard model)
Lint-free rags
Apron

(Hint: Since making the wooden version is a time-consuming project, an adult may want to do all the sawing in a home workshop or in the school woodshop beforehand. Young students can sand the pieces to give them some involvement in the initial stages. The adult may also want to do the primer and basecoat painting before bringing the pieces in for final painting and assembly at school. It all depends on time and facilities available.)

An adult or mature student should first enlarge the patterns (figures 77–79, pages 340–342), using either a photocopy machine or an opaque projector. Enlarge them to a size of your choice, though guidelines are given in the illustration. Cut out the patterns and trace around them on the 3-ply plywood. With an electric jigsaw, carefully cut out the wooden shapes. To cut out the windows, first make a hole with the electric drill large enough to take the saw blade. Insert the blade, and work from the hole to the edge of the window.

Younger students can sand the rough edges away. To remove wood dust prior to painting, rub each piece with a lint-free rag which has been lightly dipped in turpentine substitute

Paint the pieces before assembly. This is important for giving the interior of the house a finished look. Because of the size of the windows and doors, it will be almost impossible to paint the interior after assembling the constituent parts.

First, give everything a coat of white primer to seal the pores in the wood. When this is dry, use your choice of outdoor, weather-proofed paints to give a base coat. A good choice is red or green for the roof and white for the walls and eave boards, remembering that you must paint both sides. You can begin to be creative with the floor of the house now by painting in checkerboards, wavy lines, or faux carpets. Allow coats to dry thoroughly (according to instructions on the paint can) between coats, of which there should be at least two.

Now the fun begins. With fairly fine artists' brushes, paint decorations around the door and windows and on the eave boards, either in imitation of Thai art or more simply (figure 81, page 344). This could amount to nothing more than lines around all the openings and painted-on shutters. If you use more than one color, and the colors are meant to touch, paint with only color at a time and let that color dry before painting on the next color.

Experiment on paper with designs before applying them to the house. Try:

Dots of paint around the window openings (easy)
Alternating dots and lines (easy)
Diamond shapes (more difficult)
Series of semicircles (relatively easy)
Flowers (relatively easy)
Leafy vine (more difficult)

It may be easier to draw the design onto the painted wood lightly with pencil before gaining the confidence to paint freehand.

When the paint is thoroughly dry, assemble the house. If you intend to mount the house on a post and put it outside, do this first: apply wood glue to the top of the post. Center the base on top of the post and secure it with two or more 3″ or 4″ nails. Then proceed with the house assembly. Refer to the diagram (figure 80, page 343) to see how the pieces relate to one another.

1. Apply wood glue to the bottom of the floor, keeping the glue toward the center since it will flow toward the edge in the next procedure. Place the floor, right side up, exactly on the center of the base. Use a measuring stick for accuracy. Allow to dry. When dry, hammer in five 2″ nails: one in the center and one in each corner of the floor piece.

2. Apply a line of wood glue to the four edges of the floor. Position the front and rear walls, accurately centered. Use panel pins to secure them to the edge of the floor. Apply glue to the bottom and side edges of the side walls. Put them in place. Hammer in panel pins to secure them to the side edges of the floor.

3. Apply the roof, starting at the bottom. Apply wood glue to the top edges of the gable walls. Position the roof piece and hammer in a panel pin, making certain to aim the pin straight down to the wall. To maintain accuracy, measure the distance from the edge of the roof piece to the center of the plywood wall and mark with a pencil. Rather than completing one side of the roof then working on the other, apply roof pieces on each side of the gable alternately so that when they meet at the top, you can adjust the last two pieces to make a snug fit.

Continue from the bottom to the top, overlapping the five remaining roof pieces to achieve the effect of real tiles. Put a drop of wood glue on the top of each roof piece after it has been secured to give a key for the next piece.

4. Apply the eave boards. Turn the house onto its front, and apply the back eave boards first. Put wood glue along the edges of the roof pieces and put the eave boards in place. Use panel pins to secure them to the eave boards, making certain that the pins are aimed straight down to the plywood panel beneath. Repeat the procedure for the front of the house.

5. Touch up any paint, if necessary. Place a helping of wood sealant across the top of the house where the two roof pieces meet, and the house is complete.

To make a cardboard model, follow the instructions above, adapting them to the more pliable medium. Refer to instructions for making the Japanese temple light (chapter 5, page 173) and for making the adobe house (chapter 6, page 207), and for making a Noah's ark (chapter 8, page 303) for similar projects.

An Animal Investigation: Greeting Cards for Charity

Indonesia provides the last native habitat for the orangutan. Once this friendly primate roamed over the jungles and mountains of much of Southeast Asia, but in the twentieth century, human progress has removed much of the orangutan's home in the wild. The orangutan's cuddly nature and comic appearance has made it a favorite pet among residents of cities from Singapore to Kuala Lumpur. When small, the orangutans live as house pets, but when they get older, less cuddly, and too big, they are often chained in cages or sold to club owners as specialty attractions. There are now rescue projects operating in southeast Asia to return these animals to the wild, which itself is also now being preserved from further development. During the festival display books about animals in this region: the red-haired orangutans of Indonesia, the working elephants of Thailand, the jungle birds of Vietnam, the pandas of southeastern China, the monkeys and eagles of the Philippines, and the bats, snakes, turtles, frogs, and insects that inhabit this richly varied land.

Using resources in your school, make an animal activity sheet for students to complete, either for their own interest or as a festival competition—first one finished correctly wins a book, or all correct entries win a cookie. This time, instead of providing maps of the region, stimulate creative processes by asking students to draw their own, as in question six, and help them become aware of possible species extinction by questions like number seven. Create a variety of questions, such as:

1. Name five animals that live in the tree canopy of southeast Asian jungles.
2. Name five sea creatures that live in coastal waters between Burma and Bali.
3. Name five birds that nest in southeast Asia.
4. Why do some southeast Asian communities eat snakes?
5. Name five fruit trees in eastern Asia that provide food for birds and animals.
6. Draw an outline map of one of the countries of Asia. Show areas that support wild animal life and tell what kinds of mammals, birds, insects, and reptiles live there.
7. Choose one Asian wild animal and write a short essay about its life-style. Is it an endangered species? Can you find references in magazines or books to a program for rescuing this animal from human predation or destruction?
8. How many Asian animals could we find in our nearest local zoo? Is there a breeding program there? Are any animals returned to the wild?

Consider asking students to validate their answers by writing the sources in some degree of bibliographic detail at the end of each question.

If possible, organize a trip to a zoo to look at Asian animals. Even small zoos often house an endearing orangutan or two, and there are usually educational staff on hand to talk about the animals. This will be a good time to discuss the role of zoos in preserving endangered species. Ask students to think about animals in cages or compounds. Can they think of any alternatives to traditional zoos in which animals can be observed, and perhaps, preserved?

Make Animal Greeting Cards
To Aid Wildlife Preservation
(Figure 82)

What You Need:

Plain sketch paper
Plain white (and color) photocopy paper
Rulers
Pencils and erasers
Black fine-point felt-tip pens
Photocopy machine
Envelopes to fit twice-folded photocopy paper
Pictures of Asian animals (books, magazines, posters)

Round off the study of Asian wild animals with an art project that can raise funds for a local zoo, preservation project, or animal rescue. The finished projects can be photocopied, folded like professionally printed cards, and sold for a small amount, the proceeds being distributed to a good cause of your school's choice. The project can be confined to a single classroom, or it can be schoolwide, involving all ages. Student artists themselves can benefit if the teacher gives each one a copy of all the other cards (with envelopes) from their class.

Before They Begin to Draw

First, the artists decide upon the animal they want to draw, be it mammal, reptile, insect, bird, or fish. Second, they need to take some notes about the animal's life-style—where it lives, the food it eats, how many there are in the world today, and any other facts of interest to them. Third, they need to write down biographical details about themselves to add to the back of the finished card. This will include their name, age, and school address. Fourth, if appropriate, they should write down the purpose for which the card is sold. Why write down their biographies and sales intent now? To avoid mistakes when they copy it in good handwriting on the final copy!

Animal Greeting Cards: a charitable project

HOW TO DETERMINE THE SIZE FOR ARTWORK

First Fold ↓

1. Fold a sheet of photocopy paper in half, bringing top to bottom.

Second Fold →

2. Fold in half again, bringing side to side.

3. Artwork must fit a space that is one-fourth the original size.

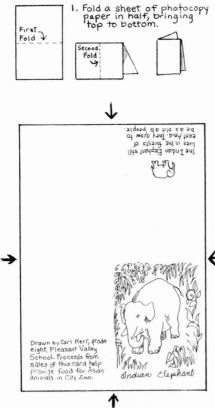

The Indian Elephant still lives in the forests of east Asia. They grow to be as old as people.

Drawn by Carl Kerr, grade eight, Pleasant Valley School. Proceeds from sales of this card help provide food for Asian animals in City Zoo.

Indian Elephant

Main artwork must fit in the lower right quarter of the paper.

← Artist's biographical details can appear on the back, which is the lower left quarter.

Short description of the animal can be written on the top right quarter.

A greeting, such as "Happy Birthday" can be drawn on the top left, but "blank" cards may be more popular.

Card will be folded on arrows. Be sure to draw and write "UPSIDE DOWN" on the two upper quarters!

Figure 82

The Drawing and Design Project

From resource materials, students find pictures of the animal they wish to draw. Better yet, sketch the animal live at the zoo, reworking into a drawing back at school. Show students how big their final sketches should be by folding a demonstration sheet of photocopy paper in half, bringing top and bottom together. Then fold it in half again. Their sketches should fit comfortably inside a quarter section of the total paper available. If a drawing is too big, try reducing it in the photocopier. When the outline drawing is done to the student's satisfaction in pencil, it should be traced onto the lower right quarter of a sheet of plain white photocopy paper with a fine-point black pen.

Depending on the size of the drawing, students can plan several designs that will include the life-style information on the front page of the card with the drawing, on the back of the card, or on the inside, along with the information about themselves: name, age, school address. They can draw on graphic borders, space permitting, to frame their sketch. Borders can be simple ruled lines, stylized vines, geometric patterns, ropes, or dots and dashes. They may leave the inside of the card blank for personal messages, or they can write "Greetings," "Happy Birthday," or "Get Well," though this limits the prospective purchasers' scope.

Photocopy the ink card masters and return them to the students to fold, insert in envelopes, and send or sell. Experiment with color photocopy paper and color envelopes. Often a simple brightly-colored envelope will dress up a black-and-white card.

Let's Eat! Prepare Singapore Steamboat

All across Southeast Asia, rice is a major component of most meals. The climate provides ideal conditions for growing it, and the population demands a steady supply. Create the flavor of the orient by using plain boiled rice as the basis for meats, seafood, and vegetables. Create a **Singapore Steamboat** that provides not only solid nourishment, but delicious soup at the end. Ideally, Singapore Steamboat can be prepared directly on the serving table, with those about to eat it seated around the pot. Each person adds his or her own prepared ingredients to the simmering kettle and removes them when they are done, adding them to a personal bowl of rice. If this is not possible, one demonstrator cook can prepare the meal in front of a seated audience and invite taste-testers to participate from time to time.

Singapore Steamboat

What You Need:

Rice

Chopped bell peppers
Onion rings
Diced potatoes
Baby sweet corn
Okra

Diced beef
Pieces of fish
Shrimp
Calamari

Salt and pepper
Hot sauce (optional)
Garlic (optional)
Herbs (oregano, oriental seaweed, thyme, marjoram) (optional)

Forks, tongs, or skewers
Boiling pot
Individual serving bowls or cups

Prepare the rice according to instructions on the package or bring sufficient water to boil, add about one-third the volume of rice, and return to boil. Simmer, covered, until water is absorbed or about twelve minutes. Keep warm over a bowl of hot water until ready to serve.

Fill a large pot just over half full of salted and peppered water and bring it to boil. (Add the optional garlic and herbs.) Arrange chopped meats, fish, and vegetables in plates around the boiling pot. With forks or tongs, drop items into the water, fondue-style. When the ingredients are cooked, remove them carefully and add to a small bowl of rice. Eat. Continue cooking in this manner, dropping in shrimp, bits of fish, meat, and vegetables. When all the ingredients have been added, withdrawn and eaten, pour some of the resulting soup into bowls and drink.

This dish is a typical Singaporean staple, served at outdoor cafes throughout the city. Westerners may find having soup at the end of the meal rather unusual, but when food is prepared in this way, most diners agree that it makes perfect sense!

For Dessert: Goreng Pisang

Banana fritters, topped with freshly grated coconut, are typically served from street vendors throughout the cities of Southeast Asia. They will add a sweet aroma to the festival when they are prepared in a cooking demonstration in the library or classroom.

What You Need:

10 bananas (to serve up to forty sample portions)
3/4 cup self-rising flour
3/4 cup rice flour
1 1/4 cup Tbsp cornstarch
1 1/4 cup water
1 pinch of salt
5 Tbsp brown sugar
1 pinch cinnamon and/or nutmeg
Oil or vegetable shortening for frying
Kitchen knife
Sifter
Mixing bowls
Clean jam jar with lid
Slotted spoon
Electric deep fryer
Paper towels

Students can help do this: peel and slice each banana into about four segments. Place segments in a large bowl. Students can certainly do this: Sift the rice flour with the self-rising flour and cornstarch into a bowl with 1 1/4 cup water. Stir until there are no lumps. Alternatively, place the flour and water in a clean glass jar with a lid, and shake vigorously. Add salt. In a separate bowl, mix brown sugar and spices.

The adult should do this: Pour about two inches of oil into the electric fryer. Heat until it smokes. One by one, dip the banana segments into the batter. First shake off excess batter and place banana segments into the hot oil with a slotted spoon.

The adult can do this with student help: When the banana segments are golden brown, remove from the oil with slotted spoon. Roll them in the spiced brown sugar, and set on paper towels to drain.

Allow the goreng pisang to cool; serve while warm. Top with coconut, ice cream, cream, or grated chocolate.

Points for Research: Exploring Eastern Philosophy and Politics

During a festival of the orient, students of all age levels should be directed to relevant print, film, and artifact resources, as well as to members of the local Asian-American community, for information and insights into this culture. While younger students can provide festival color though arts and crafts, older groups can learn about politics, racial antagonism and prejudice, immigration laws, and ancient oriental philosophies. New-found information can be shared with others through group discussion, oral reports, and written essays.

Consider these topics for thought-stimulation during the festival and, where appropriate, offer them as themes for papers to be presented to a panel of judges for prizes.

I. Chinese culture

A. *Philosophers*

1. Confucius
2. Mencius
3. Mo Tzu
4. Lao Tze

B. *Importance of the Family Unit*

1. Filial piety
2. Respect for elders
3. Ancestor worship

C. *Chinatowns*

    1. Cities within cities
    2. Chinese relax in comfortable environment
    3. Restaurants

II. Politics

A. *Communism*

    1. Origins with Marx
    2. Lenin and the Soviet Union
    3. Vietnam, China, and Cambodia
    4. The collapse of Communism

B. *Colonization of Indochina*

C. The Spanish Influence in the Philippines
D. America in Vietnam
E. Would American-style democracy work in Southeast Asia?
F. Why did the Chinese government massacre students in Peking's Tianenmen Square on June 4, 1989?

III. Refugees and Immigration

A. Why do people leave their countries?
B. Should America provide an open door?
C. What does immigration do to the balance of jobs, language, and natural resources?

Sources of Inspiration

Books by or About Southeast Asians

Fiction

Buck, Pearl S. *The Big Wave.* New York: Scholastic Books, 1973.
 A little Japanese boy reveals his true bravery when his home and family are destroyed in a tidal wave.

Chrisman, Arthur B. *Shen of the Sea.* Illustrations by Else Hasselriis. New York: E. P. Dutton, 1926.
 This Newbery medalist is a collection of stories set in China.

Clark, Ann N. *To Stand Against the Wind.* New York: Viking, 1978.
 Em, 11 years old and living in the U.S. after war destroys his home and family, begins to record his memories so that someday his children can share his Vietnam heritage.

Huynh, Quang Nhuong. *The Land I Lost: Adventures of a Boy in Vietnam.* Illustrated by Vo-Dinh Mai. New York: Harper and Row, 1982.
 This is the account of a boy's life in Vietnam before the war.

Lord, Bette Bao. *In the Year of the Boar and Jackie Robinson.* New York: Harper and Row, 1984.
 A Chinese girl leaves her native country in 1947 to join her father in New York.

Myers, Walter. *Fallen Angels.* New York: Scholastic Press, 1988.
 Richie Perry, 17 and just out of high school, enlists in the summer of 1967 and is sent to Vietnam.

Paterson, Katherine. *The Master Puppeteer.* New York: Harper and Row, 1976.
 A young puppet apprentice in feudal Japan searches for a bandit.

Say, Allen. *The Ink-Keeper's Apprentice.* New York: Harper and Row, 1979.
 A young boy is about to immigrate to America from 1940's war-torn Japan.

Uchida, Yoskiko. *Journey Home.* New York: Atheneum, 1978.
 After World War II, a Japanese-American family is released from an internment camp.

Wartski, Maureen. *A Boat to Nowhere.* Westminster, 1980.
 Vietnamese citizens set sail to escape life in their communist country.

Yep, Laurence. *Sea Glass.* New York: Harper and Row, 1979.
 After moving to a new junior high school, a Chinese-American boy has to develop self-confidence painfully.

The People

China the Beautiful Cookbook. London: Galley Press, 1989.
Photographs and easy-to-follow recipes from Beijing, Shanghai, Guandong, and Sichuan make this a valuable guide for anyone embarking on a festival of the orient.

Dooley, Thomas. *The Night They Burned the Mountain.* New York: Farrar, Straus and Giroux, 1960.
The founder of MEDICO tells how he and colleagues founded a hospital in Laos despite Communist infiltration.

Farley, Carol. *Korea: A Land Divided.* New York: Dillon, 1984.
This book for elementary schoolers shows links of trade and culture between South Korea and the United States and asks students to think about political divisions.

Fenollosa, Ernest. *Epochs of Chinese and Japanese Art.* New York: Dover Press, 1970.
From primitive Chinese and Japanese art to the present, this book also touches upon work from Tibet and Korea.

Gee, Emma. *Counterpoint: Perspectives on Asian America.* Los Angeles: U.C.L.A. Asian Studies Center, 1976.
This selection of articles, short stories, and poems presents contrasting perspectives on the past hundred years of Asian-American people.

Goldfarb, M Carolrhoda. *Fighters, Refugees, Immigrants: A Story of the Hmong.* Minneapolis: Carolrhoda, 1982.
The Hmong survivors of the Kampuchean or Cambodian holocaust gathered in a refugee camp in Thailand. This is that story, suitable for upper elementary school readers.

Hofer, Hans. *Thailand.* Singapore: Hofer Media, 1991.
Superbly illustrated, this travel handbook is readily available in the United States and Europe and offers concise histories, descriptions of temples and cities, and tells the tourist exactly what to look for.

Huynh, Quang Nhuong. *The Land I Lost: Adventures of a Boy in Vietnam.* New York: Harper and Row, 1982.
True stories recall Huynh's boyhood and his dreams of returning to the Vietnam highlands destroyed by war.

Karnow, Stanely. *Vietnam: A History.* New York: Viking, 1983.
This traces United States involvement in Vietnam from French dominion to final troop withdrawal.

King, S. W. *Chinese in American Life.* Seattle: University of Washington Press, 1962.
This well-written history also includes information about the Chinese of Southeast Asia, Canada, and Latin America.

Li, Dun. *The Ageless Chinese: A History.* New York: Scribner's, 1964.
This is a comprehensive history of the Chinese people.

Lightfoot, Paul. *The Mekong.* Englewood Cliffs, New Jersey: Silver Burdett, 1981.
Readers can take a trip down this Vietnamese river, surveying animal, floral, and human life on all sides.

Lim, John. *Merchants of the Mysterious East.* Plattsburg: New York: Tundra, 1981.
Elementary school readers can learn about several market trades in Singapore in this lively, illustrated book.

Lye, Keith. *Take a Trip to Hong Kong.* New York: Franklin Watts, 1984.
The British colony of Hong Kong passes to Chinese control near the turn of the century. This book examines the way of life there (before 1997) in text and photographs.

Lyman, Stanford. *Chinese Americans.* New York: Random House, 1974.
Lyman writes about the causes for Chinese immigration to the United States, the class structure of American Chinese society, and the anti-Chinese movement from the eighteenth century to 1910.

Mable, Margot C. J. *Vietnam There and Here.* New York: Holt, Rinehart, and Winston, 1985.
This succinct review of the Vietnam war and its related political and social issues is aimed at helping teenagers understand what happened.

Miller, Stuart C. *The Unwelcome Immigrant: The American Image of the Chinese, 1785–1882.* Berkeley: University of California Press, 1974.
This is an exhaustive study of the national antagonism to Chinese immigrants.

Passmore, Jackie. *Asia the Beautiful Cookbook.* Chicago: Weldon Owen, 1987.
Recipes and exceptionally evocative photographs from Japan, China, the Philippines, Thailand, Laos, Cambodia, Vietnam, Singapore, Malaysia, Indonesia, Burma, Sri Lanka, and India help create festival atmosphere.

Shawcross, William. *The Quality of Mercy: Cambodia, Holocaust and Modern Conscience.* London: Andre Deutsch, 1984.
Journalist Shawcross looks at the world response to disaster in Cambodia through Unicef, the Red Cross, and other relief agencies.

Sih, Paul K., ed. *The Chinese in America.* New York: St. John's University Press, 1976.
Find out about how the Chinese language is taught to school-age children in America, about America's debt to ancient oriental scholarship, and about the problems faced by Chinese communities in the United States today.

Smith, Datus C. *The Land and People of Indonesia.* New York: Harper and Row, 1983.
This brief geography and sociology book provides a glimpse of the history of this southeast Asian country appropriate for middle schoolers.

Tachiki, Amy et al. *Roots: An Asian American Reader.* Los Angeles: U.C.L.A. Asian Studies Center, 1971.
Over fifty historical and contemporary essays and other writings tell about the Asian experience in the United States.

Weglyn, Michi. *Years of Infamy: The Untold Story of America's Concentration Camps.* New York: William Morrow, 1976.
Many students will be surprised to find that Americans imprisoned naturalized Japanese Americans during World War II in concentration camps. This is a first-person account.

Wyatt, David. *Thailand—A Short History.* New Haven: Yale University Press, 1984.
Thailand, once known as Siam, evolved from petty principalities into a stable twentieth-century kingdom. This book is illustrated with maps and photographs and concludes with a bibliography.

Oriental Alphabets

Chang, Raymond, and Margaret Scrogin Chang. *Speaking of Chinese.* New York: W. W. Norton, 1978.
This book shows students that modern Chinese writing is precisely that practiced by Confucius 2500 years ago, and its pictographic style can be deciphered more easily than is readily thought.

Chiang, Yee. *Chinese Calligraphy: An Introduction to Its Aesthetic and Technique.* 3rd ed., rev. Cambridge, Massachusetts: Harvard University Press, 1973.
Chiang shows westerners how to appreciate the artistry of Chinese calligraphy.

Lai, T. C. *Chinese Calligraphy: An Introduction.* Seattle: University of Washington Press, 1973.
Calligraphic masterpieces as works of art are arranged in chronological order.

Tsien, Tsuen-hsuin. *Written on Bamboo and Silk: Beginnings of Chinese Books and Inscriptions.* Chicago: University of Chicago Press, 1962.
Tsien provides a history of Chinese writing up to the invention of paper.

Wieger, L. *Chinese Characters: Their Origin, Etymology, History, Classification and Signification.* New York: Dover, 1965.
Originally issued in 1927, this book is as artistically interesting as it is scholastically precise. It shows the development of every character in the Chinese alphabet.

Periodicals

Amerasia Journal
    Asian American Study Center
    3232 Campbell Hall, University of California
    Los Angeles, California 90024
        Since 1971 this journal, spanning many disciplines to present lively articles on arts, travel, adjusting to life in America, and culture of the homeland, has been published twice each year.

Bridge: Asian American Perspectives
    Asian Cine Vision, Inc.
    32 East Broadway
    New York, New York 10002
        Thematic cultural issues devoted to such wide-ranging topics as Asian stage and screen, Asian filmmakers, and overcoming stereotypes appear quarterly.

East Wind: Politics and Culture of Asians in the United States
    Getting Together Publications
    POB 26229
    San Francisco, California 94126
        Since 1982 this semi-annual magazine has offered issues centered around different themes, such as Asian women, immigration, and folk craft, representing many different Asian traditions.

For Further Information

Committee for Fair Immigration Legislation
c/o Center for Immigrants' Rights
2525 Broadway, Number 18
New York, New York 10025
Telephone (212) 759–1424

Indochina Refugee Action Center
1424 16th Street, N.W.
Washington, D.C. 20036
Telephone (202) 667–7810

National Immigration, Refugee, and Citizenship Forum
533 8th Street, S.E.
Washington, D.C. 20003
Telephone (202) 544–0004

Oxfam America
115 Broadway
Boston, Massachusetts 02116
Telephone (617) 482–1211

Refugee Action Group
1424 16th Street
Washington, D.C. 20036
Telephone (202) 667–7810

Chapter Ten

Hear, O Israel!
A Festival of Judaism

Along with Hinduism, the religion of the Jews has existed since time immemorial: It existed before writing developed. It began with Abraham who left his land and people in the Tigris-Euphrates valley to go to Canaan, formerly known as Palestine and today known as Israel. Jesus was born about 1700 years after Abraham settled in the land of Canaan. The prophet Muhammed began preaching five hundred years after Jesus. And nearly 1000 years after that, the prophet Nanak was born who later became the guru and leader of the Indian Sikhs.

Since earliest times, the Jewish people have suffered persecutions from their enemies: the Pharoahs, the medieval Christians, and the Nazis. Jewish people are not unfamiliar with the plight of refugees, yet wherever they have travelled, they have developed and thrived artistically, culturally, and economically, contributing their own work ethic and morality to surrounding society and—depending upon their orthodoxy—assimilating into the dominant culture around them.

363

Judaism Bookmark

Like other cultures and religions, Judaism is rich in celebrations and holidays. The Jewish year is punctuated by Old Testament feasts, the major of which are Pesach (Passover), Shavuot, and Sukkot, Rosh Hashana (New Year) and Yom Kippur (Day of Atonement). Additionally, Purim and Hanukkah, which are not Biblical in origin but date from Persian and Greco-Roman Times, are two festivals favorite of children.

Like that of the Hindus, the ancient Jewish calendar is based on the lunar cycle and depends upon leap years to keep it in rhythm with solar time and the seasons. The Jewish year begins in the autumn with the month of Tishri and is based upon the supposed date of creation, the year 3741 in the Common Era (CE, or AD). Thus 1980 (CE) was 5741 by Jewish reckoning. The year 2000 (CE) will be 5750, with 5751 beginning in the autumn.

Of all the Jewish festivals, only the weekly Sabbath is prescribed in the Ten Commandments. The Fourth Commandment requires that Jews "remember the sabbath day, to keep it holy. Six days shalt thou labor, and do all thy work; but the seventh day is the sabbath of the Lord thy God: in it thou shalt not do any work." This is the first recording in history of a public holiday. Prior to this, people had worked day in, day out, throughout the year. When the Jews threw off the yoke of slavery in Egypt, Moses, through the Commandments, required people to rest, to take refreshment. Jews keep the Sabbath on Saturday, beginning at sundown on Friday evening and concluding at sundown on Saturday.

A Table of Jewish Festivals

Jewish Month	Western Equivalent	Festival
Tishri	September/October	Rosh Hashanah (New Year Day One) Yom Kippur (Day Ten) Sukkot (Days 15–21)
Cheshvan	October/November	Hanukkah
Kislev	November/December	
Tevet	December/January	
Sheve	January/February	Tu B'Shevat
Adar	February/March	Purim
Adar II*		*Leap month (added seven) times in a nineteenth-year cycle

Nisan	March/April	Pesach
Iyar	April/May	
Sivan	May/June	Shavuot
Tammuz	June/July	
Av	July/August	
Elul	August/September	

There are a little over 15,000,000 Jews in the world today. Of that number, nearly half live in the United States, and one-fifth live in Israel. Approximately 500,000 live in the United Kingdom. Characteristic of the Jewish faith is the belief in One God and respect for scripture, and the Hebrew Bible (or Old Testament, as Christians call it), especially the first five books, called the Pentateuch. Jewish law comes from a time when morals, ritual, and custom were not separated. The commandment to abstain from pork is as important, therefore, as the commandment condemning murder.

By concentrating on four Jewish holidays especially popular with children, a festival can spread itself out over the year. Combine a traditional American Thanksgiving with a celebration of Sukkot. Hail the coming of spring with Tu B'Shevat (the "Birthday of the Trees"). To concentrate events into one Judaic Festival, celebrate the occasions out of season. If the festival is to occur during a limited time frame, different classes can study different celebrations simultaneously, with one final presentation for everybody that could include displays of artwork, oral reports on folktales, novels, history, and dramatizations. By looking at the secular manifestations of these religious holidays, non-Jewish children can gain insight into the way their neighbors live while having a good time themselves.

The Star of David: A Festival Display

What You Need:

Construction paper
Pencil
Ruler
Scissors
Felt-tip pens
Thumbtacks or staples

HEAR, O ISRAEL

EVENTS

• Folklore and Art"
  Rabbi: Ben Ezra,
  11.00 Tuesday
  Library
• Tree Planting
  3pm Monday
  Fountain Plaza
• Bagel Breakfast
  7-9 Daily, Room 5

ACTIVITIES

• Dreydels –
  How to make
  them and how
  to play.
  2pm Tuesday
  Art Room B
• Sukkot – Arts and
  Crafts
  1 pm Friday
  Art Room A

FESTIVAL OF JUDAISM

SPECIAL BOOK AND MUSIC DISPLAY: LIBRARY

Figure 83

A prominent Jewish symbol is the six-pointed Star of David (figure 83). Cut a star from construction paper and place it on a plain background with the title of the festival and a calendar of events.

If events are to be celebrated in combination with others, such as Birthday of the Trees with a spring festival, instead of using the star of David, feature a prominent symbol related to the particular holiday, such as a tree, a trellis covered with vines and fruits, or a three-cornered hat. Find out if someone in the community can write in Hebrew letters to give an authentic flavor to the title of the display.

Speakers and Visits

Besides the suggested visits and speakers listed for some of the following holiday projects, the festival organizers may wish to invite a Jewish writer, historian, or rabbi to speak to children about Judaism, synagogue worship, or family rituals. If Jewish children attend the school, ask them and their parents if they would like to talk about some aspect of their lives as Jews to a small group.

Plan a visit to a local synagogue, first having researched Jewish history and customs with the students so that they will be familiar with liturgical and ritual items and will observe proper behavior.

Holidays and Celebrations

Sukkot, The Harvest: A Craft Project

The Hebrew world *sukah* means a hut or booth and refers to the simple dwellings of the Israelites during their forty years' wandering in the wilderness. Sukkot is a harvest festival that comes five days after Yom Kippur. Some Jewish people erect *sukahs* on their lawns in which they eat their meals during Sukkot, following an instruction in the book of Leviticus (chapter 23; vv 33–44). The sukkah is decorated with plants, fruits, and colored lights. Often, four special plants, a palm branch, a sprig of myrtle, and a twig of willow, may be placed in a three-sectional holder together called a *lulay* and ceremonially waved during prayers in the synagogue and in the *sukah*. Together with a citron, they symbolize the unity and brotherhood of the human race.

At the end of Sukkot comes Simchat Torah, an occasion of feasting with wine, pastries, and good food, in honor of the holy scriptures.

Activities

1. *Make a miniature harvest booth, or Sukah* (figure 84, page 369).

What You Need:

Cardboard grocery box
Pencil
Ruler
Craft knife
Water-based paints (tempera, latex, or acrylic) in earth tones
Sponge
Construction paper
Scissors
Glue
Found objects (artificial flowers, twigs)
Handkerchief or fabric remnants

Cut away most of the sides of the box, leaving only columns in each corner. Cut away most of the top of the box. To make harvest decorations for the *sukah,* cut out green vines, branches, and fruits and vegetables from paper and glue them onto the booth. You may also use found objects, artificial flowers, and miniature plastic fruits.

Make a small table to fit inside the sukah from a smaller cardboard box or use a miniature table from a doll's house. Cover it with a handkerchief or a fabric remnant.

Since Sukkot is a time of feasting, draw picnic foods to place on the table (figure 84). Draw beverage containers, baskets, bowls of fruit, plates of sandwiches and cakes, and other good foods to eat on a small piece of folded card, making sure that the top of the drawing touches the fold. Cut out the drawing, color it on both sides, and stand it on the table.

2. *Make a large Sukah outdoors.* Decorate a trellis, a garden umbrella, or an arbor on the school campus or at someone's house. Use real fruit, flowers, and greenery. Hang outdoor lights, paper lanterns, or patio candles. Enjoy a picnic under and nearby the *Sukah.*

Hanukkah, Light: Make a Dreydel

During this eight-day festival of lights, children are given spinning tops and other presents, good food is eaten, and parties held. Hanukkah recalls the victory of the Maccabees over the tyrant Antiochus the Syrian who vowed to destroy every nation which would not bow in submission to him and worship Zeus and the other Greek gods. The Syrians defiled the Temple in Jerusalem, but after three years of bitter fighting the Maccabees won it back again. When the Temple had been cleansed, they discovered that there was not enough sanctified oil to keep the eternal lights burning. Yet through a miracle, the oil that remained kept the Menorah aflame throughout the eight day period during which new oil was being made. Hanukkah which is the Hebrew word for dedication, is a time for remembering all the tyrants of earth who oppose the weak, impose their will on others, and threaten with extinction those who resist them. Primarily, it is a time for parties, games, and eight days of gift-giving.

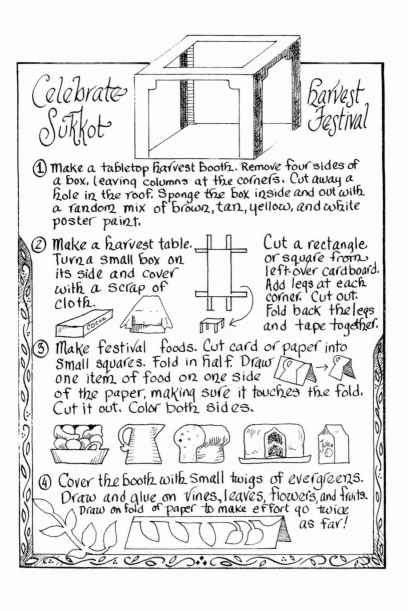

Celebrate Sukkot / Harvest Festival

① Make a tabletop harvest booth. Remove four sides of a box, leaving columns at the corners. Cut away a hole in the roof. Sponge the box inside and out with a random mix of brown, tan, yellow, and white poster paint.

② Make a harvest table. Turn a small box on its side and cover with a scrap of cloth.

Cut a rectangle or square from left-over cardboard. Add legs at each corner. Cut out. Fold back the legs and tape together.

③ Make festival foods. Cut card or paper into small squares. Fold in half. Draw one item of food on one side of the paper, making sure it touches the fold. Cut it out. Color both sides.

④ Cover the booth with small twigs of evergreens. Draw and glue on vines, leaves, flowers, and fruits. Draw on fold of paper to make effort go twice as far!

Figure 84

Activity

Play the Dreydel Game. The dreydel is a four-sided top which children are given during Hanukkah. It may be made of wood, plastic, or metal. We can make one of paper.

What You Need:

Small squares of card or cardboard
Short pencil stubs
Felt-tip pen
Treasures: Candles, nuts, pennies, or playing tokens

Make a square of card (figure 85). Divide it into quarters by drawing two diagonal lines. Pierce the card in the center with a short pencil. Spin the top by twirling the pencil.

Label each quarter with one of these Hebrew letters: The letters stand for "Nes Gadol Hayah Sham," or "A Great Miracle Has Happened," referring to the Temple lamps which burned for eight days on a one-day supply of oil.

To play, sit on the floor. Each player contributes some of his or her "treasure" to the "pot." This treasure may be candies, nuts, raisins,

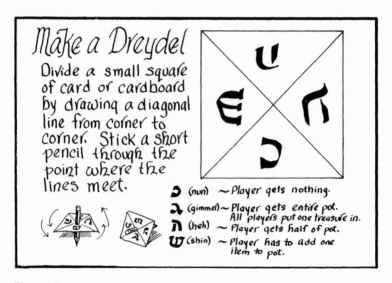

Figure 85

Figure 86

or pennies. A player spins the dreydel to see what letter it will land on.

ב (Nun) N—the player gets nothing
ג (Gimmel) G—the player gets everything in the pot
ה (Heh) H—the player gets half of the pot
ש (Shin) SH—the player is a "nerd," drops out of the game, or has to contribute more treasure to the pot in order to remain in.

Then the next player spins the dreydel and so on, until everyone has had a turn. The game may last as long as players wish.

Variation

Instead of writing Hebrew letters on the quarters of the dreydel, draw on numbers (figure 86). Instead of making up a pot of treasures, play for accumulated points during a set time period or after every player has spun an agreed-upon number of times.

Another variation asks players to take from or add to the pot. Label the quarters of the dreydel "Add One," "Add Two," "Take One," "Take Two." When the dreydel lands on "Take Two" the player may take two items from the pot, but when it lands on "Add Two" he or she must contribute two of his or her treasures. At the end of a specified time or certain number of spins, the game ends, and the person with the most number of treasures is the winner.

Purim, Deliverance: Bake Hamantashen

Just as Hindu children await the fun of Holi and Christian children the excitement of Christmas, so Jewish children look forward to Purim, a time of gift-giving, fun, and carnival. The holiday begins with the reading of the Biblical book of Esther, and the story of Ahashuerus, the King of Persia, who made Esther his queen. Through jealousy, Haman, the king's prime minister, plotted to kill all the Jews in the Persian empire, but through Esther's intervention the deceit failed, and, instead, the plotters were themselves put to death. During the reading of the story, special rattles (**groggers**) help drown out the name of Hamam whenever it is pronounced.

Purim is named after the dice which Haman used to choose the day of his revenge against the Jews. He rolled the numbers thirteen and twelve, which he felt meant the thirteenth day of the twelfth month (Adar), which is in February or March by common reckoning. When the day came, the Jews were armed and ready, due to Esther's intervention. Haman was hanged on the scaffold he had himself prepared for Mordecai, the wise man (and cousin of the Queen) who had refused to kneel before Haman as he passed through the streets.

Activities

1. **Read the story of Purim from the Book of Esther in the Bible.** When this story is read in the synagogue, children make as much noise as possible when the name of the villain Haman is mentioned. They may clap their hands, whistle, stamp their feet, beat percussion instruments, or use groggers. Encourage children to react similarly in the reading of the story at school.

Tell other stories in which a villain or monster appears and ask listeners to drown out his or her name with noise. Try "The Three Billy Goats Gruff," "Jack and the Beanstalk," or "Cinderella."

(Refer to "The Holocaust: Lest We Forget," pages 375–377 at the end of this chapter.)

2. **Make masks, crowns, and costumes** to reenact the story of Esther, Mordecai, Ahashuerus, and Haman. There are parts for many actors as Persian soldiers and Jewish people.

3. **Draw pictures to illustrate the story.** On butcher paper, a group can create a mural illustrating the entire tale.

4. A traditional food during Purim is the *Hamantashen,* or Haman's Hat, a three-cornered pastry filled with prunes or poppyseeds. Make an easy festival treat to accompany storytelling or dramatization from peanut butter and jelly sandwiches. Trim the crusts from the bread, and divide the sandwiches in half diagonally to immitate the hat which Haman traditionally wore. It is relatively easy to make Hamantashen, and children will enjoy rolling out the pastry.

What You Need:

3 cups sifted flour
1 tsp salt
1 1/4 cups shortening
3–4 Tbsp iced water
Cooked prunes (seeds removed)
Poppyseeds (optional)
Milk or water in a bowl
Extra flour
Mixing bowls, cookie tray, spoons, kitchen knife, fork
Rolling pin, pastry brush

To Make the Pastry

Youngsters can do this: Mix the flour and salt. Divide the shortening into small lumps and blend into the flour by hand, crushing the flour into the shortening with the fingers and thumb until the mixture resembles coarse corn meal. (This mixture may be made ahead and kept in a sealed container in the refrigerator.) To proceed, take a cup of the mixture and sprinkle it with the iced water, tossing lightly with a fork to blend.

Preheat oven to 425° F (225 C).

Supervise youngsters in this procedure: Dust a worksurface with flour and roll out the pastry mixture with a rolling pin until it is about 1/8 inch (3 cm) thick. Cut the pastry into 3-inch (7.5 cm) squares.

Help youngsters do this: Put one or two cooked, seeded prunes in the middle of each square and sprinkle lightly with poppy seeds. Pour a teaspoon of prune juice over the fruit.

Demonstrate once, then set young cooks to work: To make the three-cornered hat, dip a pastry brush or your finger into the bowl of water or milk. Brush the liquid along the inside edges of the pastry. Fold one corner of the pastry square over the fruit until it meets the corner diagonally opposite. Press the edges of the pastry envelope together with a fork. To glaze the top of the pastry, brush a little milk over it. Place the pastries on the baking tray and bake for 12–15 minutes, or until they are golden.

Allow to cool before serving warm or at room temperature with milk or tea.

Tu B'shevat, The Trees' New Year: Gardening Projects

On the fifteenth day of the month Shevat, which usually falls in January or February, is time to celebrate the New Year of the Trees. Since the festival originated in the warm Mediterranean climate of ancient Palestine, this festival of spring renewal comes early for much of the Northern Hemisphere.

It was the custom for parents to plant a tree on this day to honor the birth of a child, a cedar for a boy and cypress for a girl. Today, Tu B'shevat is an excellent time to recall the ecology of trees: (a) they provide food—fruit and nuts; (b) they shelter people and animals from wind and rain; (c) they provide building material; (d) they keep soil from eroding; (e) they release oxygen into the atmosphere; (f) they provide nesting sites for birds; (g) fallen leaves decompose to enrich the soil.

Activities

1. **Visit a tree farm.** Talk to nursery workers and find out how to transplant young trees successfully. Take along sketchbooks and draw young trees.

2. **Plant a sapling on campus.** Discuss soil enrichment, watering, and staking the tree to protect it from wind damage.

3. **Organize a bake sale** and contribute the profits to a local ecological organization who will plant new trees or preserve old ones.

4. **Take small cuttings from bare trees in the winter woods** and "force" them indoors by placing them in a jar of water, giving them a good shower in the sink, and watching them burst into leaf earlier than they normally would outdoors.

5. **Fill small window boxes or pots with compost and soil, and plant evergreens.** When they grow too big for the container, plant them outdoors.

6. **Make a giant fruit salad** using only fruits and nuts that have grown on trees.

The Holocaust: Lest We Forget

It is important never to forget the nightmare that faced European Jews during the years leading up to and including World War II. They, along with gypsies, political prisoners, homosexuals, the physically handicapped—any who did not fit into the Nazi ideal— were shipped to forced labor camps where millions died from hardship or were murdered in the gas chambers. The stories are harsh and do not fit easily into the happy times which schools try to create. Yet during the festival, there should be occasions when this darker side of human nature can be discussed.

There are many excellent books about the Holocaust, both histories and fiction. It is appropriate to make a special display of these materials during the festival beneath a graphic bulletin. Look at the dust jackets of the books for a display idea, or make one like figure 87: underneath a heading "Lest We Forget" place a Star of David, either drawn in barbed wire or encircled by barbed wire. Beneath the symbol, place the words "Books about the Holocaust."

Focus middle and high schoolers' attention on this black period of twentieth-century history by promoting the reading of *The Diary of Anne Frank, Schindler's Ark, When Hitler Stole Pink Rabbit, The File on Fraulein Berg,* and other books about the persecution of the Jews. Include a *public seminar* on "Books About the Holocaust" featuring students who can comment on what they have read.

Figure 87

There are still many survivors of the Nazi prison camps. Many do not wish to speak of their past, for it stirs bitter memories, while others want to share the story in order to keep the memory alive and to prevent such a thing from ever recurring. If there is someone in your community who survived a camp, escaped, or had relatives there, ask if they would be willing to talk to a class during the festival.

What events can be related to the Holocaust? Have human atrocities stopped? What is "ethnic cleansing"? Social studies classes can find out. Where on earth today are people persecuted because of their race, religion, or social differences? Make a special display area to focus on "The Continuing Inhumanities" reported in magazines and newspapers.

Sources of Inspiration

Books About Judaism

Adler, David A. *A Picture Book of Passover.* New York: Holiday House, 1982.
Following an illustrated retelling of the Israelite's journey from Egyptian bondage into the land of Canaan, there is a brief explanation of the seder and other Passover holiday customs.

Cashman, Greer Fay. *Jewish Days and Holidays.* New York: SBS, 1979.
This picture book with text explains the joys, games, and foods of Jewish holidays, from sabbath to Hanukkah to Purim.

Cederbaum, Sophia. *Rosh Ha-Shono: Yom Kippur: The High Holy Days.* New York. Union of American Hebrew Congregations, 1961.
From making honey cakes to celebrations in the synagogue, the Jews celebrate each New Year with food, prayer, and the call of the shofar.

————. *Shavuot: The Birthday of the Torah.* New York: Union of American Hebrew Congregations, 1961.
This colorful, joyful book teaches children about the origins of and respect for holy scripture in Judaism.

————. *Tu B'shevat: The New Year's Day For the Trees.* New York: Union of American Hebrew Congregations, 1961.
As trees wake up from their winter rest, young Jewish children celebrate the renewal of spring with decorations, projects in conservation and the study of plants, and parties with great bowls of fruit.

Chaikin, Miriam. *Light Another Candle: The Meaning of Hanukkah.* New York: Clarion/Houghton Mifflin, 1981.
Delicately illustrated with pen and ink drawings, this book tells the story of Hanukkah, its ancient and modern celebrations, and how it is celebrated in different countries.

Gilbert, Arthur, and Oscar Tarcov. *Your Neighbor Celebrates.* New York: Friendly House Publishers, 1957.
An excellent introduction to Jewish holiday festival celebrations for middle school readers, this book is handsomely illustrated with photographs of folkdancing, family rituals, games, and customs.

Green, Laura. *I Am an Orthodox Jew.* New York: Holt, Rinehart, and Winston, 1979.
Told from the point of view of a young Jewish-American boy, this book proudly and clearly explains ancient Jewish traditions, family life, and expectations of behavior and belief.

Greenfeld, Howard. *Bar Mitzvah.* New York: Holt, Rinehart, and Winston, 1981.
This is an illustrated history and description of the ceremony in which a Jewish boy becomes responsible for obedience to divine law.

Hannam, Charles. *A Boy in That Situation.* New York: Harper and Row, 1978.
This autobiography tells a tough, hard story, written by a man who was a Jewish boy in Nazi Germany.

Hersch, Gizelle. *"Gizelle, Save the Children."* New York: Everest House, 1980.
Sixteen-year-old Gizelle and her three sisters survive a German death camp—this is their true story.

Kushkin, Karla. *Jerusalem Shining Still.* New York: Holt, Rinehart, and Winston, 1987.
This is the 4000-year-old story of Jerusalem, its wars, invasions, pilgrims, and settlers, illustrated with wonderful woodcuts by David Frampton.

Meltzer, Milton. *Remember the Days—A Short History of the Jewish American.* New York: Doubleday, 1974.
This history, from 1654 to 1973, examines culture, life, and experience from the Jewish viewpoint.

Rosenzweig, Efraim. *We Jews: Invitation to a Dialogue.* Stroud, Gloucestershire: Hawthorn Press, 1977.
The author describes the history, religious holidays, tenets of belief, rituals, and observances, as well as the enduring character traits of Jewish people.

Rossel, Seymour. *Judaism.* New York: Franklin Watts, 1976.
Beginning with a discussion of basic Jewish beliefs, Rossel describes the denominations within Judaism, their observances, holy days, and other religious practices.

Rothschild, Sylvia, ed. *Voices from the Holocaust.* New York: New American Library, 1981.
Thirty survivors of the German holocaust recall their lives in pre-war Europe, their experiences under Hitler, and their own successful struggles in America.

Simon, Norma. *Passover.* New York: Thomas Crowell, 1965.
Passover celebrates the right of men to be free, and this book tells a story of interest to children of all faiths, of the suffering of the Jewish people under the Pharoahs, their flight from Egypt, and of how the occasion is remembered today in America and in the Middle East.

Yarden, L. *The Tree of Light—A Study of the Menorah, the Seven-Branched Lampstand.* Ithaca: Cornell University Press, 1971.
A look at the evolution and significance of the menorah as lampstand and symbol through archeological and historical study.

Fiction

Aaron, Chester. *Gideon.* Philadelphia: Lippincott, 1982.
Gideon, a Jew, smuggles supplies into the Warsaw ghetto at the risk of his own death.

Asher, Sandy. *Daughters of the Law.* New York: Beaufort Books, 1980.
Shy Ruthie copes with being the new girl in town while struggling with her parents over her bat mitzvah.

Cohen, Barbara. *Benny.* New York: Lothrop, Lee and Shepard, 1977.
In a battle of wills in 1939, Benny's father wants him to work in the family store instead of playing baseball.

———. *Bitter Herbs and Honey.* New York: Lothrop, Lee and Shepard, 1976.
Becky Levitsky loves Jewish tradition but wants to plan her own life, alienating her strict parents.

———. *King of the 7th Grade.* New York: Lothrop, Lee and Shepard, 1982.
Vic Abrams resents having to attend Hebrew School in preparation for his bar mitzvah and devises a plan for getting expelled.

Holman, Felice. *The Murderer.* New York: Scribner's 1978.
The victim of beatings and abuse by other boys in a Pennsylvania town, a Jewish youth questions life's injustices.

Ish-Kishor, Sulamith. *Our Eddie.* New York: Pantheon, 1969.
An English Jewish family emigrates to New York City in the early twentieth century.

Kaufman, Stephen. *Does Anyone Here Know the Way to 13?* Boston: Houghton Mifflin, 1985.
Myron has to chose between bar mitzvah lessons and little league.

Keneally, Thomas. *Schindler's Ark.* London: Hodder and Stoughton, 1982.
In the shadow of Auschwitz, a German industrialist risks his life to protect the Jews of Nazi-occupied Poland in WWII.

Kerr, Judith. *When Hitler Stole Pink Rabbit.* Oldham: Coward, 1972.
A young Jewish girl and her family are forced to leave Hitler's Germany to seek refuge.

Konigsburg, E.L. *About the B'Nai Bagels.* New York: Atheneum, 1979.
It was tough having your mother manage your baseball team and your brother coach, as well as preparing for your bar mitzvah.

Lasky, Kathryn. *The Night Journey.* London: Frederick Warne, 1981.
Rachel's great-grandmother tells her stories of the old days in Jewish Russia.

Lelchuk, Alan. *On Home Ground.* Orlando: Gulliver, 1987.
Nine-year-old Aaron is caught between his father's Russian heritage and his own love for American baseball.

Lingard, Joan. *The File on Fraulein Berg.* London: Elsevier/Nelson Books, 1980.
Three young girls in wartime Ireland harass their German instructor until they discover that she is the sole surviving member of her Jewish German family.

Mark, Michael. *Toba.* New York: Bradbury, 1984.
Nine short stories, set in Poland in 1910, revolve around the adventures of a ten-year-old Jewish girl.

Orgel, Doris. *The Devil in Vienna.* New York: Dial, 1978.
Two young girls, one of them Jewish, in Vienna in 1938, are devoted friends but face an uncertain future when Lieselotte's father becomes a Nazi officer.

Orlev, Uri. *The Island on Bird Street.* Boston: Houghton Mifflin, 1984.
Eleven-year-old Alex takes refuge in an abandoned building to survive on his own in a Jewish ghetto in Warsaw.

Roth, Philip. *Portnoy's Complaint.* London: Jonathan Cape, 1969.
A Jewish boy grows up in this humorous story.

Sendak, Philip. *Enemies: A Love Story.* London: Jonathan Cape, 1972.
A refugee, whose family died in the Nazi holocaust in Poland, can not overcome his wartime habits of subterfuge in New York City.

————. *In Grandpa's House.* Illustrated by Maurice Sendak. New York: Harper and Row, 1985.
Maurice Sendak's father tells of his own Polish-Jewish childhood, his journey to America, and his magic adventures through the voice of the fictional young David.

Singer, Isaac Bashevis. *The Image, and Other Stories.* New York: Farrar, Straus, and Giroux, 1985.
Twenty-two short stories by a Nobel Prize-winning author illustrate Jewish humor and sadness.

Wallace, Lew. *Ben Hur.* London: Blackie and Son, 1970.
The author's detailed knowledge of Roman and Jewish history gives this late-nineteenth-century novel a strong sense of period.

Index

383

ABOUT THE AUTHOR

ALAN HEATH is a graduate of David Lipscomb University, Nashville. He earned his master's degree from Vanderbilt University. Since 1973 he has taught at the American School in London in the library, English, theatre and graphic arts departments. In his art classes, Heath emphasizes a cross-disciplinary approach in order to link and reinforce learning. He has organized many all-school festivals using cultural, ethnic, literary, and historical themes. Heath has been active in the European Council of International Schools (ECIS) where he served as chair of its Media Services Committee and edited the *Link* magazine. He is currently book reviews editor of *The International Schools Journal*. He has regularly served on accreditation teams for Middle States Association and the ECIS in schools across Europe. He is a member of the American Art Development Committee of the British Museum, London. Heath leads many student and adult educational travel groups to Africa, the Far East, the Middle East, and to important sites in Europe to gain firsthand experience of the art, history, and culture of many ethnic and national peoples. He is also a professional artist, working mainly in pen and ink, wood carving, and acrylics. A harpist and keyboardist, he has written articles for various music and educational journals. His first book, *Off the Wall* (Libraries Unlimited, 1986), relates artwork to the development of reading enjoyment. The forthcoming *Common Threads*, Heath's second Scarecrow Press publication, is a companion volume to *Windows on the World* (1995). During his 1992–3 sabbatical year, he gained a certificate in Art History at the Royal Academy of Arts, London.